BRITISH GEOLOGICAL SURVEY

D V FROST

Geology of the country around Northallerton

Memoir for 1:50 000 Geological Sheet 42
(England and Wales)

CONTRIBUTORS

Stratigraphy
P A Rathbone

Biostratigraphy
B M Cox
H C Ivimey-Cook
G Warrington

Structure and hydrocarbons
R A Chadwick
D W Holliday

Hydrogeology
J Davies

Geophysics
J D Cornwell

London: The Stationery Office   1998

The grid used on the figures is the National Grid taken from the Ordnance Survey map with the permission of the Controller of Her Majesty's Stationery Office. Figure 1 is based on material from Ordnance Survey 1:50 000 scale maps, Ordnance Survey licence no. GD272191/1998.

ISBN 0 11 884535 7

Bibliographical reference

FROST, D V. 1998. Geology of the country around Northallerton. *Memoir of the British Geological Survey*, Sheet 42 (England and Wales).

Authors

Contributors

R A Chadwick, MA, MSc
J D Cornwell, MSc, PhD
B M Cox, BSc, PhD
D W Holliday, MA, PhD
G Warrington, DSc
British Geological Survey, Keyworth

J Davies, BSc
British Geological Survey, Wallingford

D V Frost, BSc, PhD
Newcastle upon Tyne

H C Ivimey-Cook, BSc, PhD
P A Rathbone, BSc, PhD
Formerly British Geological Survey, Keyworth

Other publications of the Survey dealing with this and adjoining areas

BOOKS

Memoirs
Geology of the country around Thirsk, Sheet 52, 1992

British Regional Geology
Eastern England from the Tees to The Wash, 2nd Edition, 1980

Mineral Assessment Reports
No. 75   The sand and gravel resources of the country around Stokesley, North Yorkshire, 1981
No. 111   The sand and gravel resources of the country around east and south-east of Darlington, Durham, 1982
No. 120   The sand and gravel resources of the country around Catterick, North Yorkshire, 1982

MAPS

1:1 000 000
Geology of the United Kingdom, Ireland and the adjacent continental shelf (south sheet), 1991

1:625 000
Great Britain North, Solid geology, 1979
Great Britain North, Quaternary geology, 1977
Aeromagnetic map (north sheet), 1972

1:253 400 or 1:250 000
Sheet 4 Geological Survey of England and Wales 3rd edition, 1970 reprint
Tyne-Tees, Solid geology, 1981
Tyne-Tees, Sea bed sediments and Quaternary geology, 1986
Tyne-Tees, Aeromagnetic Anomaly Map, 1985
Aeromagnetic map of part of Great Britain and Northern Ireland (Sheet 9)
Bouguer Gravity Anomaly map, 1978

1:50 000 or 1:63 360
Egton (Sheet 43) Solid and Drift, 1992
Stockton (Sheet 33) Solid and Drift, 1987
Thirsk (Sheet 52) Solid, 1992
Thirsk (Sheet 52) Drift, 1992

Printed in the UK for The Stationery Office
J41410   C6   3/98

Geology of the country around Northallerton

The district described in this memoir lies towards the northern part of the Vale of York; the River Tees and some of its tributaries skirt the northern boundary. It is largely low-lying and thick drift conceals underlying Permian, Triassic and Lower Jurassic strata. The Cleveland Hills form higher ground in the south-west where Middle and Upper Jurassic strata crop out. Carboniferous rocks form the basement, at about 4 to 7 km depth. This account of the area includes descriptions of the concealed strata encountered in shallow and deep boreholes (some drilled for hydrocarbon exploration), both within the district and beyond it.

During Carboniferous times the district lay in the Stainmore Trough between the Alston and Askrigg Blocks. Carboniferous strata probably exceeded 6.5 km in thickness before erosion. Dinantian rocks are estimated at 3 km or more throughout the district; Namurian rocks are over 750 m thick in places, but may be absent locally. A marked cyclicity occurs throughout the sequence with limestone and mudstone dominating in the Dinantian. Upwards, limestones become thinner and less persistent, sandstones become thicker and coarser grained and form a greater proportion of the Namurian strata where thin coals, seat-earths and cherts are more abundant. The nearest proved Westphalian rocks occur to the south, near Ripon, but it seems likely that Westphalian rocks occur at depth in the south-east of the district.

The resurvey of the district has shown a relatively uncomplicated geological structure, despite the number of tectonic episodes which are known to have affected this and adjacent areas since Devonian times. Carboniferous and older rocks were folded and uplifted during the Hercynian orogeny. This was followed by a prolonged period of weathering and erosion in hot desert conditions which has left little evidence in the sedimentary sequence of the district. Breccias and sands rest unconformably on reddened Carboniferous strata and may be of Early Permian age.

In the Late Permian, transgression of the Zechstein Sea flooded the former desert basin. The district lies astride the Cleveland High which runs east–west and separates two provinces where different palaeogeographical conditions prevailed, the Durham Province in the north and the Yorkshire Province in the south. Five main cycles of deposition are reflected in the main groups, the Don, Aislaby, Teesside, Staintondale and Eskdale groups. Where fully developed, individual cycles show an upward sequence of carbonate-anhydrite-halite-sylvite, the minerals reflecting the order of salt deposition during progressive evaporation. Collapse structures are common in the west of the district, caused by dissolution of the evaporites.

Subsidence continued through Triassic and early Jurassic times as a peripheral effect of basin development to the east. Open sea extended southwards across the area from latest Triassic times, receding southwards for most of the Middle Jurassic to re-enter the area in late Middle Jurassic times.

Triassic rocks are represented by about 350 m of the Sherwood Sandstone Group and 260 m of the Mercia Mudstone Group. These beds were laid down on a broad plain of low relief, in a semi-arid climate. The overlying Penarth Group is 12 m thick; these dark grey mudstones were deposited during a marine transgression which flooded much of south and eastern Britain.

In the Early Jurassic, fine-grained sediments of the Lias Group were deposited in shallow, shelf seas. A rhythmic pattern of alternating mudstone, siltstone and/or sandstone suggests repeated uplift and erosion of the source area. Sedimentation kept pace with subsidence in the Cleveland Basin, interrupted from time to time by an influx of silt and sand from the north-west. In the later part of this period an abundance of washed-in tree trunks and branches eventually formed jet deposits, the Jet Rock Member.

Deltaic conditions similar to those of the Carboniferous Period prevailed during the Middle Jurassic reflecting an alternation of marine and non-marine conditions. Massive sandstones are separated by mudstone, seatearths and thin coals, comprising a typical deltaic sequence. Plant remains are common and include *Ginkgoales* and fern pinnules; insect remains and reptilian footprints are also present.

The youngest Jurassic rocks show a much closer connection between the district and areas to the south than their predecessors. The beds comprise mudstone, siltstone, calcareous sandstone, limestone and oolite, and include the Oxford Clay which represents one of the most persistent and laterally extensive transgressions of the Jurassic.

About three quarters of the district is covered by a complex of glacial deposits; most are the product of an ice sheet which covered the district about 18 000 years ago and began to melt about 13 000 years ago. Older (pre-Devensian) deposits may also be present in deep buried valleys, and locally more recent Flandrian sediments overlie the Devensian deposits and modify the postglacial topography. Two major drift-filled, buried valleys cross the district; one drained northwards towards the Tees and the second drained southwards in a valley lying beneath the present-day alluvium of the River Swale. Glacial sand and gravel on the Cleveland Hills at elevations of about 300 m confirm that most of the district was once covered by ice. The region is well known in geological literature for providing evidence of the former presence of large ice-dammed glacial lakes of Pleistocene age.

Economic interest in the district, formerly an important mining area, has included alum, aggregates and building material, coal, evaporites, hydrocarbons, oil shale, ironstone and jet. An account of water resources is also given.

Cover photograph

General view of the western side of Scugdale showing the shale tips of the Jet Rock Member (Lower Jurassic) scarring the lower slopes of the valley. A marked steepening of the valley side occurs where the sandstones of the Ravenscar Group (Middle Jurassic) form a series of bench-like features. Kendall (1902) described this valley as one of several in Cleveland which, during the Quaternary, was occupied by a glacial lake, dammed by ice to the north. The Teesside plain can be seen stretching away to the north-west. (L2447)

Northern scarp of the Cleveland Hills at Busby Moor showing exposure and landslip in the Lias Group (Lower Jurassic). Calcareous and ferruginous beds and nodules in the Redcar Mudstone Formation form the resistant horizons towards the base of the scarp. The more massive beds towards the top of the face comprise fossiliferous sandstones of the Staithes Sandstone Formation [5270 0303]. (L1981)

CONTENTS

FIGURES

PLATES

TABLES

HISTORY OF THE SURVEY OF THE NORTHALLERTON SHEET

The district covered by the 1:50 000 geological map of England and Wales Sheet 42, Northallerton was originally surveyed on the six-inch County Series Sheets Yorkshire 26, 27, 28, 29, 40, 41, 42, 43, 55, 56, 57, 58, 70, 71, 72, and 73 by G Barrow, A G Cameron, C Fox-Strangways, W Gunn and H H Howell, and published in 1883 as Old Series one-inch Quarter Sheet 96 NW, in both drift and solid editions. The maps at a scale of six inch to one mile were not published, but manuscript coloured copies were deposited in the Geological Survey Office for reference. A combined memoir with the adjoining, Sheet 96 SW (Thirsk) was published in 1886. A drift edition of the Northallerton sheet was reprinted in 1959, incorporating additions made by A Strahan in 1912, and with the National Grid superimposed.

Resurvey of the district on the six-inch and 1:10 000 scale was started in 1977 by J G O Smart and C M Jones; they were joined later that year by D V Frost who undertook the major share of the work. J R Davies and P A Rathbone joined the team in 1979 and F C Cox in 1980. The surveying was completed in 1981 and the 1:50 000 Sheet was published in 1993.

Geological 1:10 560 and 1:10 000 scale National Grid maps included wholly or in part of the 1:50 000 Sheet 42 are listed, together with the initials of the geological surveyors and dates of survey. In the case of marginal sheets all surveyors are listed where overlap occurred. The surveyors were A C Benfield, A H Cooper, F C Cox, J R Davies, D V Frost, D H Land, C M Jones, D A C Mills, J H Powell, P A Rathbone and J G O Smart.

Copies of the fair-drawn maps have been deposited in the British Geological Survey libraries at Keyworth and Edinburgh for public reference and may also be inspected in the London Information Office in the Geological Museum, South Kensington. Copies may be purchased directly from the British Geological Survey as black and white dyeline sheets.

List of 6-inch or 1:10 000 geological maps:

NZ 20 NE	Dalton on Tees	DACM	1962
		DHL	1971–1973
		JGOS	1978
NZ 20 SE	Cowton	JGOS	1978
		JRD	1979
NZ 30 NW	Eryholm	DHL	1971–1972
NZ 30 NE	Hornby	DHL	1968–1972
		CMJ	1977
NZ 30 SW	Great Smeaton	JRD, PAR	1979
NZ 30 SE	Appleton Wiske	CMJ	1977
NZ 40 NW	Crathorne	DHL	1966–1967
		DVF	1977
NZ 40 NE	Hutton Rudby	DHL	1966–1967
		DVF	1977
NZ 40 SW	Rounton	DVF	1977–1979
NZ 40 SE	Potto	DVF	1979
NZ 50 NW	Stokesley	DHL	1966–1967
		DVF	1978
NZ 50 NE	Great Broughton	DVF	1978
NZ 50 SW	Carlton	DVF	1979–1981
NZ 50 SE	Cold Moor	DVF	1981
SE 29 NE	Great Langton	JGOS, JRD	1979
SE 29 SE	Leeming Bar	DVF	1979
SE 39 NW	Danby Wiske	PAR	1979
SE 39 NE	Brompton	PAR, JRD	1979
SE 39 SW	Aiderby Steeple	ACB	1979
		FCC	1980
SE 39 SE	Northallerton	DVF	1981
SE 49 NW	Osmotherley	DVF	1980
SE 49 NE	Osmotherley Moor	DVF	1979
SE 49 SW	Cotcliffe	DVF	1981
SE 49 SE	Kepwick	PAR	1979–1980
SE 59 NW	Snilesworth	DVF	1980–1981
SE 59 NE	Bilsdale	DVF	1981
SE 59 SW	Arden	PAR	1979–1980
SE 59 SE	Easterside	DVF	1981

ACKNOWLEDGEMENTS

This memoir was written largely by Dr D V Frost. Dr D W Holliday contributed to the chapters on the Carboniferous and structure and compiled the account on hydrocarbons in the Economic Chapter. Mr R A Chadwick provided the interpretation of the deep subsurface geology and structure in Chapter Six. Help and guidance given by Dr D B Smith on the difficult correlation problems of the Permian strata in this district and his expert interpretation of poorly documented boreholes is gratefully acknowledged.

British Gas Exploration and Production kindly permitted the use of seismic reflection data. Dr G Warrington has advised on aspects of Triassic stratigraphy and identified palynomorphs from the Late Permian, and from the Trias (Mercia Mudstone Group, Penarth Group and basal Lias). Dr H C Ivimey-Cook contributed greatly to the collection and identification of the Lower and Middle Jurassic faunas, Dr B M Cox identified the fauna from the Arden Hall Borehole and Dr I P Wilkinson was responsible for the identification of Jurassic microfossils.

Mr J Davies prepared the section on hydrogeology. Thanks are due to Messrs R G Crofts, J R Gozzard, D Price and J H Lovell, for their mineral assessment reports on the sand and gravel resources in the district to which useful reference was made, and to Dr P Rathbone for his written contribution of geological notes and local details for his survey area of the Cleveland Hills. Dr J D Cornwell contributed the section on geophysics.

The photographs were taken by Mr K E Thornton; a complete list of available photographs is given in Appendix 3. The memoir was edited by Mr T J Charsley and Dr A A Jackson.

I gratefully acknowledge the access and help given by the numerous farmers and landowners throughout the district during the course of the geological survey, in particular Lord Ingleby, Lord Mexborough, and the Forestry Commission who also gave permission to drill boreholes on their land; also to British Gypsum plc for their cooperation in allowing BGS to core the upper part of their Winton Manor Borehole.

NOTES

Throughout the memoir, the word 'district' refers to the area covered by the 1:50 000 series geological sheet 42 (Northallerton).

National Grid references are given in square brackets and lie within 100 km squares NZ and SE.

Numbers preceded by the letter L refer to the BGS collection of photographs; those preceded by the letter E refer to the BGS sliced rock collection.

Enquiries concerning geological data for the district should be addressed to the Manager, National Geological Records Centre, Keyworth.

PREFACE

For many centuries agriculture has dominated the sparsely populated region around the market town of Northallerton. However it was the mineral wealth of the Cleveland Hills which first gave rise to the industries of Teesside some 150 years ago, and which have now developed into the vast industrial complex some 15 km to the north-east of Northallerton.

Although these industries and the sources that they use for their raw materials have changed markedly, and particularly since the 1950s, the search for natural resources has continued. This has included resources such as oil and gas, and aggregate minerals for the construction industry — sand, gravel and limestone. Several deep boreholes were drilled to search for oil and gas at Harlsey and in the Cleveland Hills. The boreholes penetrated Carboniferous rocks to depths exceeding 1900 m, but no economically significant accumulations were encountered. Geological information is essential not only for resource assessment but also for planners and civil engineers in a district traversed by major arterial road and rail routes, and with strategic airfields as well as vital oil, gas and water pipelines. In addition, as much of the area is liable to flooding any remedial as well as remodelling work requires a detailed understanding of the near-surface geology.

This memoir is intended not only to provide basic geological data, but also to indicate where more detailed information exists in the Survey's extensive archives. It is best read in conjunction with the colour-printed 1:50 000 scale geological map, England and Wales Sheet 42, Northallerton.

The Cleveland Hills form an imposing area of upland in the southeast of the district, contrasting markedly with the adjacent, almost flatlying, agricultural land formed by the juxtaposition of the York and Teesside plains. The River Swale meanders across the south-west corner of the district. Most of the district lies in North Yorkshire, with small areas north of the rivers Tees and Leven in counties Durham and Cleveland, respectively.

Much of the Cleveland Hills area is now given over to tourism — the famous Lyke Wake Walk commences at Osmotherley, and the Cleveland Way and Coast to Coast walks also cross the district. The comprehensive studies summarised in the memoir incorporate the results of detailed mapping by the British Geological Survey as well as subsurface information from various site investigations and from exploration by the metalliferous, hydrocarbon and water industries.

The synthesis of this information throws light on the history and structure of a type area for Jurassic strata. Large areas previously mapped as sand and gravel have been demonstrated to comprise uneconomic pebbly clays but potential areas for yielding economic deposits have been highlighted. The economically valuable evaporite deposits of Durham and Cleveland extend into this district, and the presence of gypsum in the Triassic strata remains a possible source for future supply. Triassic sandstones form a reliable and important aquifer beneath much of this district. The delineation of laminated clays within the till of the lowland areas has emphasised localities where special care is required before construction is contemplated.

I am confident that this memoir — the first comprehensive account of the geology since 1886 — will play its part for many years to come, not only in facilitating the discovery and exploitation of new mineral resources, but also in aiding the planning and conservation of this attractive, unspoilt district in a manner that will meet the interests of the community as a whole.

David A Falvey, PhD
Director

Kingsley Dunham Centre
British Geological Survey
Keyworth
Nottingham
NG12 5GG

Plate 1 North bank of the River Leven near Skutterskelfe Hall, Stokesley [48345 0669] showing alluvial silts and clays overlying sand and gravel which rest on disturbed and contorted Triassic mudstones and siltstones of the Mercia Mudstone Group. (L1986)

ONE

Introduction

AREA AND PHYSICAL FEATURES

This memoir describes the geology of those parts of North Yorkshire, County Durham and Cleveland covered by the Northallerton Sheet (42) of the 1:50 000 series geological map of England and Wales. Two-thirds of the area is low lying (Figure 1), averaging between 30 and 60 m above OD, but the south-east corner, formed by part of the Cleveland Hills, rises to 435 m at Drake Howe [538 029] south-east of Carlton, with several other elevated areas around 400 m.

Most of the district drains southwards by the Swale and its tributaries but an area in the north is included in the catchment of the Tees and the Leven. All drainage is eventually discharged into the North Sea.

Much of the district is agricultural, mostly pasture on the heavy clays of the low-lying land, but where drainage has been improved and the soils are lighter, arable crops are popular on the largely level fields. The south-east corner of the district forms part of the North York Moors National Park and includes the impressive scenery of the Cleveland and Hambleton Hills which can be appreciated from the famous footpaths of the Cleveland Way, the Lyke Wake Walk and the Coast to Coast Walk. The high hills provide mostly moorland grazing for sheep, with some afforestation. The Cleveland Hills have been

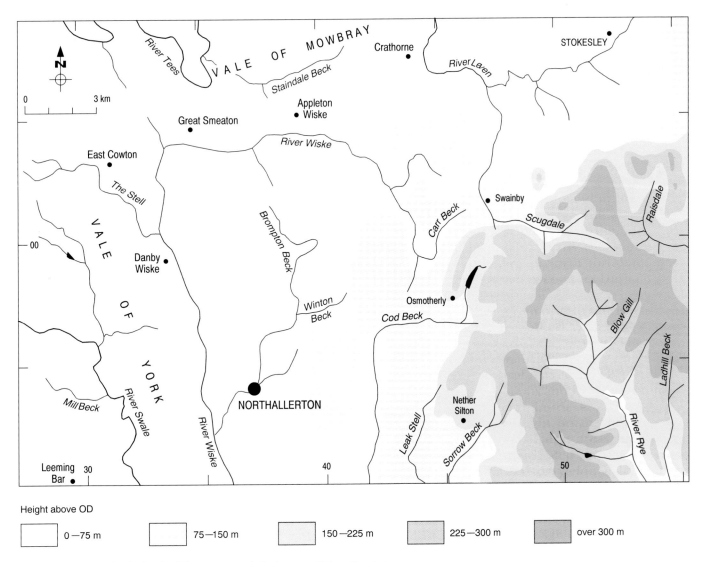

Figure 1 Principal physical features and drainage of the district.

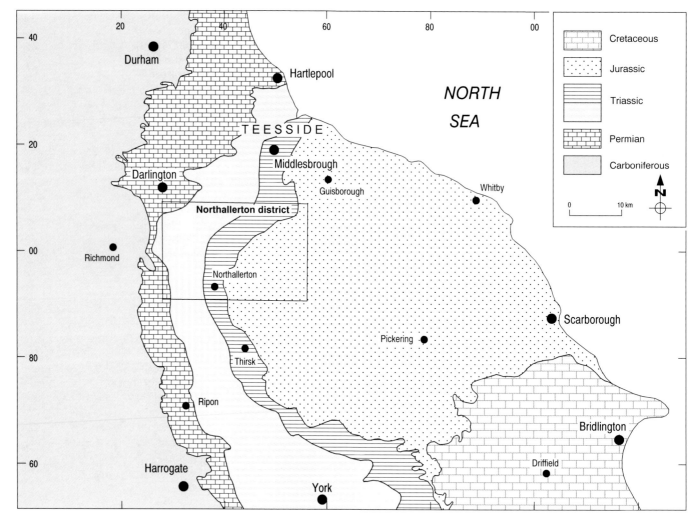

Figure 2 Geological setting of the Northallerton district.

extensively worked in the past for ironstone, alum and jet, and to a lesser extent for coal and brick clay. The sandstones have been quarried for freestone and the limestones exploited for road metal and lime, particularly in quarries at Kepwick [485 915]. The hills still retain the scars of man's activity of the past 200 years.

The Quaternary clays which cover much of the low ground have been dug, for example, at Ellerton Works [270 985] for brick and tile making, and lenses of sand and gravel within the clays worked for local building requirements, for example, in Leases Hall Sand Pit [279 910] near Leeming Bar.

There are many features of historical interest in the district, with Roman pottery discovered on the site of Holy Cross Church, Whorlton. The area was traversed by travellers between York, Piecebridge and Corbridge, with Romanby [360 930] no doubt along the route. The remains of medieval castles abound, with examples at Whorlton, Harlsey and Sigston which utilised small rises in ground level or the proximity of a river as an additional means of defence. The earliest documented event was the Battle of the Standard in 1138 [368 981] near

Danby Wiske and the abundance of standing stones marking land boundaries suggests that the higher Cleveland Hills area was often disputed territory. It was, however, a favoured area for burials — tumuli abound and the Wain Stones overlooking Stokesley are noted by locals for their magical and mystic properties. Some of the dead were, however, carried 42 miles along the Lyke Wake Walk from Osmotherley [458 972] to the Yorkshire coast for the benefit of their souls.

Mount Grace Carthusian Priory [449 985] was founded in 1398, and cultivation terraces [255 941] near Kirkby Fleetham are probably of a similar age. In more recent times, the region became peaceful and prosperous, with the building of many halls, manor houses and granges.

PREVIOUS RESEARCH

Reference to the geology of the district can be found in a few early observations on the agriculture and water supply (Willan, 1782; Tuke, 1794) but the first geological map, surveyed by William Smith, was published in 1821.

It was followed in 1853 by a geological map of Yorkshire, at a scale of 5 miles to an inch, by John Phillips. By then, the range of strata from Late Permian to Late Jurassic had been detected by both surface observations and borehole provings (Figure 2).

Important ironstone discoveries were recorded in detailed papers by Marley (1857), Sorby (1857), Phillips (1858), and Bewick (1861), and the presence of rock salt in the Triassic of the Middlesbrough area reported on by Marley in 1864.

The geological literature on north-east Yorkshire has been dominated by research on the stratigraphy and palaeontology of the Jurassic strata, particularly that exposed on the coast, with the work of Simpson (1855) and Buckman (1915) being of historical importance. Passing reference was made, however, to inland exposures within the district or to those proved in the mining and quarrying processes. The most detailed work was by Tate and Blake (1876) on the Yorkshire Lias, but the most comprehensive account of the district was provided ten years later by Fox-Strangways, Cameron and Barrow (1886) in a memoir describing both the Northallerton district and the adjoining area of Thirsk to the south.

More recently Rayner and Hemingway (1974) edited and contributed to *The geology and mineral resources of Yorkshire*, and the district is also included in *British Regional Geology: Eastern England from the Tees to The Wash* (Kent, 1980b).

Advances in rock thin-sectioning and research using the petrological microscope enabled Hallimond (1925), Smithson (1934, 1941, 1954), Dunham (1951) and Chowns (1966, 1968) to develop ideas on the likely depositional environments of the ironstones. From these studies, a new impetus was given to publication, in the 1970s, of the sedimentary history of the other Jurassic lithologies, which in turn led to the refining of the stratigraphy of the district.

An appreciation of the wider geological context of the district was given by the publication of the 1:250 000 Tyne-Tees geological map showing the details of the Continental Shelf of the North Sea.

Exploratory boreholes drilled for the oil industry at Harlsey and in the Cleveland Hills have extended our knowledge of the underlying Carboniferous rocks of the district, and recent geophysical and seismic traverses have enabled interpretations to be made regarding the basement structures.

Four boreholes were drilled in the Cleveland Hills by the British Geological Survey specifically to provide new stratigraphical and palaeontological information of the Jurassic strata, and to enhance the geological map (Ivimey-Cook, 1992c; Rathbone, 1987b). Agreement between British Gypsum plc and BGS enabled the top part of the Winton Manor Borehole to be cored, so that a continuous sequence of the Penarth Group could be obtained and described.

TWO

Carboniferous

At the end of the Devonian Period, north-east England was a peneplain formed mostly of Lower Palaeozoic and early Devonian rocks. These strongly folded and faulted basement rocks are assumed to underlie the whole of the district at depths exceeding 4 km.

The varied stability and rigidity of the basement during early Carboniferous extension resulted in the development of basin (trough or gulf) and block (or shelf) facies. In the basinal areas, the sequence of rocks is thick, mostly without stratigraphical breaks and commonly folded, whereas those of equivalent age on the blocks are thinner, incomplete, and structurally simpler. The boundaries between the two are commonly marked by major fault zones, which probably formed as major compressive features during the Caledonian continental collision, and were subsequently reactivated (Chadwick and Holliday, 1991) in Carboniferous and later times. The district lies to the north-east of Askrigg Block, within the Stainmore Trough; it is bounded to the north by the Stainmore Syncline (Kent, 1966, p.327). The east–west-trending Stainmore Trough swings southwards into the Cleveland Basin and merges with the Bowland Trough in the Skipton–Harrogate–York area (Figure 3).

The total thickness of Carboniferous sedimentary rocks in the Stainmore Trough is not proved but the Cleveland Hills Borehole, made by Gulf Exploration Co. in 1940, penetrated 745 m of predominantly marine shales, ranging in age from lower Namurian to upper Dinantian. Up to about 5500 m of Dinantian strata are estimated to occur in the Stainmore Trough compared with only 300 m on the Askrigg Block. The total thickness of Carboniferous beds in the trough probably exceeded 6500 m before partial removal by erosion. Geophysical evidence suggests that the base of the Carboniferous in the Cleveland area is at a depth of more than 5000 m below OD.

Beyond the limits of the district, the Askrigg Block is bounded to the west by the Dent fault system and to the south by the Craven Fault System. The eastern limit of the block is less clearly defined; the contrast between the Carboniferous facies proved in the Harlsey and Cleveland Hills boreholes led Kent (1966) to suggest that the boundary lay in the intervening ground, perhaps coincident with major north–south-trending faults passing through the villages of East Harlsey, Sigston and Cotcliffe. However, this has not been confirmed by seismic reflection data which reveals that Dinantian rocks are 3000 m or more in thickness throughout the district. The eastern boundary of the block is probably gradational, and located towards the south-west of the district.

Stratigraphy

Provings of Carboniferous rocks are limited to two deep boreholes drilled for hydrocarbon exploration, one in the Cleveland Hills and the other at Harlsey. Therefore, the following generalisations are based on data from adjoining areas.

There are three main divisions in the Carboniferous rocks of northern England. The lowest division, mostly of Dinantian age, contains limestones interbedded with mudstones and sandstones; the middle division is of Namurian age and consists mainly of sandstones and grits with subordinate mudstones; the upper division is of Westphalian age and comprises, mudstones, siltstones and sandstones with subordinate coals and seatearths. The rocks of the Carboniferous Period broadly represent, therefore, a major marine transgression, followed by delta progradation and a gradual withdrawal of the sea, so that towards the end of Westphalian times a land surface of continental proportions was established. Neither the marine transgression nor the following regression was uniform, and both phases were subject to many minor fluctuations in sea level which resulted in a marked cyclicity in the deposits. This is especially marked in the Britantian and Lower Namurian rocks of both the block and basinal sequences, and allows a close correlation. Each cycle consists of rhythmic sequences, in ascending order, of limestone, mudstone, sandstone, seatearth and/or coal.

The top of the Dinantian is drawn at the base of the Great or Main Limestone, which forms an excellent stratigraphical marker throughout northern England. The overlying Namurian strata are designated as the Stainmore Group and extend up to the Subcrenatum Marine Band, which delineates the base of the Westphalian or Coal Measures strata. The rhythmic sequence of lithologies continues above the Main Limestone but with increasing modification. Limestones become progressively thinner, less persistent and more argillaceous, and are interbedded with calcareous fossiliferous mudstones (shell beds). Mudstones become more silty, with increasing interlamination of siltstone and sandstone. Sandstones are thicker, of coarser grain and form a greater proportion of the total rock assemblage. Their bases are commonly erosional. Thin coals and seatearths are more abundant than in the lower strata. Chert, both bedded and in nodular form, is more typical than in the underlying Dinantian or in the overlying Westphalian strata.

Seismic data suggests that the Namurian rocks of the district vary from 100 to over 750 m in thickness and may be absent locally.

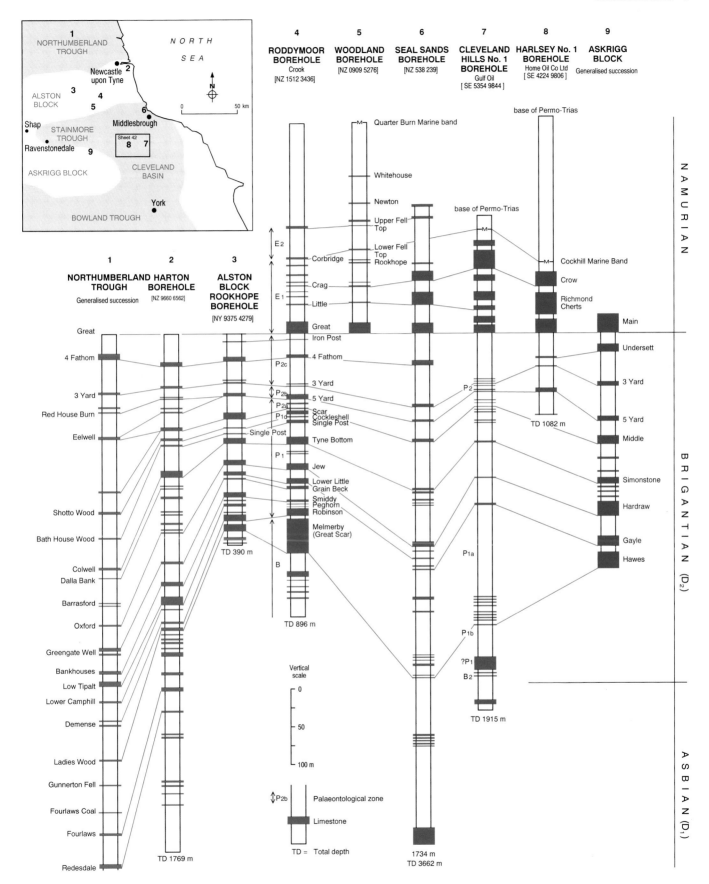

Figure 3 Correlation of Carboniferous strata proved in deep boreholes in the Northallerton district and surrounding areas.

Westphalian strata were probably deposited over the district, but have been removed during the Variscan orogeny. The nearest proved Westphalian strata occur to the south, near Ripon, and to the east, near Whitby. However, it seems probable, from seismic data, that early Westphalian rocks occur locally at depth in the south-eastern part of the district.

DETAILS

Cleveland Hills No. 1 Borehole [5354 9844]

NAMURIAN   From the detailed account of this borehole by Fowler (1944) it may be concluded that Carboniferous strata were penetrated at 1159 m depth, 158 m above the base of the Main Limestone (Figure 3). Cores yielded *Eumorphoceras bisulcatum*, indicating a Namurian (E_2) age for mudstones 11 m below the top of the Carboniferous strata, probably marking the position of the Cockhill (*Cravenoceras cowlingense*) Marine Band. Between 1201.83 m and 1315.51 m depth, grey and dark grey siliceous and nodular cherty limestones with subordinate mudstone beds and partings are common. This sequence is broadly similar to that at Richmond where the Crow Limestone, the Richmond Cherts and the Little and Main limestones have comparable lithology and thickness (Fowler, 1944; Dunham and Wilson, 1985).

DINANTIAN   Between 1317 m and 1415 m depth, the sequence is largely arenaceous. Pale grey micaceous sandstone is common, with interbedding and interlamination of carbonaceous micaceous silty mudstones. The strata between 1415 m and 1509 m comprise an alternation of mudstones and thin limestones with sporadic sandstones. A P_2 age is indicated at the top of these beds, suggesting a correlation with the Three Yard, Five Yard, Scar and Eelwell limestones of other areas (Figure 3). A grey crinoidal limestone, 5 m thick at a depth of 1517 m, yielded *Eomarginifera tissingtonensis*, a productoid brachiopod typical of the mudstones overlying the Hardraw and Jew limestones. Mudstones predominate between this limestone and 1744 m, with an horizon near the P_2a/P_1b junction indicated, that is near the top of the D_1 Subzone. A 30 m limestone with its base near 1860 m was dated as possibly P_1 or B_2. The contained brachiopods, of late Asbian aspect, were similar to those in the Draughton Limestone of the Bowland Trough. A slightly lower limestone at a depth of 1902 to 1907 m yielded *Productus redesdalensis* and *P. hemisphaericus*, forms typical of the early part of the late Asbian in the Northumberland Trough, for example Redesdale Ironstone Shale and Limestone. Dark grey mudstones were proved to a depth of 1915 m, at which level the hole was abandoned. The base of the Carboniferous probably lies at least 3000 m below final depth.

Harlsey No. 1 Borehole [4224 9806]

This borehole, drilled by Home Oil Co. Ltd in 1965, entered the Carboniferous at a depth of 707 m. The topmost 200 m of Carboniferous strata consists largely of sandstone, with interbedded black silty mudstone and minor sandstone interbeds. The sandstones are grey, fine to medium grained, well cemented, with carbonaceous, micaceous partings. The mudstones yield ironstone nodules at 757 m and 761 m. Sporadic, pyritic, plant fragments are poorly preserved; productoid brachiopods and *Lingula* sp. were also found at this level.

A 0.30 m-thick coal was proved at 822 m depth, and 0.60 m of coal and shale were proved at 908 m depth. Mudstones with high gamma-ray values between 896 and 902 m probably correlate with a goniatite-bearing bed, thought to be the Cockhill Marine Band, in Cleveland Hills Borehole.

The highest calcareous horizon in the borehole is present in mudstones at a depth of 848 m but the main sequence of limestones occurs between 907 m and 980 m. The limestone is generally grey and brown in colour, finely crystalline, partly crinoidal and variably siliceous. Some of the sequence is completely replaced by chert. Grey and black pyritic shale beds separate the limestone into three units, which are correlated with the Crow Limestone, the Richmond Cherts, and the Little and Main limestones (Figure 3). Small goniatites, recorded below the limestone at 984 m, are probably indicative of the E subzone.

Dark grey calcareous shales with thin grey-brown shaly limestone occur between 984 m and 1027 m. A limestone, between 1008 and 1012 m depth, probably correlates with the Undersett Limestone.

Two sandstones (at 1031–1043 m and 1061–1073 m depth), with contrasting black micaceous/carbonaceous shale interbeds, are fine to very fine grained, usually with a silica cement. Both sandstones are overlain by limestones, 3 m and 11 m thick respectively, in which crinoids are the only recorded fossils.

Studies of the fossil assemblages in the Harlsey and Cleveland Hills boreholes by Dr N J Riley show a greater preponderance of shelf-derived, Yoredale-type faunas in the Harlsey Borehole, supporting some of the conclusions of Kent (1966). This reflects the closer proximity of Harlsey to the Askrigg Block, which probably supplied much of the bioclastic debris to the Stainmore and Cleveland basins.

Precise correlation of Harlsey No. 1 Borehole is difficult. but an equivalence of the chert and limestone-rich horizons with those in Cleveland Hills No. 1 Borehole is implied (Figure 3.).

THREE

Permian

The stratigraphy of the Permian rocks of north-east England has been known since early in the last century, based on the pioneering work of Sedgwick (1829), King (1850) and Kirkby (1861). Detailed correlation has proved difficult, due to lateral variation, the penecontemporaneous alteration of the rocks, and the resultant partial destruction and obliteration of some of the contained fossils. The presence of evaporite deposits in various forms at several stratigraphical levels, together with their dissolution in places, has complicated stratigraphical interpretation.

A classification of the strata (Table 1) has been established from surface mapping and from detailed logs of boreholes drilled for hydrocarbon and mineral exploration, to the east of the district, and offshore in the North Sea. The strata can be correlated closely with those of north Germany and Holland (Smith, 1980). The nomenclature used here follows Smith et al.

(1986); the palaeogeography of the region has been interpreted by Smith (1989) and Smith and Taylor (1992).

Permian rocks are not exposed within the district because of a thick cover of superficial deposits. They are, however, interpreted from sparse borehole evidence at subcrop in two small areas, totalling some 11 km², in the north-west near Dalton-on-Tees, and in the south-west near Leeming Bar. Because the borehole records from north Yorkshire are either very old or have inadequate lithological descriptions, several additional boreholes were drilled by the British Geological Survey to establish the detailed Permian stratigraphy of the area. These included Hurworth Place Borehole [2901 0953], 200 m to the north of the district (Smith and Moore, 1973), Halnaby Borehole [2607 0717] 800 m to the west of the district, and Aiskew Bank Farm Borehole [2667 8888] 1200 m to the south (Pattison, 1978).

Table 1 Classification of Permian strata.

	Groups	Cycles	Previous nomenclature	Present nomenclature		
				Durham Province		Yorkshire Province
UPPER PERMIAN	Eskdale	EZ5	Upper Marls	Roxby Formation (Transgressive from the south)		Roxby Formation
	Staintondale	EZ4		Sherburn Anhydrite Upgang Formation* Rotten Marl Formation		Sherburn Anhydrite Formation Upgang Formation Rotten Marl
	Teesside	EZ3		Boulby Halite Formation Billingham Anhydrite Formation Seaham Formation		Boulby Halite Formation Billingham Anhydrite Formation Brotherton Formation
			Upper Magnesian Limestone			
	Aislaby	EZ2	Middle Marls	Seaham Residue* Roker Dolomite* and Concretionary Limestone*	Edlington Formation (in south and east of province)	Fordon Evaporites (Kirkham Abbey Formation down dip to the east)
	Don	EZ1		Hartlepool Anhydrite*		Hayton Anhydrite Formation
			Lower Magnesian Limestone Hampole Beds Lower Magnesian Limestone Marl Slate	Ford Formation		Cadeby Formation — Sprotbrough Member / Wetherby Member
				Raisby Formation Marl Slate Formation		Marl Slate Formation
LOWER PERMIAN			Basal Sands and breccia	Yellow Sands and Breccias		Basal Permian Breccia

* Not proved in this district.

Farther east, hydrocarbon exploration boreholes, although drilled to considerable depths, were not cored continuously, and the description of strata in some, such as the Cleveland Hills [5354 9844] and East Harlsey No. 1 [4233 9976] boreholes within the district, and Kirkleatham No. 1 Borehole [5878 2128], to the north near Middlesbrough, is based solely on cuttings samples.

From an assessment of the Permian rocks, both at outcrop and in many boreholes in the surrounding districts, Smith (1970) postulated two main depositional provinces for the English Late Permian (Zechstein) — these are the Durham Province in the north, separated by the east–west-trending Cleveland High, from the Yorkshire Province in the south (Figure 4). The Northallerton district straddles the Cleveland High, on each side of which Late Permian sedimentation, up to the base of the Teesside Group (Table 1) took place under appreciably different palaeogeographical conditions. Boreholes which penetrated the Durham Province succession include Kirkleatham No. 1 Oil, Hurworth Place and Halnaby boreholes: those proving Yorkshire Province successions include Leeming Bar (Mowbray Brewery, 1886 and 1909), Aiskew Bank Farm and Kirklington [SE 2879 0913] boreholes (Figure 4). The Cleveland Hills No. 1 (Fowler, 1944) and Harlsey No. 1 [4224 9806] boreholes lie close to the Cleveland axis, but are described within the Yorkshire Province as they provide details, both at depth and down dip, in the Cleveland and east Yorkshire areas (Figure 4).

Hercynian earth movements resulted in faulting, folding and uplift of Carboniferous and older strata. Subsequent weathering and erosion occurred over a period of some 40 million years, before the start of accumulation of the first extensive, thick, postorogenic deposits, in the Late Permian. In the Early Permian, the land surface lay near the western margin of a major inland drainage basin, the floor of which was perhaps 250 m below world sea level (Smith, 1970; Glennie, 1972). This landlocked basin extended across the North Sea, east-north-eastwards into the Baltic and eastwards into Germany and Poland. During the Permian, the British Isles gradually drifted northwards from the equatorial belt into the semi-arid belt of the northern tropics (Scotese and McKerrow, 1990).

Lower Permian

During the Early Permian, the palaeogeography of the region featured a slightly elevated rock pediment, where patches of angular gravel, and wind-blown and water-laid sand accumulated (Smith, 1989; Smith and Taylor, 1992). The western edge was formed by a more elevated rocky ridge, the Proto-Pennines. Dune sands, that drifted across the rocky surface under the influence of prevailing north-easterly winds (Steele, 1981; Chrintz and Clemmensen 1993), have not been recorded in the district, where the lowest Permian rocks of any extent or thickness are of Late Permian age and rest directly upon basal breccias.

BASAL PERMIAN BRECCIA

In Hurworth Place Borehole (Figure 4), the basal breccia is 0.41 m thick and consists of clasts up to 0.05 m long, in a tough matrix of fine- to medium-grained sandstone. The clasts are mainly of Carboniferous limestone, with a few pebbles of sandstone, siltstone and mudstone. Pyrite is abundant, both as a replacement and as a matrix mineral. The breccia rests upon pale grey Carboniferous mudstone, stained purple in places and with ironstone nodules that show considerable reddening; a narrow neptunian dyke, about 2 m deep, contains rounded grains of wind-blown sand.

Reddened Carboniferous strata were also recorded in the Cleveland Hills and Harlsey boreholes and in the latter the basal breccia is 3 m thick. The reddening provides an indication of proximity to the junction between Carboniferous and Permian rocks, or the presence of a former cover of Permian rocks (Smith, 1970, 1974).

In Halnaby Borehole, the basal breccia, about 6.5 m thick, consists of clasts of dolomitised Carboniferous limestone in a gypsum/dolomite matrix. The clasts become coarser towards the base. Interbeds of pebbly dolomite and pebbly dolomitic sandstone with gypsiferous mudstone and siltstone, 2.70 m thick, occur at about 2.60 m above the base.

South-west of the district, at Aiskew Bank Borehole, the basal breccia is only 1.17 m thick, but here too the dominant clast lithology is dolomitised Carboniferous limestone.

Upper Permian

The Late Permian tropical Zechstein Sea was formed by flooding of the former desert basin (Smith, 1970). A complex history of sedimentary infill has been outlined by Smith (1980, 1989) who showed that, as in Germany, there were four main cycles (EZ1–EZ4) of deposition, together with the minor EZ5 cycle and several subcycles. The strata are assigned to five groups (Table 1). Where fully developed, individual cycles show an upward sequence of carbonate–anhydrite–halite–sylvite, the minerals reflecting the precipitation of successively more soluble salts in an evaporitic environment. The deposits of the first two main cycles almost filled the original topographic depression. They are characterised by marginal belts of thick carbonate rocks followed, in the second cycle, by thick basin-centre evaporites. Deposits in cycles EZ3 and EZ4 are chiefly evaporites with a persistent, relatively thin, carbonate wedge in Cycle EZ3. The cycle and group boundaries are not all coincident.

DON GROUP (EZ1)

Over much of north-east England, the basal beds of the Don Group, the **Marl Slate Formation**, comprise grey, laminated, argillaceous dolomite, in beds 0.30 m to 1.5 m thick. They yield carbonaceous plant fragments

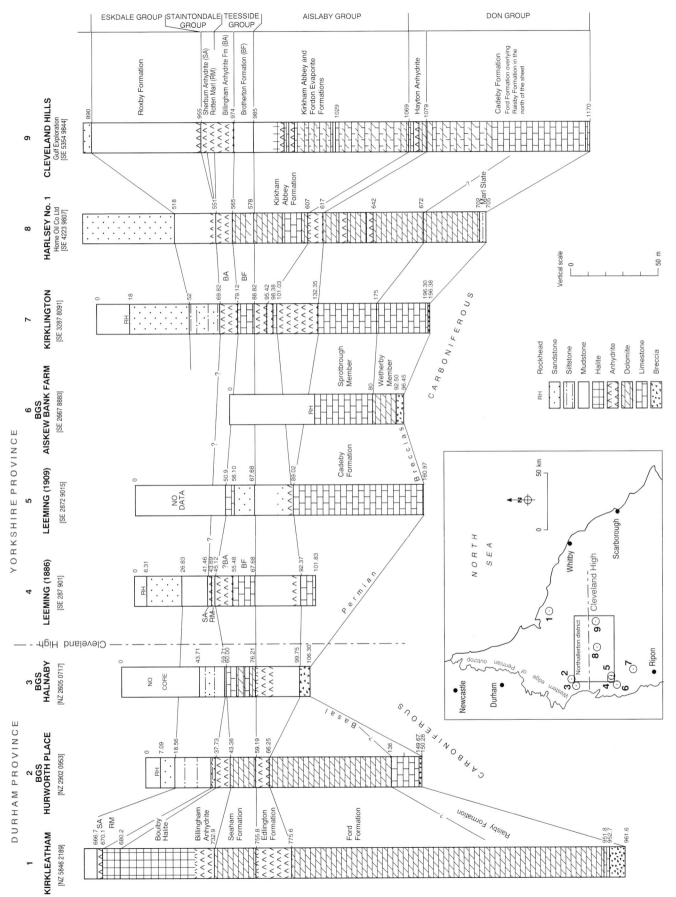

Figure 4 Correlation and classification of boreholes in the Permian strata of the Northallerton district and surrounding areas.

and a distinctive fauna including foraminifers, *Lingula* sp. and fish debris. These beds are the first fully marine deposits laid down after the Zechstein transgression. However at this time, much of the district consisted of an elevated rocky surface, well above the level of the encroaching Zechstein sea, and the Marl Slate is only patchily represented. It may be present in the eastern part of the district; for example in Harlsey No. 1 Borehole, cuttings samples from between 701 and 703 m (2300 and 2309 ft) are described as 'shale, black-brown bituminous', but these are mixed with other lithologies.

The remainder of the first cycle of the Upper Permian rocks of north-east England consists largely of grey and buff dolomites and dolomitic limestones with sporadic calcareous mudstone partings. The dolomite has a saccharoidal texture (sand grade); small pyrite-lined cavities after secondary anhydrite, and veins with galena, occur sporadically throughout, and small numbers of foraminifers and bivalves are present.

Identification of the top of the first (EZ1) cycle is particularly difficult in poorly documented boreholes where the EZ1 carbonates are overlain by EZ2 carbonates. Smith (1989) suggests that EZ2 deposits are over 75 m thick over most of the district, but die out westwards in the East Cowton [31 03] and Great Langton [30 96] areas.

Durham Province: Raisby and Ford formations

The Raisby and Ford formations (formerly the Lower and Middle Magnesian Limestones respectively) (Table 1) were proved in Hurworth Place Borehole, just to the north-west of the district. The Raisby Formation is 14 m thick and is overlain by about 70 m of the Ford Formation; limestones in the latter are distinguished by having a greater proportion, and general predominance, of ooliths.

Yorkshire Province: Cadeby Formation

In Leeming Bar (1886) Borehole, grey limestone between 92.37 and final depth at 101.83 m (Figure 4) has been assigned to this formation (formerly the Lower Magnesian Limestone) by Smith (personal communication, 1992); the Leeming Bar (1909) Borehole proved a thickness of 71.95 m, above the final depth at 160.97 m.

Cleveland Hills No. 1 Borehole proved a total Permian sequence of 280 m, but only 13 per cent was cored, with a recovery of only 40 per cent. The lithologies are comparable with those in other boreholes in the district, although the thicknesses are almost double. Fowler (1944) identified the 158 m of strata between 1012 and 1170 m depth (3322 and 3840 ft) in this borehole as 'Lower Magnesian Limestone'. The lower 65 m consist of grey limestone and are overlain by 93 m of grey and light brown dolomite with anhydrite. Fowler also included, as the topmost beds of the 'Lower Magnesian Limestone', 14 m of dolomite with replacement anhydrite, but these beds are now considered to belong to the Hayton Anhydrite Formation (Smith, 1974, p.130).

In Harlsey No. 1 Borehole, the majority of strata classified as Permian comprise buff to dark brown dolomite. Between 617 and 702 m strata with gypsum and

anhydrite belong to the Cadeby Formation. About 4.4 m of anhydrite between 637.2 to 641.8 m (2090 and 2105 ft) may be a correlative of the Hayton Anhydrite (Smith, 1989, p.297, fig. 8). Smith considers that a further 30 m of beds above this anhydrite, which are also reported to contain anhydrite, may also be classified as Hayton Anhydrite.

In Aiskew Bank Farm Borehole, just to the south-west of the district, strata between rockhead, at 45.2 m, and 92.40 m are assigned to the Cadeby Formation. Unfossiliferous, pale yellow, grey and brown dolomite is present above 68.7 m, and grey dolomite with a moderately rich fauna (Pattison, 1978) occurs between 68.7 m and 92.40 m. Smith (personal communication, 1992) subdivides the formation into two members (Wetherby and Sprotbrough members) at 79.11 m, below a 0.004 m bed of dark grey mudstone, and correlates this boundary with the Hampole Discontinuity (Smith 1968). This discontinuity is not recognised north of the Cleveland High though there is some evidence of shallowing, at the top of the Raisby Formation (Smith, 1989).

Yorkshire Province: Hayton Anhydrite

The Hayton Anhydrite is the topmost unit of the Don Group and the lateral correlative of the lower part of the Edlington formation (Smith et al., 1986). It has been proved in Harlsey No. 1 Borehole (607 to 617 m depth) and in Cleveland Hills Borehole (1069–1079 m) (Figure 4). In Kirklington Borehole to the south of the district, it is recorded between 103.29 and 132.35 m depth (Powell et at., 1992) and is bluish grey in colour, with some dolomite and gypsum in the lower part. It is overlain by a thin breccia and passes up into dolomitic limestone and anhydrite of the Kirkham Abbey Formation.

AISLABY GROUP (EZ2)

In this district, the Aislaby Group, about 40 m thick, comprises marine carbonates and the epicontinental deposits that were formerly the upper part of the Middle Marls (Table 1). The marls were laid down on shelf areas, in a dwindling complex of hypersaline lagoons, restricted shallow shelf seas, sabkhas and salt flats (Smith, 1989, p.299). Farther east, where subsidence was more rapid, carbonates up to 200 m thick formed, together with evaporites. Extensive primary and secondary evaporites were formed towards the end of the cycle, when the rate of halite precipitation exceeded the rate of subsidence and halite filled much of the Zechstein basin. Fluctuation in the position of the boundary between areas of mudstone and carbonate deposition resulted in considerable interfingering of these lithologies.

Durham Province: Edlington Formation

In Hurworth Place Borehole (Figure 4), this formation occurs between 59.19 and 66.25 m depth, and consists of dull grey silty mudstone with rare interbeds of buff grey dolomite, generally interspersed with veins, lenses and nodules of gypsum and anhydrite. Towards the base of the formation, the mudstone contains an increasing amount of disseminated dolomite which shows weak banding. The banding is contorted, with dips of up to 35°. The lowest part of the formation consists of 2.25 m of gypsum.

The Edlington Formation passes eastwards into some or all of the equivalents of the Hayton Anhydrite Formation, the Kirkham Abbey Formation and the Fordon Evaporite Formation (Smith, 1974).

In Halnaby Borehole (Figure 4), between 76.21 and 99.75 m depth, the formation consists of grey mudstone with veins, nodules and beds of gypsum, anhydrite and dolomite. Palynological samples have been examined by Dr G Warrington. Samples MPA 14425 and 14427, from depths of 76.25 and 77.80 m respectively, yielded very sparse organic residues from close to the top of the unit; these include only very sporadic indeterminate bisaccate pollen. Samples MPA 14430, 14432, 14434 and 14436, from depths of 81.10, 89.00, 92.60 and 94.60 m respectively, yielded slightly richer residues that include small assemblages of determinable miospores (spores and pollen of land plants) (Table 2). These assemblages are dominated by saccate pollen that reflect a parent vegetation of conifers. Specimens are most numerous in the lowest sample (MPA 14436); this yielded an assemblage in which bisaccates are the dominant pollen type. The younger assemblages are sparser and in these a monosaccate pollen (*Perisaccus granulosus*) is a more prominent component. The assemblages are comparable in composition with those reported from the Zechstein succession elsewhere in eastern England (Clarke, 1965; Warrington *in* Smith et al., 1973). The presence of *Lueckisporites virkkiae* is indicative of a Late Permian (Kazanian to Tatarian) age (Warrington *in* Smith et al., 1974), within the interval of about 260 to 250 Ma (Forster and Warrington, 1985).

Yorkshire Province: Edlington Formation

A description of 'grey shale, gypsum and clay', between 71.48 m and 90.22 m in the Leeming Bar (1886) Borehole (Figure 4) suggests a correlation with the Edlington Formation. The record of about 9 m of 'amber limestone' between 79.55 and 88.70 m depth suggests the presence of anhydrite (possibly the Hayton Anhydrite) at this locality.

Identification of the correlatives of the Edlington Formation within the sequence of Hayton Anhydrite, Kirkham Abbey and Fordon Evaporite formations, proved in the uncored hydrocarbon exploration boreholes, is difficult. Anhydritic limestone and dolomite present between the depths of 578 and 607 m in Harlsey No. 1 Borehole (Figure 4) are considered by Smith to have similarities with the Kirkham Abbey Formation. In the Cleveland Hills Borehole, Fowler (1944, p.199) considered that the 'Middle Permian Marls' are 29 m thick and occur between the depths of 984 and 1013 m (3228 and 3322 ft). These beds comprise:

	Thickness m
Mudstone, anhydritic, dolomitic	3.2
Halite	5.9
Anhydrite, with thin red marl beds	10.1
Anhydrite and gypsum interbedded with grey dolomitic mudstone	9.8

Table 2 Miospores from the Permian of the Halnaby Borehole.

Miospore taxa	Preparation (MPA) numbers			
	14436	14434	14432	14430
Taeniaesporites labdacus	+			
Falcisporites zapfei	?			
Protohaploxypinus sp.	+			
Protohaploxypinus jacobii	?			
Striatopodocarpites sp.	?			
Crustaesporites globosus	?			
Taeniaesporites angulistriatus	+			
Vittatina hiltonensis	+			
Labiisporites granulatus	+		+	
Lunatisporites sp.	+	+	+	+
Protohaploxypinus chaloneri	+		cf.	+
Protohaploxypinus microcorpus	?	cf.	cf.	+
Klausipollenites schaubergeri	+		+	+
Lueckisporites virkkiae var. A	+	+	+	+
Lueckisporites virkkiae var. B	?		+	+
Perisaccus granulosus	+	+	+	+
Striatoabieites sp.			+	
Striatopodocarpites antiquus			?	?
Taeniaesporites albertae				?
Paravesicaspora splendens				+
Converrucosisporites sp.				?
indeterminate bisaccates	+	+	+	+

However, Smith (personal communication, 1992) considers that 10 m of 'blue grey anhydritic marlstone' that overlie these beds, and dolomite and dolomitic limestone with inclusions of anhydrite that underlie them, may also be correlated with the Edlington Formation.

TEESSIDE GROUP (EZ3)

The Zechstein Sea was probably only 5 to 20 m deep in this area during EZ3 deposition (Smith, 1989). Sedimentation was more uniform than at any time previously during the Late Permian, occurring on a broad shelf, in a tideless tropical inland sea, and with the shoreline lying an estimated 15 km west of the district. The carbonate rocks, mainly thin-bedded limestone and dolomite, are 11 to 16 m thick, and are unusual in displaying little lithological and faunal variation. Apart from a slight thinning across the Cleveland High, they do not differ appreciably between the Durham and Yorkshire provinces. Sedimentary structures, such as low-amplitude ripples and small-scale cross-lamination, suggest environmental conditions of low to moderate energy levels. However, widespread sheets of algal (*Calcinema*) and bivalve debris may have been produced by periodic storms.

The carbonate rocks are overlain by an evaporite sequence, which formed as the salinity of the Zechstein Sea increased in response to further shallowing. The main evaporite, the Billingham Anhydrite, is 7 to 9 m thick over much of the district. Its approximate western margin in north-east England coincides with the western limit of the district.

Durham Province: the Seaham Formation

This formation (formerly part of the Upper Magnesian Limestone; Table 1) comprises grey, pale grey and buff-grey, fine-grained dolomite and limestone. The rock is thinly bedded, with sporadic cross-lamination. Bedding planes show thin laminae of dark grey carbonaceous and/or argillaceous dolomite. Gypsum occurs locally, but pyrite is common and is associated particularly with scattered, poorly preserved shells of bivalves, such as *Liebea* sp. and *Schizodus* sp.; *Calcinema permiana* is fairly common. In Hurworth Place Borehole (Figure 4), the Seaham Formation occurs between 43.36 and 59.19 m depth, and has clearly defined lower and upper boundaries. In the Halnaby Borehole, the formation lies between 60.00 and 76.21 m, and consists mainly of grey and buff, fine-grained, partly oolitic dolomite and limestone; it contains *Calcinema* and abundant bivalves.

The **Billingham Anhydrite Formation** rests on the Seaham Formation in Hurworth Place Borehole and is 7.6 m thick (Figure 4; Smith and Moore, 1973). It comprises pale grey, translucent, finely crystalline anhydrite underlain and overlain by grey-brown gypsum; some interbedding also occurs. In Halnaby Borehole, the Billingham Anhydrite is represented by a residue comprising 0.30 m of mottled, red, brown and grey, partially brecciated limestone.

Yorkshire Province: Brotherton Formation

In Leeming Bar (1886) Borehole, grey limestone between 55.48 and 67.68 m is attributed to this formation (Smith, personal communication 1992). The overlying 10 m of 'conglomerate, gypsum and shaly stone' may represent the sulphate phase of EZ3, represented by the Billingham Anhydrite Formation.

In the Cleveland Hills Borehole, the 'Upper Magnesian Limestone' (Brotherton Formation) was described by Fowler (1944, p.199) as a 'brown earthy dolomite', lying between 973.17 m to 984.14 m (3192 and 3228 ft). The succeeding 10 m of anhydrite with dolomitic mudstone and limestone may be a correlative of the Billingham Anhydrite Formation.

The Harlsey No. 1 Borehole proved 12.5 m of dolomite and limestone of the Brotherton Formation, overlain by 9 m of grey and white, finely crystalline anhydrite belonging to the Billingham Anhydrite Formation (Figure 4).

Although halite deposits have been proved in the Cleveland area their lateral extent is not known, and the western boundary of the EZ3 **Boulby Halite** in north-east England may coincide with the north-east of the district (Smith, 1989).

STAINTONDALE GROUP (including EZ4)

The rocks of this group in north-east England have been classified (Smith et al., 1986) into several formations (Table 1), but the **Rotten Marl** and the **Sherburn Anhydrite** are the only formations tentatively recognised within this district. The higher formations of the group are transgressed by the Roxby Formation.

Yorkshire Province

In the Leeming Bar (1886) Borehole, some 1.30 m of 'red shaly stone with gypsum, red clay and 'Fuller's Earth'' are interpreted by Smith (personal communication, 1992) as a possible representative of the Rotten Marl Formation. The overlying 15 m, described as 'red hard stone' with 'gypsum', he interprets as a possible equivalent of the Sherburn Anhydrite Formation.

ESKDALE GROUP (including EZ5)

In the final (EZ5) phase of Zechstein deposition in north-east England, there was a basinwards expansion of the marginal plains which had flanked the Zechstein Sea throughout most of the Late Permian. Mainly water-laid silts, clays and subordinate sands, forming the Roxby Formation, extended towards the basin centre. In time, coarser sediments gradually prograded diachronously into these areas to form the Sherwood Sandstone Group. In the absence of biostratigraphical evidence the position of the Permian–Triassic system boundary cannot be identified within this continental succession. Smith (1989, p.308) considers that it lies within the proximal clastic rocks of the Sherwood Sandstone Group in the Yorkshire area, but that farther north and east in Durham and Cleveland it passes basinwards into the finer grained distal beds of the Roxby Formation. In this district, the Roxby Formation–Sherwood Sandstone Group transition is considered to approximate to the Permian–Triassic boundary.

ROXBY FORMATION

The dominant lithologies comprise dull red mudstone and siltstone, formerly referred to as Upper Permian Marls in the Yorkshire Province.

Durham Province

In Hurworth Place Borehole (Figure 4), the Roxby Formation comprises some 17 m of dark red, tough, micaceous mudstone with thin partings of fine-grained micaceous sandstone, overlying 2 m of red sandstone and siltstone (Smith and Moore, 1973). Clay flakes and desiccation cracks are common and gypsum veins and sporadic nodules also occur. The mudstone is marked by grey-green reduction spots. Gypsum veins and rare anhydrite nodules are present towards the base. The top of the formation is gradational by intercalation of sandstone into the Sherwood Sandstone Group.

Halnaby Borehole proved over 16 m of red-brown silty mudstone, with subordinate red-brown siltstone and fine-grained sandstone. This lithology is typical of the gradational boundary between the Staintondale and Eskdale groups.

The top of the Roxby Formation is difficult to define because of the gradational nature of the passage between the 'red marls' and the Sherwood Sandstone Group.

Yorkshire Province

In Cleveland Hills No. 1 Borehole, Fowler (1944) attributed 47 m of 'red marls' to the 'Upper Permian Marls'.

Some 21 m of 'red marl, maroon shale and sandstone laminae together with gypsum', are classified in the Harlsey Borehole as belonging to the Roxby Formation.

COLLAPSE STRUCTURES

In the south-west of the district, between Leeming Bar [290 900] and Kirkby [280 960] (Figure 5), numerous depressions occur on surface drift deposits and some contain water after periods of heavy rain. They range in size from a few metres to some 300 m in length, and up to 100 m across. Some are up to 10 m deep and are reported by local farmers to be sinking sporadically. Such features have been described elsewhere in north-east England by Cameron (1881), Kendall and Wroot (1924), Smith (1972), Cooper (1986; 1995), Powell et al. (1992) and Cooper and Burgess (1993). They have been interpreted as collapse structures caused by dissolution of the evaporites within the Edlington and Roxby formations. In this district, the majority of the collapse hollows occur over the subcrop of the Brotherton Formation. They extend down dip and some small hollows are found on the lowest beds of the Sherwood Sandstone Group.

The juxtaposition of porous sands and gravels in a topographic low, such as the valley of the Scurf Beck near Leeming Bar, provides the optimum conditions for movement of groundwater in the phreatic zone in the Upper Permian strata of this district. It is there that many collapse structures were noted.

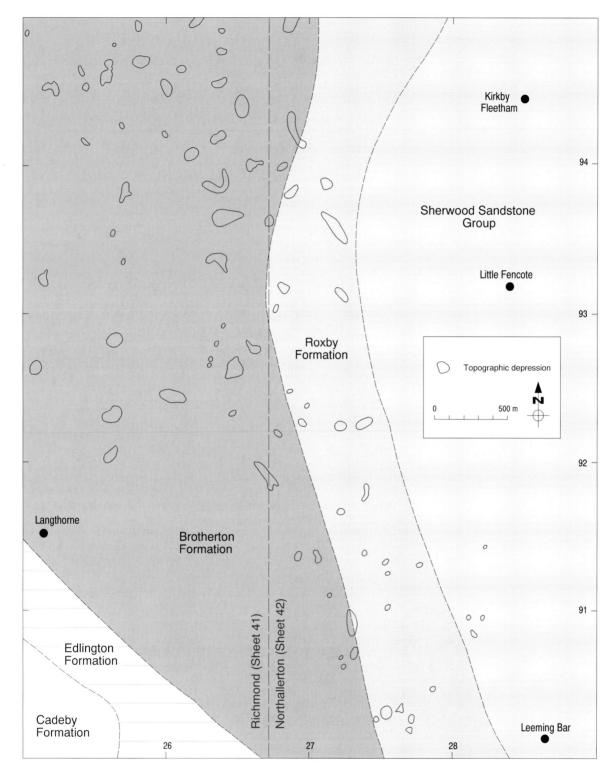

Figure 5   Topographic depressions caused by dissolution of evaporites south-west of Catterick.

FOUR

Triassic

The Triassic deposits of the district accumulated along the western margin of the epicontinental North Sea Basin (Warrington and Ivimey Cook, 1992). Sedimentation began around 250 million years ago and continued intermittently for some 45 million years (Forster and Warrington, 1985). Although underlying most of the district and forming rockhead in over 50 per cent of the area, the Triassic rocks are largely obscured by drift deposits and therefore poorly documented. They have been partially proved by numerous boreholes drilled for water, but their total thickness in the district has been proved only by Harlsey No. 1 and Cleveland Hills No. 1 boreholes.

The British Trias includes three groups: in ascending order, the Sherwood Sandstone Group, the Mercia Mudstone Group, and the Penarth Group (Warrington et al., 1980). In this district, the Sherwood Sandstone Group (formerly the Bunter and the Keuper Sandstone), consists of up to 350 m of red, yellow and grey fine-grained sandstone. The Mercia Mudstone Group (formerly the Keuper Marl) is some 260 m thick and comprises mostly red, purple, green and grey silty mudstone and siltstone. Gypsum veining and banding together with sporadic gypsum nodules is common. The Penarth Group (formerly the Rhaetic) is 12 m thick and was proved in the Winton Manor Borehole which was specially cored for the purposes of the Northallerton resurvey, and in several boreholes near Stokesley. The highest beds assigned to the Trias comprise the basal part of the Lias Group, below the lowest occurrence of the ammonite *Psiloceras* (Cope et al., 1980a; Warrington et al., 1980).

Macrofossils are unknown from the Sherwood Sandstone and Mercia Mudstone groups of the district but miospores (spores and pollen of land plants) have aided correlation in the Mercia Mudstone Group. A miospore assemblage from beds about 1 km north-west of Hutton Rudby is indicative of an early Mid-Triassic (Anisian) age. An assemblage from beds higher in the succession, 1.5 km east of Hutton Rudby, may be of late Ladinian or early Carnian age (late Mid to early Late Triassic). Miospores of Rhaetian (late Late Triassic) age occur, with marine organic-walled microplankton, in the Penarth Group and basal Redcar Mudstone Formation (Lias Group) in the Winton Manor Borehole.

The boundary between the Permian and Triassic systems cannot be precisely defined. The arbitrary dividing line adopted in the district is between the dominantly arenaceous beds of the Sherwood Sandstone Group and the dominantly argillaceous beds of the underlying Roxby Formation.

SHERWOOD SANDSTONE GROUP

The subcrop of the group beneath the drift deposits is some 9 km wide and extends from the western margin of the district to the outskirts of Northallerton. Near Little Smeaton, the crop swings north-eastwards through Appleton Wiske and Crathorne where the highest beds are exposed in the banks of the River Leven. Farther east, in Harlsey No. 1 Borehole, 248 m of red micaceous sandstone was proved. This thickness increases to 277 m in the Cleveland Hills No. 1 Borehole towards the eastern margin of the district.

Sediments of the Sherwood Sandstone Group accumulated on a broad plain of low relief; periods of desiccation and exposure alternated with shallow-water deposition in a semi-arid continental climate (Warrington, 1974, p.150). They are a finer-grained equivalent of the 'Bunter Pebble Beds' of Yorkshire and the East Midlands, and were referred to as 'Keuper Sandstone' by Fox-Strangways et al. (1886). The dominant direction of sediment transport was towards the north-east (Smith and Francis, 1967).

Details

The thick superficial deposits of the York and Teesside plains have restricted the exploitation of the Sherwood Sandstone Group to one quarry within the district. This quarry [348 921] on the west bank of the River Wiske, on the western outskirts of Northallerton, has been used as a refuse tip, but at the time of the original survey red sandstone was recorded. The few remaining exposures are limited to where the rivers Tees and Leven have cut down through the superficial deposits.

Red, fine-grained, cross-bedded and thinly bedded sandstone occupies much of the bed of the River Tees near Sockburn [341 089]. The dip is slight and variable, and the strata here are near the base of the group.

Strata near the top of the Sherwood Sandstone Group are exposed in the banks of the River Leven north-east of Crathorne. Red-brown, fine-grained, massive, cross-bedded sandstone crops out beneath 3 m of river deposits near Crathorne Hall [4469 0835]. The sandstone is over 3 m thick, and contains numerous red mudstone clasts.

Two kilometres upstream adjacent to Middleton Wood [4590 0960], just north of the district, a section exposes the boundary between the Sherwood Sandstone Group and the overlying Mercia Mudstone Group. Mr D Land recorded the details which were classified by Smith (1980); he assigned these passage beds to the Seaton Carew Formation.

The section shows:

	Thickness m
MERCIA MUDSTONE GROUP	
Mudstone, pale purplish red, silty, micaceous; green in lowest centimetre	2.74
Unconformity	

	Thickness m
SEATON CAREW FORMATION	
Sandstone, pale bluish green; scattered, large, wind-rounded grains; stellate crystals of malachite (green)	0.30
Gap – ? Unconformity	0.30
SHERWOOD SANDSTONE GROUP (UNDIVIDED)	
Sandstone, red, fine-grained; cross-bedding trends north-west–south-east	1.22

MERCIA MUDSTONE GROUP

The outcrop of the Mercia Mudstone Group is between 4 and 5 km wide, stretching from Northallerton in the south to Stokesley in the north-east of the district. The strata are largely concealed by superficial deposits, but some 200 m have been proved in Cleveland Hills No. 1 Borehole (Figure 6) and in Harlsey No. 1 Borehole. The Blue Anchor Formation occurred at the top of the group (p.18).

The base of the group is unconformable on the underlying Sherwood Sandstone Group and this boundary has been correlated with the Hardegsen Disconformity (Warrington, 1970) which occurs in the Middle Bunter succession of Germany and is recognised elsewhere in the British Isles. It marks an abrupt change in deposition from the largely arenaceous and fluvial beds of the Sherwood Sandstone Group to the mainly argillaceous and evaporitic deposits of the Mercia Mudstone Group. The dominant non-fluvial facies of the Mercia Mudstone Group were deposited in water of marine origin which had access to the former continental basins of Germany and the North Sea region (Warrington, 1970). Remoteness from the marine source in southern Europe resulted in the depositional environments in the basin being subject to continental as well as marine influences.

The Mercia Mudstone Group consists predominantly of red-brown, purplish red and sporadically grey-green mottled silty mudstone. It may be massive or finely laminated, or more commonly the two bedding varieties are interbedded. Clay minerals typically form up to 80 per cent of the mudstone, and include illite, chlorite and smectite — an association indicating deposition in fairly tranquil basic saline or hypersaline water (Jeans, 1978). Sporadic rainfall on the low-lying land areas resulted in arenaceous sediment being carried into the basin to form thin siltstones and sandstones, referred to as 'skerries' (Smith, 1910).

Gypsum and anhydrite occur as thin beds, nodular masses and ramifying secondary veins in the red mudstones. A particularly thick bed of gypsum, only a few metres below the top of the group, was worked near Brompton. These beds, which correspond to the Newark gypsum of east Nottinghamshire (Warrington, 1974), may provide future reserves in the district.

In the Cleveland Hills No. 1 Borehole, Fowler (1944, p.195) recorded a conglomerate 1.5 m thick, some 60 m above the base of the group. However, this lithology has been re-examined and is now considered to consist of chippings from a cement plug, probably associated with the borehole casing.

Details

Natural exposures of the Mercia Mudstone Group are largely limited to small sections in the River Leven near Hutton Rudby (Plate 1). Where immediately overlain by a few metres of glacial or river deposits, these strata commonly show contorted bedding which is attributed to cryoturbation during the Pleistocene. Where normally bedded, the dip is slight and generally to the south-east, but small-scale faults with hades of between 30 and 40° have been noted.

The most westerly section [4631 0709] in the banks of the River Leven exposes a massive green siltstone, 0.30 m thick, overlying red and green mudstones. A sample [MPA 17813] from the siltstone was processed for palynomorphs, and a small organic residue dominated by miospores was recovered. Associated detrital organic matter comprises brown and black material, including structured woody phytoclasts. The miospores are yellow to yellow-brown in colour and are mostly rather poorly preserved; the following were observed by Dr G Warrington: indeterminate trilete spore (granulate), *? Tsugaepollenites oriens*, *Alisporites* sp., *A.* cf. *circulicorpus*, *A. grauvogeli*, *A. toralis*, *Voltziaceaesporites heteromorpha*, *Sulcatisporites* sp., *Protodiploxypinus fastidiosus*, *Illinites* sp., *Triadispora staplini*, *?Angustisulcites gorpii*, *A. grandis*, *Lunatisporites* sp., *L.* cf. *discrepans*, *Striatoabieites balmei* and indeterminate bisaccate pollen.

This assemblage consists almost exclusively of bisaccate pollen. The association of *Angustisulcites* spp. with *?Tsugaepollenites oriens* is indicative of an early Mid-Triassic (Anisian) age, and of a correlation with the Kirkham Mudstone Formation in the Mercia Mudstone Group succession of west Lancashire (Wilson and Evans, 1990, fig. 14).

An exposure [4642 0682] 1 km west of Hutton Rudby, is unusual in that the dip is up to 8° towards the north-east. The section shows:

	Thickness m
Siltstone and sandstone, pale green (skerry)	0.05
Mudstone, red, and green siltstone; interlaminated	0.30
Mudstone, green, silty	0.30
Mudstone, red, silty, massive; irregular pale green patches	1.50
Gap	c.0.05
Mudstone, red, silty, massive	1.50
Mudstone, green, silty; with fine siltstone laminae at base	0.30
Mudstone, red, silty	1.00

About 1 km to the east of Hutton Rudby, a section [4815 0619] in the south bank of the River Leven exposes 4.98 m of beds towards the top of the Mercia Mudstone Group. These beds are mostly finely laminated and show penecontemporaneous deformation at several levels. The section is as follows:

	Thickness m
Mudstone, red, silty, massive; rare green reduction spots	2.00
Mudstone, red, silty, massive; interbedded and interlaminated with green siltstone and mudstone, sporadically showing contorted laminae	2.98

A section [4832 0640], in the north bank of the River Leven, near Horsepark Wood, exposes 1.5 m of pale grey,

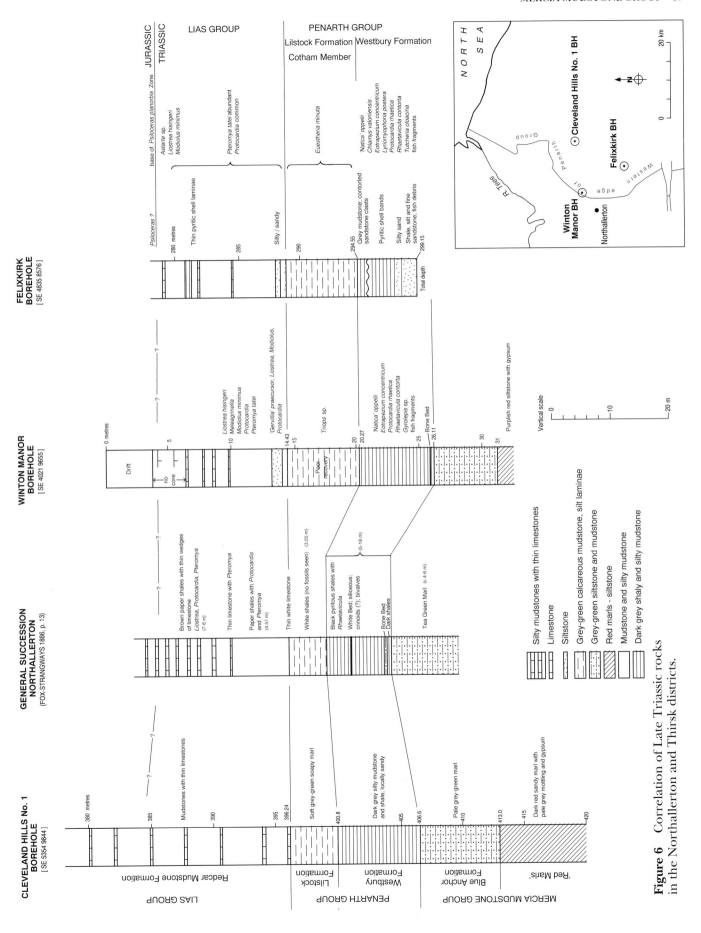

Figure 6 Correlation of Late Triassic rocks in the Northallerton and Thirsk districts.

green and red mudstone underlying a metre of river deposits. A sample [MPA 17817] from the mudstone was processed for palynomorphs and yielded a small organic residue dominated by miospores; associated detrital organic matter comprises yellow, brown and black material, including structured woody phytoclasts. The miospores vary from yellow to very dark brown in colour; Dr G Warrington recorded the following, though the generally poor standard of preservation impedes satisfactory determination in many cases: indeterminate trilete spores, ?*Kuglerina meieri*, ? cf. *Vallasporites* sp., ?*V. ignacii*, *Alisporites* sp., *A. grauvogeli*, *A. toralis*, cf. *Klausipollenites schaubergeri*, *Protodiploxypinus* sp., ?*P.* cf. *fastidiosus*, *Ellipsovelatisporites plicatus*, ?cf. *Quadraeculina* sp., ?*Vesicaspora fuscus*, ?*Triadispora* sp., ?*T.* cf. *plicata*, ?*Angustisulcites* sp., ?*A klausii*, *Lunatisporites* sp., *Striatoabieites* sp, *S. balmei* and indeterminate bisaccate pollen.

The trilete spores are extremely scarce and include virtually opaque specimens that may be reworked from Carboniferous deposits. Many specimens in the remainder of the assemblage, which consists predominantly of bisaccate pollen, are not satisfactorily determinable. This component has, however, a post-Anisian aspect, and may be late Ladinian or early Carnian (late Mid- to early Late Triassic) in age, on the basis of the occurrence of *Ellipsovelatisporites plicatus* with possible specimens of *Vallasporites*, *Angustisulcites* and *Parillinites*. The material recovered from this sample does not permit a more satisfactory dating.

The highest beds of the Mercia Mudstone Group crop out in irregular drift-free patches along the rising ground east of Northallerton and Brompton. There are no exposures, but hand-auger holes penetrated a metre or so of brown silty clays which overlie red and green weathered mudstones.

The area between Highfields Farm [385 964] and Hill House Farm [394 964] is pitted with numerous depressions marking disused gypsum workings, which date from the middle of the last century.

Near the top of the Mercia Mudstone Group, a pronounced change in the overall colour from red to green marks the base of the **Blue Anchor Formation**. The formation has not been mapped in the district, but is 4.89 m thick in Winton Manor Borehole (Figure 6). It comprises pale grey-green mudstones and siltstones with thin, dark grey, shaly and pyritic mudstone partings. The distinctive colour allows recognition of the formation in drift-free soil and subsoil east of Northallerton, near Helmersdale Farm [3871 9238], Bank Close [3882 9374] and Rabbit Hill [4135 9700]. One metre of green mudstone was recorded in the backwall of a landslip [3888 9473] near Harrogate House. The top of the formation is a disconformity with evidence of weathering and erosion prior to deposition of the succeeding Westbury Formation of the Penarth Group (Raymond, 1955).

The Blue Anchor Formation has not yielded fossils but, from its position beneath the Rhaetian (Late Triassic) Penarth Group and some distance above the beds that are of late Ladinian–early Carnian age, it is assessed as Late Triassic, possibly Norian–Rhaetian. Palynology samples from Winton Manor Borehole (Table 3) proved barren, in contrast with those from the succeeding Westbury Formation.

PENARTH GROUP

This group comprises deposits that reflect a marine transgression which established marine conditions throughout much of Britain during the latest Triassic. The group is divided into the Westbury Formation, with dark grey silty mudstones, siltstones and very thin limestones, and the overlying Lilstock Formation, which contains more calcareous beds represented by the Cotham Member (Lott and Warrington, 1988).

From scarce exposures to the east of Northallerton, Fox-Strangways et al. (1886) compiled a succession which compares closely with that of the Winton Manor Borehole and other boreholes farther east (Figure 6).

Westbury Formation

Dark grey silty mudstones up to 6 m thick, with siltstones, thin sandstones and very thin limestones, dominate this formation, which penetrates downwards into fissures on the weathered and eroded surface of the underlying Blue Anchor Formation (Raymond, 1955). Some of the Westbury Formation mudstones are shaly and may be laminated. Low in the sequence a 0.02 m-thick bed of micaceous, sandy siltstone with abundant fish fragments was recorded as a 'Bone Bed' (Fox-Strangways et al., 1886); such beds are common in the British Isles around this level but are probably not contemporaneous. The formation contains a marine bivalve fauna dominated by *Rhaetavicula contorta*, together with *Eotrapezium concentricum* and *Protocardia rhaetica*, and mudstones yield fish fragments, especially in the lower part of the formation. In Winton Manor Borehole some fragments of '*Natica*' *oppelii* were identified; this small gastropod is commonly preserved as a pyritic film. Dark grey laminated silty mudstones crop out [4099 9646] near Winton and 'paper-shales' were recorded [4136 9809] near Harlsey Castle. One of the few Mesozoic cores taken in the Cleveland Hills No. 1 Borehole proved the Westbury Formation, which showed a lithology and fauna very similar to those in the Winton Manor Borehole.

Lilstock Formation, Cotham Member

These beds, which are up to 6 m thick, are characterised by pale grey to greenish grey, calcareous mudstones, commonly with paler, off-white, silty and micaceous partings and thin lenses. The mudstones contain some swelling micas, and slump structures occur. Fossils are generally very rare; in Winton Manor Borehole a specimen of the rare notostracan arthropod *Triops* sp. was recorded but no estheriids were seen. Estheriids are common in these beds in the Felixkirk Borehole (Ivimey-Cook and Powell, 1991) to the south of the district (Figure 6), but they were not recorded from Cleveland Hills No. 1 Borehole. The member is interpreted as representing a more 'lagoonal' phase of sedimentation than the earlier beds.

LIAS GROUP

Redcar Mudstone Formation

The basal 10 m or so of these beds are of Triassic age, but the formation continues into the Jurassic and they are therefore described with the remainder of the Lias Group (Chapter 5).

Table 3 Distribution and relative abundances of palynomorphs in the Penarth Group and basal Lias Group, Winton Manor Borehole.

Depth in borehole (metres)

Palynology sample horizons and preparation (MPA) numbers

MIOSPORES:

Leptolepidites argenteaeformis
Granuloperculatipollis rudis
Geopollis zwolinskae
Rhaetipollis germanicus
Chasmatosporites apertus + C. magnolioides
Lunatisporites rhaeticus
Ovalipollis pseudoalatus

Microreticulatisporites fuscus
Vitreisporites pallidus
Acanthotriletes ovalis + A. varius
Deltoidospora spp. + Concavisporites spp.

Quadraeculina anellaeformis
Alisporites spp.+ indeterminate disacciatriletes

Ricciisporites tuberculatus

Classopollis torosus + C. sp.

Gliscopollis meyeriana

Vesicaspora fuscus
Cingulizonates rhaeticus
Carnisporites anteriscus + C. lecythus + C. spiniger
Protohaploxypinus cf. microcorpus
Camarozonosporites golzowensis
Densosporites sp.
Perinosporites thuringiacus
Limbosporites lundbladii
Lycopodiacidites rhaeticus + L. rugulatus
Convolutispora microrugulata + C. sp.

Converrucosisporites luebbenensis
Polycingulatisporites bicollateralis
Protodiploxypinus sp.
Tsugaepollenites ? pseudomassulae
Semiretisporis gothae + S. maljavkinae
Kraeuselisporites reissingeri

Aratrisporites cf. palettae
Perinopollenites elatoides
Cyathidites australis + C. minor
Kyrtomisporis laevigatus + K. speciosus
Porcellispora longdonensis
Calamospora mesozoica

Todisporites major + T. minor
Osmundacidites wellmanii + Baculatisporites sp.
Verrucosisporites sp.
Cyadopites sp.
Retitriletes austroclavatidites + R. sp.
Contignisporites problematicus
Granulatisporites sp.
Nevesisporites bigranulatus
Zebrasporites interscriptus

ORGANIC-WALLED MICRO-PLANKTON AND OTHER REMAINS

Rhaetogonyaulax rhaetica
? Beaumontella caminuspina
Dapcodinium priscum
Micrhystridium lymense + M. sp.
Beaumontella langii
Cymatiosphaera polypartita
Tasmanites sp.
Crassosphaera sp.
Foraminifer test linings
Botryococcus

RELATIVE ABUNDANCE OF MIOSPORES (WHITE) TO OTHER PALYNOMORPHS (BLACK)

LITHOSTRATIGRAPHY

Key

○	0-1%
●	>1%-5%
⊢⊢⊢⊢ 50%	>5% (BAR SCALE)
?	Questionable record
cf.	Comparable form present
P	Present (not counted)

BLUE ANCHOR FORMATION	WESTBURY FORMATION	LILSTOCK FORMATION		REDCAR MUDSTONE FORMATION
			COTHAM MEMBER	
MERCIA MUDSTONE GROUP	PENARTH GROUP			LIAS GROUP

Palynology of the Penarth Group

Dr G Warrington documented the palynology of this sequence from Winton Manor Borehole. Samples from this section yielded palynomorph assemblages comprising miospores (spores and pollen of land plants) and smaller numbers of marine organic-walled microplankton (Table 3).

Miospore associations from the Westbury Formation are characterised by the presence of *Ricciisporites tuberculatus* (dominant), with *Classopollis* spp., *Gliscopollis meyeriana*, *Ovalipollis pseudoalatus*, *Rhaetipollis germanicus*, and disacciatriletes, including *Alisporites*; other taxa occur in small numbers (e.g. *Geopollis zwolinskae* and *Lunatisporites rhaeticus*) or less consistently (e.g. *Quadraeculina anellaeformis* and *Acanthotriletes* spp.). An increase in diversity in the miospore associations in the upper part of the formation reflects the appearance, in small numbers, of representatives of a number of trilete spore genera. This trend continues upwards into the Cotham Member, assemblages from which lack *Rhaetipollis germanicus* and have fewer *Ovalipollis pseudoalatus* and *Ricciisporites tuberculatus* than those from the Westbury Formation. Disacciatrilete pollen are, however, more abundant in Cotham Member assemblages which are characterised by the presence of fairly numerous *Acanthotriletes* spp., *Baculatisporites* spp., *Calamospora mesozoica*, *Cingulizonates rhaeticus*, *Concavisporites* spp., *Convolutispora microrugulata*, *Cyathidites* spp., *Deltoidospora* spp. and *Osmundacidites wellmanii*, together with smaller numbers of other trilete spores such as *Carnisporites* spp., *Kyrtomisporis* spp., *Limbosporites lundbladii*, *Lycopodiacidites* spp. and *Todisporites* spp.

The upward change in the composition of the miospore associations reflects a change from a parent flora dominated by conifers, that produced the pollen taxa which dominate the Westbury Formation assemblages, to one with a greater proportion of pteridophytes which produced the trilete spores that are more prominent in Cotham Member assemblages. The appearance and diversification of miospore associations in the Penarth Group reflects the response of the contemporary land flora to geographical changes and climatic amelioration associated with a marine incursion into the region in latest Triassic times. The absence of miospores in the Blue Anchor Formation and their presence in the succeeding Westbury Formation provides evidence of a decrease in aridity from Mercia Mudstone Group to Penarth Group times. More specifically, the presence of a bryophyte spore (*Porcellispora longdonensis*) in some Cotham Member assemblages testifies to the existence of damp terrestrial environments; this is further indicated by the increase in abundance and diversity of trilete spores derived from other plants, such as ferns, that required damp habitats.

The presence of *Quadraeculina anellaeformis* and *Tsugaepollenites? pseudomassulae*, in association with taxa including *Rhaetipollis germanicus*, *Ovalipollis pseudoalatus* and *Ricciisporites tuberculatus*, is indicative of a latest Triassic (Rhaetian) age. Evidence of marine incursion at this time is provided by the organic-walled microplankton present in the Penarth Group palynomorph assemblages. These include dinoflagellate cysts, principally *Rhaetogonyaulax rhaetica*, and the acritarchs *Cymatiosphaera* and *Micrhystridium*, which indicate marine aqueous environments. Tasmanitid algae and a colonial alga (*Botryococcus*) also indicate aqueous depositional environments, though the latter may signify brackish conditions.

The palynology of the Penarth Group in eastern England has also been documented from Felixkirk Borehole, some 10.5 km farther south, in the Thirsk district (Warrington *in* Powell et al., 1992), and from the Cockle Pits and Blyborough boreholes, 84 and 113 km to the south-east respectively, in the Humberside area (Lott and Warrington, 1988; Warrington *in* Gaunt et al., 1992). The Winton Manor assemblages are comparable in composition with those documented from these sections. However, a decrease in the abundance of organic-walled microplankton relative to miospores is apparent from the sections in the Humberside area, northwards to those in the Thirsk and Northallerton districts. This trend may reflect an approach towards the margin of marine influence in more northerly districts, (Warrington and Ivimey-Cook, 1992).

FIVE

Jurassic

The Jurassic rocks crop out in the south-east of the district and extend westwards as far as Northallerton. They form an eastwards-tilted block that has been folded into a series of elongate basins and domes; the most important of these is the Cleveland Anticline. The oldest beds in the west comprise soft mudstones, commonly masked by drift deposits in the lower ground. The younger Jurassic strata contain more resistant sandstones, limestones and ironstones interbedded with the shales. These higher beds form the high moorlands of the Cleveland and Hambleton hills (Plate 2). They give rise to bold, north and west-facing scarps, and to spectacular cliff scenery where they reach the east coast between Staithes and Filey.

Recent geological exploration has proved that Jurassic rocks extend beyond the North Yorkshire coastline and crop out on the floor of the North Sea over a larger area than that known onshore in the Cleveland area. In Teesside and Cleveland areas, the Jurassic rocks are some 700 m thick. The overall classification adopted here to describe these Jurassic beds is shown in the table inside the front cover. The relative ages and former names attributed to different parts of the sequence are shown in Tables 4 and 5; some of the names still in use were introduced by William Smith nearly 200 years ago, in the pioneer days of English stratigraphy. Much of the subsequent refinement of lithostratigraphical and biostratigraphical nomenclature and the correlation of strata has been done by study of sections exposed along the coast. Inland exposures are more fragmentary and are commonly inaccessible. Studies of the successive faunas in these rocks and their comparison with other areas has produced a biostratigraphical framework, based principally on the occurrence of one group of marine cephalopods, the ammonites. These were evolving rapidly and are of great use in establishing age correlation in the Lower Jurassic, and in the late Middle and Upper Jurassic rocks of this area. Units of correlation (zones and subzones), with a resolution averaging less than 0.5 million years, are recognised.

Other taxa of animals and plants are now being studied, and used for refining parts of the biostratigraphical sequence so producing parallel zonations. These can be particularly important where ammonites do not occur or are rare, as in much of the local early Mid Jurassic, and in boreholes where ammonites may not be recovered. They also provide some insight into the environment of deposition and palaeogeography.

Early research by Young and Bird (1822, 1828), Sedgwick (1826), Phillips (1829, 1858), Simpson (1855), Wright (1860) and Blake (1872) was summarised by Tate and Blake (1876) and Fox-Strangways (1892). In this century, commerical drilling for gas, oil and other minerals has added to our knowledge of the sequence (Arkell, 1929–1937; Howarth, 1955; Wright, 1968). Studies of microfossils have enabled other divisions to be made. The ammonite zones were established from specimens collected from the excellent exposures of the

Plate 2 Raisdale and Cringle Moor [5350 0300]. The valley is floored by mudstones and sandstones of the Lower Jurassic. The skyline is dominated by an outlier of the Middle Jurassic Ravenscar Group in which sandstone is the dominant lithology.

Table 4   Classification of the Lower Jurassic (Lias Group) strata of the Northallerton district.

Series	Stage	Yorkshire coast				Northallerton district
		Fox-Strangways and Barrow (1915)	Hemingway (1974)	Cope et al. (1980a)	Powell (1984) and Knox (1984)	
MIDDLE JURASSIC	AALENIAN	*Dogger*				
LOWER JURASSIC	TOARCIAN	UPPER LIAS — Blea Wyke Series; Alum Shale Series	UPPER LIAS — Blea Wyke Sands; Striatulus Shales; Peak Shales; Cement Shales; Main Alum Shales; Bituminous Shales; Jet Shales	Blea Wyke Sands; Striatulus Shales; Peak Shales; Alum Shales Formation; Jet Rock Formation (LIAS GROUP)	Blea Wyke Sandstone Formation — Yellow Sandstone Member, Grey Sandstone Member, Fox Cliff Siltstone Member; Peak Mudstone Member; Whitby Mudstone Formation — Alum Shale Member, Jet Rock Member	not present; Whitby Mudstone Formation (Jet Rock Member)
		Jet Rock Series; Grey Shale Series	Grey Shales	Grey Shales Formation	Grey Shale Member	
	PLIENSBACHIAN	MIDDLE LIAS — Ironstone Series; Sandy Series	MIDDLE LIAS — Cleveland Ironstone Formation; Staithes Formation	Cleveland Ironstone Formation; Staithes Formation	Cleveland Ironstone Formation; Staithes Sandstone Formation	Cleveland Ironstone Formation; Staithes Sandstone Formation
		Bb; Ba	Ironstone Shales; Pyritous Shales	Ironstone Shales; Pyritous Shales	Redcar Mudstone Formation — 'Ironstone/Pyritous Shales'	Redcar Mudstone Formation (undivided)
	SINEMURIAN	LOWER LIAS — Ab; Aa	LOWER LIAS — Siliceous Shales	Siliceous Shales; Calcareous Shales	'Siliceous Shales'; Calcareous Shales	'Calcareous Shales'
	HETTANGIAN					
TRIASSIC	RHAETIAN					

Table 5   Fauna of the Ironstone/Pyritous shales at Tom Gill

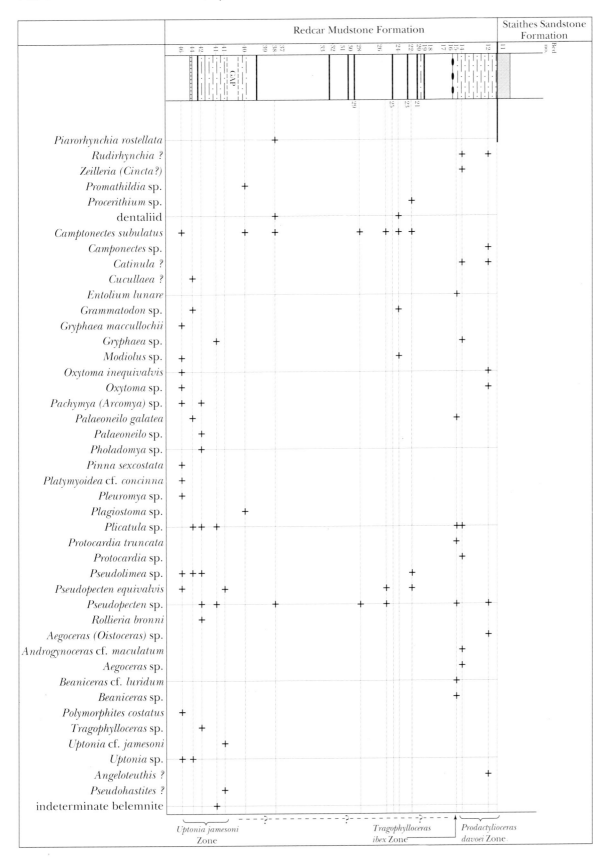

Redcar Mudstone Formation

Staithes Sandstone Formation

Piarorhynchia rostellata
Rudirhynchia ?
Zeilleria (Cincta?)
Promathildia sp.
Procerithium sp.
dentaliid
Camptonectes subulatus
Camponectes sp.
Catinula ?
Cucullaea ?
Entolium lunare
Grammatodon sp.
Gryphaea maccullochii
Gryphaea sp.
Modiolus sp.
Oxytoma inequivalvis
Oxytoma sp.
Pachymya (Arcomya) sp.
Palaeoneilo galatea
Palaeoneilo sp.
Pholadomya sp.
Pinna sexcostata
Platymyoidea cf. concinna
Pleuromya sp.
Plagiostoma sp.
Plicatula sp.
Protocardia truncata
Protocardia sp.
Pseudolimea sp.
Pseudopecten equivalvis
Pseudopecten sp.
Rollieria bronni
Aegoceras (Oistoceras) sp.
Androgynoceras cf. maculatum
Aegoceras sp.
Beaniceras cf. luridum
Beaniceras sp.
Polymorphites costatus
Tragophylloceras sp.
Uptonia cf. jamesoni
Uptonia sp.
Angeloteuthis ?
Pseudohastites ?
indeterminate belemnite

Uptonia jamesoni Zone   Tragophylloceras ibex Zone   Prodactylioceras davoei Zone

Yorkshire coast, or those inland in a few large clay, shale or ironstone pits. Unfortunately, natural exposures inland are poor and fossils appear less abundant than at the coast; for this reason it has been necessary, in the Northallerton district, to use borehole information to supplement detailed geological surveying in order to fill the gaps in the stratigraphical and palaeontological knowledge of the Jurassic strata. Despite these problems, the Jurassic rocks are perhaps the best known, and have been studied in greater detail than those of any other system. The names used in this account are based on those by Hemingway and Knox (1973), with later modifications by several authors.

Palaeogeography

The Cleveland Basin, in which the Jurassic rocks of north and east England were deposited, lies near the western margin of the much larger Mesozoic North Sea Basin. It is bounded to the south by the Market Weighton Block, and to the west by the Askrigg Block and Stainmore Trough. The northern boundary of the basin lies mainly offshore and has not been defined. The palaeogeography of the area in Jurassic times is well known (Bradshaw et al., 1992). Open sea covered the area in both latest Triassic and early Jurassic times, receded southwards for most of the early and middle part of the mid-Jurassic and re-entered the area in Callovian times. An ever-changing, rapidly evolving and migrating fauna, particularly ammonites, lived in the surface waters. Other groups useful for zonation include foraminifera, ostracods and dinoflagellate cysts.

In the Early Jurassic, sediments of the Lower Lias Group were deposited in shallow, muddy shelf seas, commonly inhabited by bottom dwellers such as molluscs. These quiet conditions of sedimentation kept pace with subsidence of the Cleveland Basin floor, and were interrupted in late Pliensbachian times by an influx of silts and sands from the north-west. A rhythmic alternation of mudstone, siltstone and/or sandstone suggests repeated uplift and erosion of the source area. The sediments of the Staithes Sandstone Formation were deposited in a shallow, marine, inshore environment, judging from the rich (in numbers of individuals) fauna and abundant evidence of burrowing activity.

The Cleveland Ironstone Formation was also deposited in a shallow-water marine environment, which maintained a prolific, thicker shelled fauna, including oysters and pectens, some burrowing bivalves, cephalopods and crinoids.

During Toarcian times, more variable marine conditions prevailed. Washed-in tree trunks, which eventually formed the jet deposits in the Jet Rock Member, suggest that there was land nearby.

At the end of the Early Jurassic, earth movements caused uplift and gentle folding in north-east Yorkshire, and a phase of marine erosion ensued. The character of the Middle Jurassic sedimentary rocks implies an alternation of marine and nonmarine conditions, similar to those which prevailed during the Carboniferous Period;

massive sandstones are separated by mudstones, seatearths and thin coals, comprising a typical deltaic sequence.

There is evidence that the sea encroached from the south onto the delta flats on several occasions. The first was during deposition of the Eller Beck Formation in late Aalenian times, and later the Scarborough Formation was formed when a more extensive transgression in mid-Bajocian times left calcareous deposits rich in bivalves, gastropods and echinoids.

The Scalby Formation indicates that deltaic conditions were established again in late Bajocian and Bathonian times, and muds, silts and sands were built up to sea level. Plant remains are common and include Ginkgoales and fern pinnules; insect remains and reptilian footprints are also present.

The youngest Jurassic rocks show a much closer connection between Yorkshire and areas to the south than their predecessors. The Cornbrash was deposited in seas which transgressed into Yorkshire, probably from the west. Although thin, this deposit has a wide lateral extent and the Middle Jurassic strata over which it transgressed must have been uniformly flat. A further 100 m of Jurassic beds overlie the Cornbrash. They comprise mudstones, siltstones, calcareous sandstones, limestones and oolites, and include the Oxford Clay which represents one of the most persistent and laterally extensive transgressions of the Jurassic.

Lower Jurassic

Marine conditions prevailed throughout the Early Jurassic in the Cleveland Basin, although water depths and lithologies varied. This variation was reflected in the former lithostratigraphical division, into Lower, Middle and Upper Lias (Table 4). The Middle Lias was subdivided into a lower Sandy Series and an upper Ironstone Series (Fox-Strangways et al., 1886; Fox-Strangways, 1908). Hemingway (1974) redefined the Middle Lias and introduced the Staithes Formation and overlying Cleveland Ironstone Formation. A BGS cored borehole (Powell, 1983, 1984) at Felixkirk, some 5 km south of the district, confirmed the presence of all the Lower Jurassic stages and the majority of the constituent zones (Ivimey-Cook and Powell, 1991). The Lower Jurassic is renamed the Lias Group and additional formational names proposed for mapping purposes (Table 4). The Redcar Mudstone Formation is equivalent to the Lower Lias, and the Whitby Mudstone Formation equivalent to the Upper Lias of this district.

The first appearance of the ammonite *Psiloceras*, which has been used to define the base of the Jurassic System (Cope et al., 1980a), has been proved in the Felixkirk Borehole, about 10 m above the base of the Lias Group; consequently the lowest strata in the group are of Triassic age.

LIAS GROUP

The group, which is estimated to be about 350 m thick, is subdivided into four formations that can be traced throughout the district. In upwards sequence, these are the Redcar Mudstone, Staithes Sandstone, Cleveland Ironstone and Whitby Mudstone (Table 4).

Strata of the Redcar Mudstone Formation mostly subcrop beneath the drift deposits, and form an arcuate belt, some 2 to 3 km wide, stretching from near Stokesley in the north-east to Thornton-le-Beans in the south; exposures are rare and restricted to sporadic small stream sections and temporary excavations. Exposures of the Staithes Sandstone Formation are more abundant, usually in the form of natural scarps, facing between north and west, and overlooking the Teesside and York plains. The Cleveland Ironstone Formation is represented by a 'slack', or slight depression in the topography, at the top of the Staithes Sandstone Formation scarp, and, although drift free in most of the district, is rarely well exposed. The overlying Whitby Mudstone Formation comprises largely argillaceous strata and is poorly exposed. However, it is subject to landslips and the arcuate scars forming the backwalls of these features are sufficiently fresh in places to expose the formation. The Jet Rock is the only resistant lithology and makes a small landform feature, but in most places this has been masked by shale tips of the waste from old levels, driven into the hillsides to mine the jet.

Redcar Mudstone Formation

The formation is about 230 m thick, and consists of mainly dark grey fissile mudstone and siltstone. In excellent coastal sections, these beds were divided by the early workers (e.g. Buckman, 1915) into, in ascending order, Calcareous, Siliceous, Pyritous and Ferruginous shales according to their lithological character.

To the south, Powell (1984) recognised these divisions in the Felixkirk Borehole but they cannot be mapped at surface within the district. Some 230 m of the Redcar Formation were recorded in the Cleveland Hills No. 1 Borehole. A few metres of the oldest beds were also proved in the Winton Manor Borehole.

The formation contains about 10 m of beds of Triassic age, deposited prior to the appearance of the ammonite *Psiloceras* which indicates the base of the Jurassic (Cope et al., 1980a). The Felixkirk sequence provided evidence that all the zones of the standard sequence from the *planorbis* to *ibex* zones (inclusive) are present; however, the ammonite sequence was too imperfect to prove all the subzones and some may be missing (e.g. part of the *bucklandi* Zone). Details of the sequence are given in Ivimey-Cook and Powell (1991) and the data is summarised in Figure 6.

The lithological units of Buckman (1915, p.61), Calcareous, Siliceous, Pyritous and Ironstone shales, are used here as informal descriptive terms, but the dating of the units does not agree with Buckman's age attributions or with those used by Van Buchem and McCave (1989). Powell (1984), and Ivimey-Cook and Powell (1991) review their use in the Felixkirk Borehole and suggest that, by comparison with the Acklam boreholes to the south (Gaunt et al., 1980), the base of the

Siliceous Shales may be earlier in this borehole than farther south. There is also evidence that there was greater total sedimentation in the north than farther south. However, this may not account fully for the difference in thickness between the Felixkirk and Cleveland No. 1 boreholes, part of which may be due to taking the base of the Staithes Sandstone Formation at a slightly higher level, in the chippings samples, of the latter borehole. Other aspects of the conditions of sedimentation in this basin are considered in relation to the sequence in Robin Hood's Bay by Van Buchem and McCave (1989) and Van Buchem et al. (1992).

Details

The basal unit, the Calcareous Shales, contains locally pyritic, calcareous mudstones with shell-rich layers and thin beds of shelly limestones; it is nearly 90 m thick in Felixkirk Borehole.

Sporadic exposures of this unit occur in the area around Harlsey and Potto. Many more were recorded by Fox-Strangways et al. (1886) but these are now overgrown. An old well [4235 9970], at the southern edge of East Harlsey village, proved a 'hard shelly rock with *Gryphaea* sp.' some 3.86 m thick, beneath a metre of made ground. This, and similar records, is likely to indicate beds of latest Hettangian or younger age. The arable fields east of Harlsey Castle contain numerous ferruginous limestone fragments, some containing *Gryphaea* sp. An old landslip scar [420 943] bordering Cod Beck, near Kirby Sigston, exposed the following section:

	Thickness m
Clay, red-brown, sandy, with small pebbles	0.30
Mudstone, grey	0.30
Limestone and mudstone, grey, interbedded, *Gryphaea* sp. common	0.50
Mudstone, grey	0.50
Limestone, with *Gryphaea* sp.	0.20
Total	1.80

Similar lithologies are exposed [4240 9550] in a small tributary of the Cod Beck south of Foxton.

A small stream in the Bullamoor area, immediately east of Northallerton, cuts down through thin superficial deposits into dark grey laminated mudstone. Limestone fragments are found [397 923] west of Sowerby Grange and at the head of Harrogate Gill [393 944]. No diagnostic zone fossils have been found.

In the Winton Manor Borehole [4021 9656], 10.77 m of Calcareous Shales were proved (Figure 6). The top 2.74 m were not cored but are recorded as shales and limestones. The underlying beds consist of laminated/fissile, micaceous, silty and shelly grey mudstones and variably silty, micritic or shelly limestones; near the base is a 0.86 m-thick siltstone of which the basal 0.3 m is massive and virtually noncalcareous. The macrofauna recovered includes *Cardinia?*, '*Gervillia*' *praecursor*, *Liostrea hisingeri*, *Meleagrinella fallax*, *Modiolus laevis*, *M. minimus*, *Plicatula* sp., *Protocardia philippiana*, *Pteromya tatei*, echinoid test fragments and diademopsid spines. *Liostrea*, *Modiolus*, *Protocardia* and *Pteromya* dominate this fauna within shell-rich layers. There is no sign of any *Psiloceras* so all these beds are assigned to the Triassic. Their thickness is less than the 10 m of similar beds found below *Psiloceras* in the Felixkirk Borehole; the base of the Jurassic in Winton Manor was probably penetrated at about 6 m depth.

Palynomorphs recovered from this sequence by Dr G Warrington comprise miospores (spores and pollen of land plants), and marine organic-walled microplankton (Table 3). An assemblage from the base of the formation is similar in composition to that from the top of the underlying Cotham Member of the Penarth Group. However, those from higher in the Redcar Mudstone Formation are less diverse and are dominated by bisaccate pollen, including *Alisporites*, and representatives of the circumpolles group (*Classopollis* spp. and *Gliscopollis meyeriana*); the trilete spore *Kraeuselisporites reissiingeri* is also prominent but other taxa are only sparsely represented.

The assemblages occur in beds that are considered to lie below the level at which *Psiloceras* appears and are, therefore, assigned a latest Triassic (Rhaetian) age. They are comparable with those known from the Lias Group of that age in the Cockle Pits and Blyborough boreholes in the Humberside area (Lott and Warrington, 1988; Warrington *in* Gaunt et al., 1992).

The organic-walled microplankton component of the assemblages comprises sporadic dinoflagellate cysts and acritarchs; tasmanitid and colonial algae, and linings of foraminifer tests, are also present.

Fox-Strangways et al. (1886, p.17) record '*Gryphaea incurva*' in a roadside cutting near Potto Hill Farm and interpreted it as belonging to Tate and Blake's (1876) '*bucklandi* Zone'; however that 'Zone' was a broad concept that encompassed both the *bucklandi* and *semicostatum* zones of current usage. Tate and Blake (1876, p.67) also claimed that beds of their '*bucklandi* Zone' were exposed in the roadside between the church at East Harlsey and Morton Grange [c.425 998]. Both these exposures could have been in the Calcareous Shales. The exposure at the ford [427 967], below Ellerbeck Mill, is now overgrown, but Tate and Blake (1876, p.67) recorded shales with limestones yielding a fauna including *Cardinia, Gryphaea, Lucina,* a nautiloid, *Arnioceras semicostatum* and belemnites; this suggests a late Early Sinemurian age near the top of the unit.

The overlying Siliceous Shales consist of silty mudstones, siltstones and fine-grained, calcareous sandstones; calcareous concretions occur and the beds are commonly bioturbated. They are very poorly known locally. In Felixkirk Borehole, they are about 35 m thick, the lower boundary is gradational, and is placed at the highest bioclastic limestone of the Calcareous Shales which approximates to the base of the *turneri* Zone. The unit passes up into the Ironstone/Pyritous Shales of the late *raricostatum* Zone.

Fox-Strangways et al. (1886, p.17) record 'soft shales with *Ammonites armatus*' in a railway cutting [4784 0247] west of Whorl (presumably 'Wholton') Castle. This ammonite suggests the presence of the Siliceous Shales.

The term 'Pyritous Shales' was used by Buckman (1915, p.61) for beds of late *raricostatum* to *jamesoni* Zone age and 'Ironstone Shales' was used for beds of *valdani* to late *davoei* Zone age on the Whitby coast. Powell (1984), and Ivimey-Cook and Powell (1991) concluded that no satisfactory division could be made between these units from the evidence in the Felixkirk Borehole, where both sideritic concretions and pyritous burrows are present throughout 70 m of beds. No other suitable criteria for this division were observed. This combined unit is seen in stream gullies below the Staithes Sandstone, for example at Tom Gill, Halliday Slack and Harten Gill. It lacks the sandstones of the underlying unit, and consists of grey mudstone and siltstone with small pyritous nodules and beds of siderite concretions. Van Buchem and McCave (1989) introduced a tripartite division for the Whitby coast sequence at about this level, but their divisions have not been identified in the district. The top of this unit, and of the Redcar Mudstone, is taken at the first bed of sandstone of the Staithes Sandstone Formation.

The section at Tom Gill [5274 0336] shows over 50 m of intermittent exposure of silty mudstone alternating with more shaly horizons and with nodular ironstone. The mudstone varies in silt and sand content, and also in the amount of calcareous or ferruginous cement present, and weathers into an alternation of more or less resistant horizons up the cliff face. The sequence is shown in Table 5 together with the fauna collected. The beds between 41.5 to 51 m below the Staithes Sandstone are silty mudstones with a diverse, bivalve-rich fauna that contains ammonites, including *Uptonia* cf. *jamesoni, Uptonia* sp., *Polymorphites* cf. *costatus* and *Tragophylloceras* sp.; these indicate the higher part of the *Uptonia jamesoni* Zone. The junction between the two higher subzones probably lies between the occurrence of *Polymorphites* and the *U*. cf. *jamesoni* near the base of the section.

Higher in the gully, the shales yielded bivalves, dominantly *Camptonectes* and *Pseudopecten*. No ammonites were found so the *jamesoni*/*ibex* zonal boundary cannot be located. The highest 7.5 m of beds are again more silty, and yielded a more diverse fauna including *Rudirhynchia*?, *Zielleria* (*Cincta*)?, bivalves and several taxa of ammonites. The ammonites probably indicate both the top of the *ibex* Zone and a condensed *davoei* Zone. The presence of *Beaniceras* cf. *luridum* suggests the *luridum* Subzone at 7.5 m below the Staithes Sandstone. This taxon is, however, almost immediately followed by *Androgynoceras* cf. *maculatum*, indicating the top of the *maculatum* Subzone (Phelps, 1985), and an *Aegoceras* (*Oistoceras*) sp. close above may be either from late in the *capricornus* Subzone or from the succeeding *figulinum* Subzone. This suggests that the early part of the *davoei* Zone is condensed and part may be absent.

In the stream gully at Halliday Slack [5545 0355], beds of late *jamesoni* Zone age can be proved in a partially exposed section totalling about 6 m; the beds are very similar to those at the base of Tom Gill in both lithology and fauna. Additional taxa present here include *Tetrarhynchia* cf. *dunrobinensis, Antiquilima, Gresslya, Parainoceramus, Polymorphites lineatus* and *Pseudohastites* cf. *charmouthensis*. The presence of further *Polymorphites* low in the sequence strengthens the correlation of these beds with the *polymorphus*/*brevispina* Subzone, the overlying beds with *Uptonia* probably correlate with the *jamesoni* Subzone.

In Harten Gill [5460 9934], close below the Staithes Sandstone, 2 m of shaly beds are exposed at the base of the valley. These beds yielded *Camptonectes subulatus, Gryphaea gigantea, Modiolus* and *Pseudohastites*. The fauna is not zonally diagnostic but probably indicates a late *ibex* Zone age.

In Felixkirk Borehole, the combined Pyritous Shales and Ironstone Shales are represented by only 35 m of shaly and silty mudstone, ranging in age from basal *jamesoni* Zone into the *luridum* Subzone of the *ibex* Zone. Few ammonites were recovered and the details of the zonation remain unclear. The lithology and faunas are comparable with those at Tom Gill.

Staithes Sandstone Formation

The Staithes Sandstone forms a well-defined topographic feature across the district (Figure 7); it is commonly the steepest section of the lower face of the scarp in both the Cleveland and Hambleton Hills. Natural sections occur at Harten Gill [545 992] in Raisdale, at Halliday Slack [544 035] east of Carlton Bank, and in Tom Gill [527 035] under Carlton Bank. There are also more obscure

Figure 7 Geological sketch map of the Cleveland Hills showing important localities.

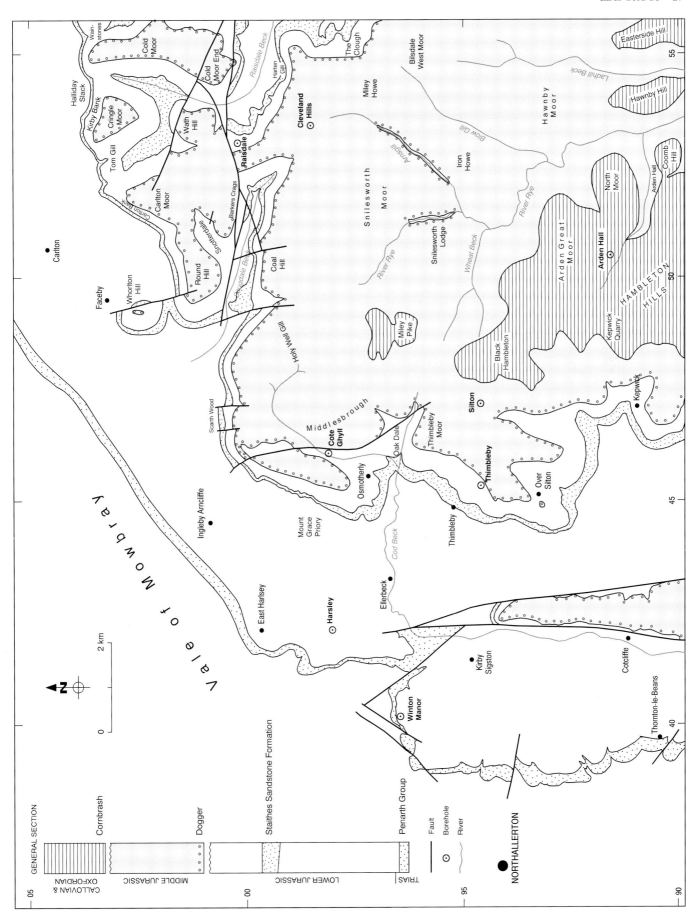

sections along the banks of Cod Beck [458 965] and its tributaries in the vicinity of Osmotherley.

Howard (1985, p.262) redefined the base of this unit, taking it at the base of an 'Oyster Bed', 0.15–0.30 m thick. This bed consists of calcareous and ferruginous sandstone and is packed with *Gryphaea gigantea*, *Oxytoma* and *Pseudopecten*. It is Bed 5 of Buckman (1915) at Hawsker Bottoms, equivalent to Bed 14 of Tate and Blake (1876) at Cowbar Nab, Staithes, which Howard considered to be laterally persistent throughout the Cleveland Basin.

The formation varies in thickness between 20 and 26 m, and consists predominantly of pale grey to brownish grey, fine- to medium-grained sandstone, which is commonly micaceous and locally calcareous and ferruginous. In boreholes cores, it appears blotched with dark brown iron stains. In exposures, it is commonly yellow-brown on weathered surfaces and blue-grey where unweathered. Cross-bedding, ripple cross-lamination and intense bioturbation are common. The tops of some sandstone beds show erosive scours infilled by sandstone, which may also incorporate mudstone clasts, carbonaceous material and shell-rich layers. In this district, there were at least five major pulses of sediment influx. The formation thins southwards within the Cleveland Basin, suggesting a northerly or north-westerly source for the sediment. There is an abundant bivalve fauna, but ammonites are generally scarce.

The top of the formation is marked by a change in lithology, to mudstone and ironstone of the Cleveland Ironstone Formation. Howard (1985) defined this as at the base of Bed 24 at Staithes which coincides with a change from argillaceous siltstone to shale with sporadic nodules of siderite mudstone.

Lithological and faunal characteristics suggest that the formation was deposited in shallow marine water, possibly including intertidal conditions, and was subjected to periodic storms. Winnowing of finer sediment from amongst shell material may have concentrated the bivalves.

The Staithes Sandstone Formation was deposited in a comparatively short span of time. In this district, ammonites are rare, but dates of late *davoei* Zone for the top of the Redcar Mudstone Formation at Tom Gill and *subnodosus* Subzone for part of the overlying Cleveland Ironstone Formation in both the Felixkirk and Thimbleby boreholes show that most was deposited during the *figulinum* Subzone of the *davoei* Zone and the *stokesi* Subzone of the succeeding *margaritatus* Zone. *Aegoceras* (*Oistoceras*) sp. is quite common in the base of the Staithes Sandstone at Tom Gill and occurs at a similar level in Harten Gill confirming a probable *figulinum* Subzone age for these beds. Above this, ammonites are very sparse.

Details

The Staithes Sandstone Formation is probably the best exposed formation within the district, especially along the northern flank of the outcrop between Osmotherley and Cold Moor. The lithological details are therefore illustrated by reference to three localities where the entire section may be examined. These localities are at Tom Gill, in the north, Osmotherley in the west and Harten Gill in the south.

At Tom Gill [527 035], 24.99 m of strata are exposed; the topmost 6 m forms a nearly vertical face. The section shows:

	Thickness m
Sandstone, yellow-brown, fine-grained, micaceous, flaggy, with interlamination of silty and sandy mudstone; *Chlamys?*, *Gryphaea?*, *Oxytoma inequivalve*, *Protocardia truncata*, balanocrinoid columnals	6.10
Sandstone, yellow-brown, flaggy	0.46
Sandstone, interbedded with mudstone	1.83
Sandstone, grey-brown, calcareous ferruginous concretions; serpulids 1.8–2.4 m from base of bed, *Gryphaea*, *P. truncata* and crinoid fragments; 0.6 m up — *Tetrarhynchia*, *Camptonectes*, *Gryphaea gigantea*, *Plicatula*, *Protocardia truncata*, *Pseudolimea*, *Pseudopecten*; at the base — *Tetrarhynchia subconcinna*, *G. gigantea*, *O. inequivalve*, *Plicatula numismalis*, *Protocardia truncata*, *Pseudopecten*	3.66
Mudstone, grey; silty at top with *Tetrarhynchia*, *Camptonectes*, *G. gigantea*, *Mactromya?*, *Meleagrinella*, *Pleuromya costata*, *Pseudopecten equivalvis*, *Protocardia truncata*, and belemnites	0.91
Sandstone, brown, flaggy; *Tetrarhynchia?*, *G. gigantea*, *P. truncata*, *Pseudopecten*	0.76
Mudstone, grey, silty; 2.4 m up — *Lucina*, *Aegoceras* (*Oistoceras*) sp.; 1.2 m up — *Oxytoma*, *A.* (*Oistoceras*) sp. and crinoid fragments; at base — *G. gigantea*, *O. inequivalve*, *Pseudopecten*	5.18
Sandstone, brown; mudstone partings; ironstone nodules at base; top sandstone — *G. gigantea*, *O. inequivalve*, *Pseudolimea*, *Protocardia truncata*; lower part — *O. inequivalve*, *Palaeoneilo galatea*, *A.* (*Oistoceras*)	1.83
Sandstone, brown, flaggy, calcareous; *G. gigantea*, *Pleuromya costata*	0.91
Mudstone, grey, silty	0.91
Sandstone, massive, calcareous, shelly; *Rudirhynchia?*, *Camptonectes?*, *G. gigantea*, *O. inequivalve*, *P. equivalve*, *A.* (*Oistoceras*)	2.44

on REDCAR MUDSTONE FORMATION

East of Tom Gill, further exposures [5295 0342], on a gentler slope, show the following 12.60 m thick sequence.

	Thickness m
Sandstone, buff, fine-grained; sporadic cross-bedding	2.70
Siltstone and sandstone interbedded; bioturbation common, including *Rhizocorallium?*	2.00
Sandstone, buff, fine- to medium-grained, thinly bedded mudstone clasts; plant and shell fragments	1.10
Siltstone and sandstone, weakly cemented, bioturbated	1.50
Ironstone, calcareous, shelly	0.10
Sandstone, massive, ferruginous, shelly; top bioturbated, lower part with current structures	2.80
Sandstone, poorly cemented, bioturbated, pectenids and belemnites common	1.40
Sandstone, buff, shelly; ferruginous lenses	1.00

on REDCAR MUDSTONE FORMATION

Farther east along the escarpment, at Halliday Slack [545 035], exposures of a prominent 0.10 m-thick ironstone, the Osmotherley Seam, mark the base of the Cleveland Ironstone Formation. The underlying 3 m is obscured but intermittent exposures indicate a further 21 m of typical Staithes Sandstone Formation with bivalve faunas; the base is marked by a prominent massive calcareous sandstone 2.4 m thick.

To the south-east, in the south bank of Raisdale, is the exposure in Harten Gill [545 990]. The sequence in the lower part of this valley shows 21.66 m of these beds:

	Thickness m
CLEVELAND IRONSTONE FORMATION (Base)	
STAITHES SANDSTONE FORMATION	
Sandstone, yellow-brown, fine-grained, interbedded mudstones, partly calcareous	2.50
Mudstone, grey, silty	0.30
Sandstone, brown, fine-grained, flaggy, cross-bedded; *Camptonectes*, ostreids, *Oxytoma inequivalve*, *Pseudolimea*, *Pseudopecten*, belemnites and crinoid columnals	1.20
Siltstone and sandstone, interbedded; *Camptonectes*, *Goniomya hybrida*, *Pachymya* (*Arcomya*), *Plicatula*, *Protocardia truncata*	1.30
Mudstone, grey, silty	1.00
Sandstone, brown, fine-grained, massive, shelly, flaggy at base	0.50
Siltstone and mudstone, interlaminated	1.60
Sandstone, brown, fine-grained, massive, ferruginous and calcareous	1.00
Mudstone and siltstone, interlaminated	0.80
Sandstone, brown, fine-grained, flaggy, calcareous and ferruginous, shelly lenses	1.50
Mudstone, grey-brown, ferruginous, partly obscured	3.05
Sandstone and siltstone, interlaminated	0.15
Mudstone, grey, silty	1.00
Sandstone and siltstone, interlaminated	0.20
Mudstone, grey, silty	1.50
Sandstone and siltstone interlaminated; *Goniomya hybrida*, *Gryphaea gigantea*, *O. inequivalve*, *P. truncata*, *Pseudopecten equivalvis*	0.50
Siltstone, grey, sandy, laminated and burrowed	2.40
Sandstone, brown, massive; *Camptonectes*, *Goniomya hybrida*, *Gryphaea gigantea*, *O. inequivalve*, *Pleuromya costata*, *Protocardia truncata*, *Pseudolimea pectenoides*	0.40
Mudstone, grey, silty, large ironstone lens; *Rudirhynchia huntcliffensis*, *Camptonectes*, *G. gigantea*, *Oxytoma*, *Pseudolimea*, *Pseudopecten equivalve*, *Aegoceras* (*Oistoceras*), crinoid fragments	0.66
Sandstone, fine-grained, flaggy, bioturbated; top yielded *Rudirhynchia*, *G. gigantea*, *O. inequivalvis*, *P. equivalvis*; lower part yielded *Gibbirhynchia*?, *Rudirhynchia*?, *G. gigantea*, *O. inequivalve*, *Pholadomya* and belemnites	1.30
on REDCAR MUDSTONE FORMATION	

In the exposures along the upper tributaries of Cod Beck, e.g. below Oak Dale [between 4625 9645 and 4621 9645], about 13.5 m of dominantly sandy beds occur in the valley-side cliffs. Neither top nor base of the unit is clear and the faunas are again dominated by *Oxytoma inequivalve*, *Protocardia truncata* and *Pseudopecten equivalvis* with some serpulids, *Camptonectes*, *Cardinia* and crinoid columnals present in the sandstones and shaly siltstones.

In the northern tributary below Whitehouse Farm [4615 9698], about 3.5 m of sandy shales and sandstones yield a similar, bivalve-dominated fauna, occurring here with *Cardinia laevis*, *Pleuromya costata*, *Plicatula* and belemnites.

A borehole drilled for BGS in 1981 in Raisdale, near Chop Gate [5320 0012], proved over 14 m of Staithes Sandstone Formation below 18.29 m and the final depth of 32.56 m. The sequence consists of siltstones, fine-grained massive sandstones and silty mudstones; some are bioturbated and others are thinly bedded.

The Thimbleby Borehole [4541 9469] proved some 9.9 m of Staithes Sandstone, assuming the ironstone between 35.58 and 35.64 m is equated with the base of the Cleveland Ironstone Formation. The sequence contains massive, pale grey sandstone, interbedded with grey to yellow-brown, intensely bioturbated siltstone and fine sandstone; these contain dark brown ferruginous stains, commonly as haloes around burrow-fills. The sequence includes several thin and rather diffuse ferruginous sandstones, and yields a sparse fauna dominated by *Protocardia* and *Pseudopecten*. No ammonites were recovered, so no subzonal position can be assessed.

In the Felixkirk Borehole, some 5 km to the south of the district, a 24.75 m-thick sequence of the Staithes Sandstone Formation was penetrated. It consists of very fine- to medium-grained calcareous sandstone with subordinate siltstone. Shell-beds yield *Liostrea*, *Modiolus*, *Oxytoma*, *Palmoxytoma*, *Protocardia*, *Pseudopecten*, rare rhynchonellids and belemnite fragments, together with trace fossils including *Chondrites*, *Diplocraterion* and *Rhizocorallium* and indeterminate burrowers. In the lowest part, the sequence shows an upward-coarsening cycle which may have begun slightly earlier than farther north, in very late *ibex* Zone times but no ammonites were recovered from this part of the core so no substantive zonal assessment can be made (Ivimey-Cook and Powell, 1991).

Cleveland Ironstone Formation

The formation is some 15 m thick, comprising a succession of marine shale (laminated silty mudstone), ironstone (sideritic and chamositic), argillaceous siltstone, fine sandstones and shell bed. The ironstones, in places oolitic, have not been as extensively worked as farther to the east. Exposures are poor in this district, accounting for the scarcity of literature pertaining to this north-west part of the Cleveland Basin.

The Yorkshire coastal sequence was first described in detail by Young and Bird (1822) from a section in Boulby Cliff, 3 km west of Staithes. They assigned the name 'Kettleness Beds' to the upper part of the formation, leaving the lower part unnamed. Phillips (1829) named the entire sequence the 'Ironstone Series' a term subsequently adopted by Fox-Strangways et al. (1886) and which remained in use until the Cleveland Ironstone Formation was introduced by Chowns in 1968 and adopted by Hemingway (1974) (Table 4).

At the type section at Staithes, Chowns defined the base of the formation at the base of Bed 27, thus excluding the Osmotherly Ironstone Seam. However, Hemingway (1974) lowered the boundary to include the Osmotherly Seam and about 1 m of strata below it. Howard (1985) agreed with this position and defined it as coinciding with Bed 24 (of Staithes).

The top of the formation is defined by the base of the overlying Whitby Mudstone Formation. This is however a transitional boundary, and there is much local lateral facies change. Howard (1985, p.268) has proposed that the boundary is 'either at the top of the highest oolitic ironstone or at the top of the hard siderite mudstone nodules (ironstone doggers) overlying the highest Type 2 Cycle, whichever is the stratigraphically higher in any particular section'. This level is readily recognisable in sections and boreholes in north-east Yorkshire. In the Northallerton district, it is drawn at the top of the Main Seam oolitic ironstone.

Chowns (1968) demonstrated a southward descending unconformity at about the *margaritatus–spinatum* Zone boundary, cutting out successively older beds below the Main Seam. In the Thirsk district the Main Seam, rests on beds which include only the Avicula Seam and Osmotherly Seam (Powell et al., 1992). Howard (1985) used this unconformity to separate the formation into two members. The lower, Penny Nab Member, comprises up to four, mostly argillaceous, upward-coarsening sequences capped by ironstones. The overlying Kettleness Member comprises chamositic and sideritic oolitic ironstone which interfingers with, and passes laterally into, siliciclastic silty shale, siltstone and subordinate very fine sandstone. Up to six minor upward-coarsening cycles, each capped by nodular sideritic mudstone, are developed in the siliciclastic facies.

In this basin, the Cleveland Ironstone Formation is of late Pliensbachian age; it ranges from the *subnodosus* Subzone of the *margaritatus* Zone up into the *hawskerense* Subzone of the *spinatum* Zone. In the Northallerton district, the *hawskerense* Subzone is not proved above the Main Seam, but in the Felixkirk Borehole *Pleuroceras* sp. occurs just above the Main Seam in interbedded siltstone and fine sandstone, which are transitional between the Cleveland Ironstone and Whitby Mudstone formations.

Deposition of the formation took place in successive parasequences (Van Wagoner et al., 1990), bounded by marine-flooding surfaces. There is extensive fine cross-lamination in the arenaceous beds indicating deposition in a shallow-water environment. The marine fauna is dominated by suspension feeding and nektonic taxa, principally of bivalves and cephalopods. Howard (1984) proposed that a barrier system, with offshore sediment transport from the north and west during storm events, was the most probable depositional environment. The sediment source cannot be determined.

The oolitic cross-bedded ironstones were once considered to be the alteration products of limestones percolated by iron-bearing solutions (Sorby, 1857; 1906). However, Hallimond (1925) maintained that they were inorganic chemical precipitates. They are now considered to be deposits formed during a period of rising sea level, but in water depths of less than 50 m (Howard, 1984). The source of the iron has been discussed elsewhere (Chowns, 1966; Hemingway, 1974). The limestones originally consisted of berthierine-rich, ooidal mud which, during early diagenesis, became strongly sideritised. The formation of the ooids in an anoxic environment, at the same time as the deposition of aerobic, deltaic-type sediments, has not been resolved.

Details

The formation is largely covered by drift deposits between Kepwick and Thimbleby, but it is estimated to be about 12 m thick. The Thimbleby Borehole [4541 9469], drilled in 1981 by BGS to establish the stratigraphy of this area, proved the formation to be 13 m in thickness (Figure 8). *Amaltheus* cf. *gibbosus* at 26.5 m depth, and *Amaltheus subnodosus* at 31.06 m, indicate the presence of the *gibbosus* and *subnodosus* subzones respectively. The Main, Avicula and Osmotherly ironstone seams were therefore confirmed and a correlation with the Pecten, Two Foot and Raisdale ironstone seams suggested (Figure 8). The lower part of the formation is lithologically comparable with the Staithes Sandstone Formation.

Sporadic exposures of the formation occur in Cod Beck and Oakdale Beck, south and east of Osmotherly, from which an outline of the complete sequence may be built up (Figure 9). The Main Seam is exposed [4694 9645] below the dam for the Oak Dale Reservoir. Some 0.45 m of ironstone are separated by 0.60 m of grey silty mudstone, from a further underlying 0.25 m ironstone seam. The lower beds are underlain by silty mudstone, rich in large ironstone nodules, and yield abundant *Palmoxytoma cygnipes*, *Protocardia truncata* and *Pseudopecten*.

A further 4 m lower in the sequence, the following section was recorded [4639 9644].

	Thickness m
Mudstone with ironstone nodules	0.10
Ironstone, massive	0.15
Mudstone, grey, silty, ferruginous	0.12
Ironstone, massive	0.20
Mudstone, grey	0.12
Mudstone, grey, silty, with ironstone nodules, shelly	0.15
Mudstone, with small ironstone nodules	2.00

The ironstones are correlated with the Avicula Seam.

The Osmotherly Ironstone, some 30 cm thick, was recorded [4625 9652] about 5 m beneath the Avicula Seam.

A similar section in Cod Beck [461 970], below the Old Wier, proved the following sequence.

	Thickness m
CLEVELAND IRONSTONE FORMATION	
Ironstone	0.10
Mudstone, grey-blue, laminated	0.80
Ironstone (Osmotherly Seam)	0.30
Mudstone, grey, silty, laminated, with a sandstone lens, 0.15 m thick, 0.50 m beneath the ironstone	1.60
STAITHES SANDSTONE FORMATION	
Sandstone, fine-grained, cross-bedded	0.30
Mudstone, grey, bivalves	0.50
Sandstone	0.30
Mudstone, grey	0.80
Sandstone	2.00

Sporadic exposures [4580 9993] of grey silty mudstone, with calcareous-ferruginous lenses up to 2 m long and 0.40 m thick, occur within the confines of landslip in the scarp face of the Cleveland Hills above Arncliffe Hall. Nearby [4584 9998], grey siltstones and fine-grained sandstones contain shelly ironstone concretions which are considered to lie within the Cleveland Ironstone Formation.

Farther east, in Scarth Wood [4670 0050], an exposure of two ironstones, 0.30 and 0.40 m thick, separated by 6 m of shales was recorded by Fox-Strangways (1886, p.24). He corre-

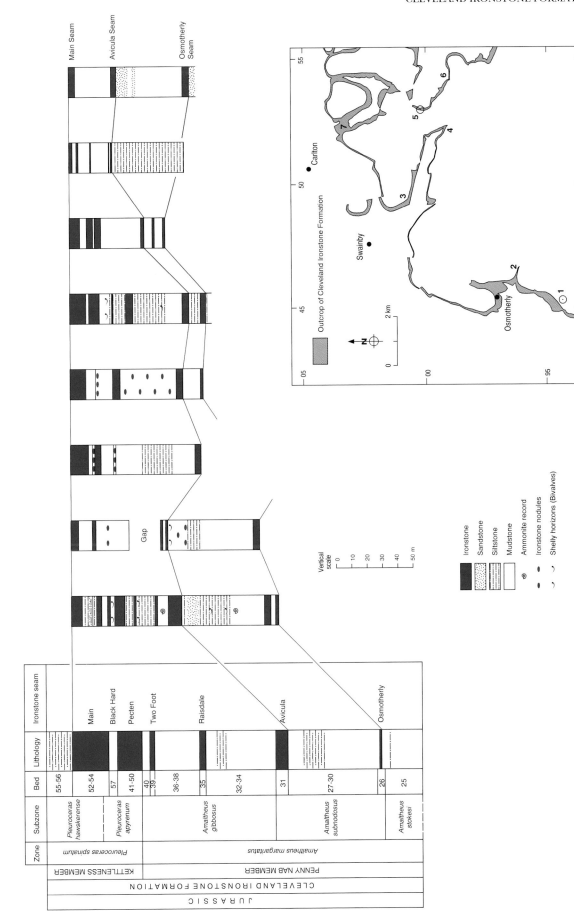

Figure 8   Correlation of the Cleveland Ironstone Formation.

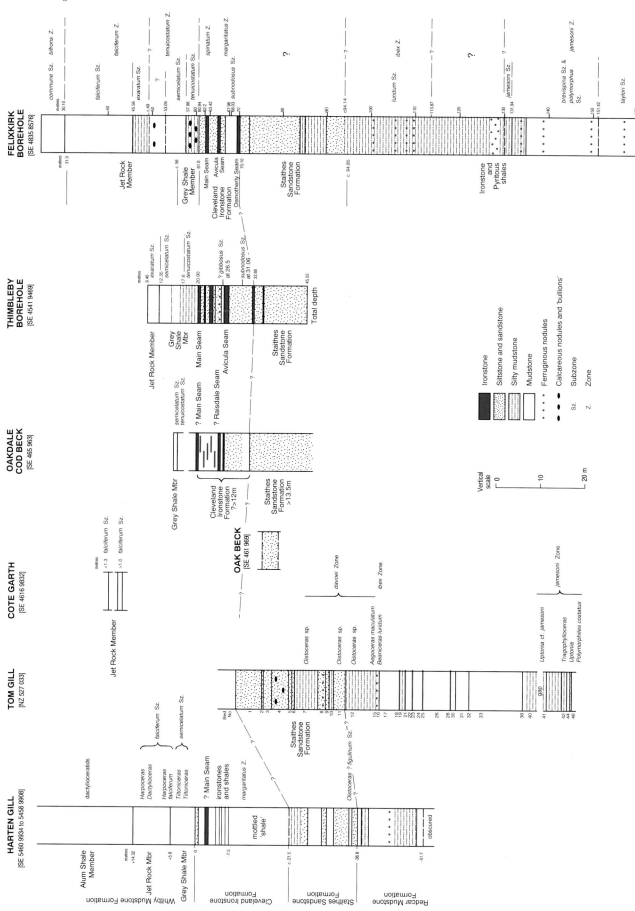

Figure 9 Sections in strata of Pliensbachian and Toarcian age.

lated the upper seam with the Two-Foot and the lower seam with the Avicula horizon. Their location, within a large area of landslip, makes the correlation difficult to assess.

A large spoil tip [4795 0062] in Clain Wood provides evidence of ironstone workings at the entrance of Scugdale, where drifts worked the Main Seam, but it was considerably thinner than in the Swainby Mine [4947 0080] nearby, and was soon abandoned.

The Swainby Mine was worked by a drift near Huthwaite Green. The section in the worked seam showed:

	Thickness m
Ironstone (Main Seam)	1.00
Shale	0.25
Ironstone	0.56

A further trial drift [5215 9996] was made for the Main Seam east of Scugdale Hall.

At the head of Scugdale, a section [5253 9911] on the south bank of Scugdale Beck exposes 12.14 m in the following sequence.

	Thickness m
Mudstone, grey, silty, laminated, tough, with yellow ferruginous bed at base (Sulphur Band)	2.00
Ironstone (partially exposed) (Main Seam)	c.0.90
Mudstone, grey, laminated	0.60
Ironstone, nodular	0.07
Mudstone, grey, laminated	1.06
Ironstone, massive (?Raisdale Seam)	0.45
Mudstone, grey, laminated, with large ironstone nodules	3.65
Ironstone, massive (Avicula Seam)	0.30
Mudstone, grey, silty	1.22
Ironstone, shelly	0.07
Mudstone, grey, silty	1.82

The 0.45 m massive ironstone was classified by Fox-Strangways as the Two-Foot Seam but was correlated by Chowns (1968) with the Raisdale Seam.

Only 2 km due east of the Scugdale Head section lies Harten Gill [5445 9900], on the south bank of Raisdale, which provides an almost continuous natural exposure of beds from the Staithes Sandstone Formation up into the Middle Jurassic. The Cleveland Ironstone Formation is here about 20 m thick and was recorded as follows.

	Thickness m
Mudstone, black, carbonaceous, pyritic, laminated	0.01
Mudstone, grey, weathering to pale grey	0.20
Ironstone, oolitic (Main Seam)	0.60
Mudstone, grey, laminated	0.40
Ironstone	0.40
Mudstone, grey, laminated	0.10
Ironstone	0.30
Mudstone, grey, laminated	1.00
Ironstone, nodular	0.20
Mudstone, grey, laminated	1.40
Ironstone (Two-Foot, of Fox-Strangways)	0.20
Mudstone, grey, laminated	0.40
Ironstone	0.10
Mudstone, grey, laminated	0.60
Ironstone, nodules with pectenoids	0.10
Mudstone, grey, laminated	0.30

Ironstone, nodular	0.10
Mudstone, mottled grey, yellow and red-brown, laminated (Chowns, 1968, recorded the Avicula and Osmotherley ironstone seams in this part of the sequence); *Amaltheus margaritatus* occurs with *Camptonectes*, *Entolium?*, *Protocardia truncata*, *Pseudolimea*, and *Pseudopecten* some 9 to 10 m from the base	c.14.00

About 1 km north of Scugdale Head, near High Crosslets, the Raisdale Borehole [5320 0012] was drilled by BGS in 1981 in an attempt to clarify the lower boundary of the Cleveland Ironstone Formation (Figure 8). A concentration of ironstone beds occur between 8.80 m and 18.29 m depth and include the Main Seam near the top, and possibly the Osmotherley Seam at the base. A further 14 m of siltstone, sandstone and mudstone were penetrated in this hole; the arenaceous beds showed bioturbation but ferruginous lithologies are rare, and the beds are typical of the Staithes Sandstone Formation. The evidence here confirms the condensed sequence of the West Cleveland area (Howard, 1985; Powell et al., 1992) where the Cleveland Ironstone Formation ranges between 9 and 14 m thick.

The most northerly exposures of the formation occur on the northern scarp of the Cleveland Hills at Busby Moor. Here exposures are sporadic but the ironstones make small bench features in the Green Bank area [526 032] and to the south and south east of Tom Gill [529 032].

A general section built up from the scarp [5295 0342] east of Tom Gill is as follows.

	Thickness m
Ironstone, white, oolitic	0.10
Mudstone, silty, ferruginous, laminated	0.20
Ironstone, oolitic (Main Seam)	0.56
Mudstone, orange, ferruginous	0.70
Ironstone	0.08
Mudstone, grey, laminated	1.10
Ironstone	0.06
Mudstone	0.15
Ironstone, interlaminated with mudstone, shelly at top	0.12 to 0.20
Mudstone, silty	10.50
Mudstone, dark grey, silty	3.80
Ironstone. nodular (?Osmotherley Seam)	0.20
Total	17.65

Isolated trackside outcrops above the stream gully at Halliday Slack [5455 0340] expose fine-grained brown, micaceous sandstones with a bivalve fauna including *Oxytoma inequivalve*, *Protocardia truncata* and *Pseudolimea acuticostata*, with *Pleuroceras* sp. indicating the *spinatum* Zone; patchily abundant crinoid fragments also occur.

Whitby Mudstone Formation

These shales and silty shales, formerly known as the Upper Lias (Table 4), were earlier divided into six lithological units based on the excellent exposures along the Yorkshire coast to the east (Hemingway, 1974). Cope et al. (1980a), Powell (1984) and Knox (1984) revised this nomenclature, defining five members in the Whitby Mudstone Formation. In ascending order, these are the Grey Shale, Jet Rock, Alum Shale, Peak Mudstone and

Fox Cliff Siltstone, overlain by the Blea Wyke Formation. Due to late Toarcian erosion, only the lower three members are present in this district. The Jet Rock Member is the only one of these named on the map, but its delineation separates the Grey Shale Member from the Alum Shale Member. All three of these are early Toarcian in age.

The Whitby Mudstone Formation is up to 60 m thick but natural exposures are rare. The Thimbleby Borehole (Figure 9) proved 13 m of the Grey Shale Member which yielded a diagnostic assemblage of ammonites, largely of *Dactylioceras* (*Orthodactylites*) *tenuicostatum* Zone age.

The Jet Rock Member is sporadically exposed, but its general position is rarely in doubt because of the numerous adits and spoil tips which mark its past exploitation for saleable 'hard jet' extracted from the Jet Shales (Hemingway, 1974). The overlying Alum Shale Member comprises largely unfossiliferous silty mudstones. It has been quarried locally and a few faces remain, for example above Carlton Bank and near Thimbleby, but most are now overgrown or covered by slipped rock.

The conditions of sedimentation of the Whitby Mudstone Formation were similar to those of the earlier Redcar Mudstone Formation. Current structures in silt and sand grade lithologies are rare, and the scarcity of bottom-living faunas suggests less suitable conditions for life, possibly in deeper waters. Mobile nektonic faunas, including cephalopods and some bivalves, are only common locally. The Jet Rock Member was deposited under stagnant anoxic conditions, which resulted in the accumulation and preservation of bitumen (Bituminous Shales of earlier authors) and of drifted araucarian wood fragments. These fragments had previously been trapped and eroded on sand bars or beaches, drifted away, delignified and are now found as jet (Hemingway, 1974).

GREY SHALE MEMBER

This lower part of the Whitby Mudstone Formation comprises grey and pale grey silty well-laminated mudstones. Sporadic ferruginous and calcareous beds and concretions are also present. Pyrite mineralisation is common, as numerous small cubes on bedding planes, or in disseminated form as pyritised plant and fossil fragments. Bioturbation structures are usually preserved in pyritic silt. There are few natural exposures of this member.

DETAILS

The Thimbleby Borehole (Figure 9) proved the Grey Shale Member, between 12.00 and 20.90 m; it yielded an ammonite fauna proving the two upper subzones of the *Dactylioceras* (*Orthodactylites*) *tenuicostatum* Zone. There is no evidence for the presence of the two earliest subzones of this zone, but they could be present between about 18.00 and 20.90 m depth, where the mudstone is more silty. The basal 1.40 m contain sporadic pyrite in burrow fills and more ironstone nodules than the beds above. The bivalve dominated fauna includes *Tetrarhynchia?*, *Astarte*, *Camptonectes*, *Eotrapezium?*, *Grammatodon*, *Pseudolimea acuticostata*, *Pseudolimea* sp, *Pseudopecten*, a

Dactylioceras (s.l.) at 18.00 m, and also belemnite fragments. The top of the Main Seam, at 20.90 m, may be of *hawskerense* Subzone age. Between 17.70 and 17.86 m, laminated silty mudstones are rich in *D.* (*O.*) *tenuicostatum*, proving its nominal Subzone; *Astarte* and *Steinmannia?* are also present. Beds of *semicelatum* Subzone age occur between 12.35 and 17.35 m; the lowest part, below 17.0 m, is dominated by *Dactylioceras* (*Orthodactylites*) *semicelatum* together with a bivalve fauna including *Chlamys?*, *Eotrapezium*, a nuculid, *Oxytoma* and *Pseudomytiloides dubius*. The upper part is rich in the harpoceratid ammonite *Tiltoniceras antiquum*, also some aptychi, the large thin valved *Pseudomytiloides dubius*, *Steinmannia bronni* and fish remains. The top of the Grey Shales is taken at 12.00 m at the top of a unit of well-laminated mudstones. The age of the top 0.35 m of these beds is uncertain as they yielded only indeterminate harpoceratids.

Farther north, in Oakdale Beck [465 964], approximately 1.5 m of grey mudstone are seen, about 4 m above the Cleveland Ironstone. These shales yielded *Astarte* sp., *Dactylioceras* (*O.*) cf. *semicelatum*, *D.* (*O.*) cf. *tenuicostatum* and *Dactylioceras* sp., suggesting beds approximately at the junction of the *semicelatum* and *tenuicostatum* subzones of the *tenuicostatum* Zone; these approximate in horizon to the beds at about 17 m depth in Thimbleby Borehole.

In Raisdale, near the top of the steep-sided valley of Harten Gill [5446 9900], about 6 m of grey, silty, laminated mudstone occur above the Cleveland Ironstone Formation. Between 2.7 and 3.6 m above the ironstone, these beds yield *Pseudomytiloides dubius*, *Steinmannia bronni*, *Steinmannia* sp., harpoceratids indet., *Tiltoniceras* sp. and fish fragments, indicative of beds near the top of the *semicelatum* Subzone of the *tenuicostatum* Zone.

In Raisdale Borehole [5320 0012], 5.10 m of Grey Shales, comprising pale grey to yellowish buff silty, shaly mudstone, were proved below the superficial deposits. The beds are deeply weathered but yield dactylioceratid fragments at about 4.0 and 8.60 m depth.

The *tenuicostatum* Zone is proved to be nearly 11 m thick in Felixkirk Borehole [4835 8576]; only the lowest 5 m of this is of Grey Shales Member lithology, consisting of grey mudstone and siltstone with calcareous concretions. The higher beds are comparable with the Jet Rock Member, with darker, bituminous mudstone present above 56 m depth (Ivimey-Cook and Powell, 1991). This indicates that more euxinic depositional conditions were initiated earlier in this area than elsewhere in the basin.

JET ROCK MEMBER

In the type area, between Hawsker Bottoms and Saltwick Bay on the Yorkshire coast, the Jet Rock Member (formerly known as Jet Shales) comprises some 31 m of tough, finely laminated, fissile, bituminous, brown silty mudstone with 5 or 6 beds containing more or less continuous calcareous concretions or 'doggers'. The 'Jet' occurs principally about 5 m from the base, immediately below the Top Jet Dogger. These beds are overlain by bituminous shales (formerly the Bituminous Shales) which contain several beds of concretions; the topmost bed (Ovatum Band) is a double row of sideritic concretions (Bed 48 of Howarth, 1962).

South of this district, the member totals 24.7 m in thickness in the Felixkirk Borehole (Powell et al., 1992). Within the district, an estimated 9 m of grey mudstone are comparable in lithology and thickness to the Jet Shales of the type area. This tough brown mudstone forms a distinctive feature and has been mapped where possible. Mining regulations specified that levels driven into the hillside for the purpose of jet extraction were at least 60 yards apart so there are numerous small shale tips containing representative lithologies of the Jet Rock Member. The mudstone usually weathers to a purplish brown colour but still remains a tough flexible shale reminiscent of an oil shale. A few fragments of brittle, black, bituminous jet may still be found.

DETAILS

In the Kirby Sigston–Cotcliffe graben, old workings [4210 9289], indicated by spoil tips of grey-brown fissile mudstone in Landmoth Wood, mark the probable position of the Jet Rock Member beneath landslip on the west side of this major fault system (p.60).

In Thimbleby Borehole, only 2.60 m of the Jet Rock Member were cored immediately beneath drift deposits (Figure 9). The mudstone is grey-brown in colour, slightly silty and markedly laminated. Many small calcareous nodules, up to 0.04 m in length, are present, and are commonly associated with comminuted bivalve shells and fish fragments. Calcareous beds up to 0.02 m thick, are not uncommon. The fauna of the beds between the depths of 9.50 and 12.00 m includes *Parainoceramus?*, *Pseudomytiloides dubius*, *Pseudomytiloides* sp., *Eleganticeras* sp. and harpoceratids. This indicates a position in the lower third of the *Cleviceras exaratum* Subzone of the *Harpoceras falciferum* Zone.

At the top of Halliday Slack [5463 0340], sporadic sections occur along the track to the shale tips of the jet workings.

A small valley-side cliff, west of Cote Garth [4616 9832], near the Osmotherley reservoir, provided two exposures of the upper part of the member. Near the southern end, about 1 m of shale yielded possible plant fragments, *Meleagrinella* sp., *Modiolus?*, *Pseudomytiloides dubius*, *Pseudomytiloides* sp., *Steinmannia?*, *Dactylioceras* sp., indeterminate harpoceratids, *Hildaites* sp. and fish scales; a small exposure over 2 m higher in the cliff yielded *Dactylioceras* sp.. Both exposures are in the upper part of the member (Bituminous Shales) and are probably of *Harpoceras falciferum* Subzone age.

In Raisdale, some 9 m of grey fissile ferruginous mudstones are exposed in the higher parts of Harten Gill [5444 9898]. The valley sides are extensively slipped. Material estimated to lie between 7.6 and 9 m above the base of the member yielded the ammonite *Harpoceras falciferum*, in addition to *Striactaeonina* sp., *Lucina* sp., *Pseudomytiloides dubius* and fish fragments. This ammonite indicates the *falciferum* Subzone; the material is probably from the upper part of the Jet Rock Member.

ALUM SHALE MEMBER

The Alum Shale, overlying the Jet Rock is the top-most member of the Whitby Mudstone Formation which is represented in this district. It is about 40 m thick in the south and west of the district near Osmotherley. It is partially exposed in an old quarry north-east of Thimbleby [4640 9630] where the shale was once dug for alum (p.79), and was classified as Alum Shales by Fox-Strangways (1886).

DETAILS

North-east of Thimbleby [4640 9630], the quarry section recorded during this survey is as follows:

	Thickness m
SALTWICK FORMATION	
Mudstone, black, carbonaceous	c.0.60
Sandstone, brown, fine-grained, base containing carbonaceous, micaceous and coaly partings	c.1.80
Mudstone, grey, with silty laminae	0.70
Mudstone, dark grey, carbonaceous	0.02
Sandstone, pale brown, fine-grained	0.04
Mudstone, olive-grey, with ironstone nodules	0.50
Sandstone, brown, flaggy, with mudstone partings; top massive, siliceous and ferruginous	1.50
WHITBY MUDSTONE FORMATION	
Mudstone, grey, with ironstone nodules and lenses	1.00
Ironstone; thin silty and sandy laminae, shell debris	0.20
Mudstone, grey	1.00
Ironstone nodular bed	thin
Mudstone, grey, laminated, fossiliferous	0.30
Ironstone bed	thin
Mudstone, grey, laminated; sporadic ironstone nodules	20.30

Fox-Strangways et al. (1886, p.32) recorded the overlying Dogger Formation as about 0.48 m thick near the top of this excavation and stratigraphically above this sequence in the Alum Quarry. The top 5 m or so of the section however are typical lithologies of the Middle Jurassic Saltwick Formation. Such a stratigraphical juxtaposition presumably results from local erosion cutting into the Lias in a channel-like form. The carbonaceous mudstones provide a channel fill of Middle Jurassic strata but the margins are not exposed.

Along the Northern scarp, at Carlton Bank [5210 0272], the junction between the Lower and Middle Jurassic strata is well exposed, and recorded as follows:

	Thickness m
MIDDLE JURASSIC, SALTWICK FORMATION	
Sandstone, yellow-brown, fine to medium-grained, massive	10.00
LOWER JURASSIC, WHITBY MUDSTONE FORMATION	
Ironstone with mudstone partings and lenses (probably reworked)	0.23
Mudstone, pale grey, leached	1.20
Mudstone, dark grey, slightly silty, laminated	40.00

The main exposure in the Alum Shales results from diggings for alum at Carlton Bank [520 028]. Fox-Strangways (1886) reported 'characteristic fossils' which were 'rare compared with the coastal sections'. The north-facing quarry is now deeply weathered and collecting is difficult; material from about 3 m above the Jet Rock contained *Lucina*, *Pseudomytiloides dubius*, *Steinmannia?* and an indeterminate ammonite. A similar thickness of Alum Shale Member is exposed 2 km down dip in Thackdale [5153 0097] where dactylioceratids were recovered.

Dactylioceras sp. was found some 11 m below the top of the succession on the north face of Cringle Moor [537 033].

In Raisdale, at Harten Gill [544 990], some 25 m of Alum Shales are exposed in steep and slipped exposures; above this, there is a gap of about 16 m between the top of the exposures and the massive basal sandstones of the Saltwick Formation. The fauna from the lowest few metres includes *Lucina*, *Meleagrinella*, *Pseudomytiloides*, *Dactylioceras* and *Harpoceras*; strata between 15 to 20 m from the base yield fragments of *Modiolus*, *Parainoceramus?*, *Pseudomytiloides* and dactylioceratids, and beds from the top of the exposure, about 24–25 m above the base, yield *Discinisca*, *Meleagrinella*, *Modiolus*, nuculanids, and *Pseudomytiloides*? These taxa indicate an early Toarcian age.

An erosive channel was interpreted by Fox-Strangways (1886, p.28) to cut down some 30m into the 'Upper Lias' strata at the south end of Cold Moor [5499 0015] in Raisdale. The channel passes through into Bilsdale and, although exposures are poor, it is filled by the lower beds of the Saltwick Formation [5565 0085].

The Whitby Mudstone Formation is exposed sporadically on the south side of Scugdale, and at Blue Scar [5130 9935], some 8 m of blue-grey laminated mudstone of the Alum Shale Member crop out immediately beneath the Dogger Formation of the Middle Jurassic.

On the extreme eastern edge of the district near Chop Gate in Bilsdale, sporadic exposures of Alum Shales are present beneath the massive sandstone crags of the Saltwick Formation. The most extensive exposure [5512 9894] forms the back face of a landslip and shows some 6 m of grey laminated mudstone.

In Kirby Sigston–Cotcliffe Graben, sporadic exposures are present in Sigston and Landmoth Woods [4220 9273], and a well-defined exposure [4207 9112] occurs at the rear of Cotcliffe Lodge where some 1.50 m of grey-brown laminated mudstone underlies the Dogger Formation.

Middle Jurassic

Towards the end of the Toarcian, the Lower Jurassic of the Cleveland Basin was gently folded and eroded, and the upper part of the Lias Group, present elsewhere in the region, is absent. The succeeding Middle Jurassic rests unconformably on the Whitby Mudstone Formation and there is evidence of channels cutting down nearly to the Jet Rock Member (Hemingway, 1974). The Middle Jurassic of the district reflects a wide range of depositional environment and include beds of fluvial, deltaic, paralic and fully marine origin.

The oldest Middle Jurassic unit present in the district is the highly variable, marine Dogger Formation of early Aalenian age (Table 6). This is overlain by the Ravenscar Group which ranges from Bajocian to Bathonian in age (Hemingway and Knox, 1973). This group comprises nonmarine sandstone, siltstone and shale, together with thin coals and ironstones; this 'estuarine or deltaic' sequence is divided by thin marine units. Locally, the group rests directly on the Lias. It is overlain by the Osgodby Formation of Callovian age; the Cornbrash, which occurs elsewhere in the region, has not been proved within the district.

Dogger Formation

This formation commonly contains a thick basal conglomerate with well-rounded pebbles, up to 70 mm diameter. Limestone, sandstone, and shale also occur. The formation is up to 8 m thick and occupies depressions eroded in the underlying Whitby Mudstone Formation. The Dogger is developed widely within the district but in general is too thin to be shown at 1:50 000 scale. It is overlain by the erosive base of the Saltwick Formation, which locally oversteps the Dogger to rest on strata of the Lias Group. Fossils include corals,

bryozoans, molluscs and echinoderms, as well as many derived from Toarcian concretions.

Details

Near Beacon Hill, in Kirby Sigston–Cotcliffe graben, a 1 m-thick ferruginous limestone [4260 9383], resting on the Alum Shale Member, was recorded by Fox-Strangways (1886, p.33). This unit was traced along the west of the hill to Cotcliffe Lodge where an exposure of the Dogger Formation was recorded, following the collapse of a retaining wall [4208 9112]. The Dogger rests with apparent conformity on grey-brown laminated mudstones of the Whitby Mudstone Formation and passes upwards into rubbly, ferruginous, fine-grained, yellow-brown sandstones of the Saltwick Formation. The section is as follows:

	Thickness m
SALTWICK FORMATION	
Sandstone, fine-grained, ferruginous, rubbly, with irregular bedding	0.30
Mudstone, grey-brown, laminated	0.20
Sandstone, conglomeratic, ferruginous, shelly, calcareous	0.30
Mudstone, grey-brown, ferruginous, laminated	0.10
DOGGER FORMATION	
Limestone, conglomeratic, ferruginous, partly oolitic	0.25
Mudstone, grey-brown	0.30
Limestone, conglomeratic, ferruginous, shelly	0.20
Mudstone, grey-brown	0.10
Limestone, conglomeratic, massive, oolitic, ferruginous, shelly pockets	0.30
Mudstone, grey-brown, laminated	1.30
WHITBY MUDSTONE FORMATION	

The rubbly, ferruginous, calcareous dogger horizons were rich in bivalves and ammonites and a large collection was made by Mr P G Ensom for the Yorkshire Museum in York.

The Dogger crops out at the base of the escarpment south of Kepwick [470 909] and is about 3.5 m thick.

Trial adits below Atlay Bank [4667 9056 and 4665 9051] were recorded by Fox-Strangways et al. (1886, p.32). In the northern adit, two ferruginous limestone beds and an iron-stone bed are each separated by shale.

The upper limestone yielded chamositic ooids interbedded with lenses of shelly sideritic oolite, calcareous ironstone and pale grey bioclastic limestone with bryozoan and brachiopod debris. Dr H C Ivimey-Cook (written communication, 1985) reports that specimens collected in 1976 by Dr R F Youell from this area yielded a simple coral, *Lopha* sp., *Propeamussium* sp. and an indeterminate trigoniid.

The Dogger Formation is not exposed along the scarp east of Nun House but sandstones at Carlow Hill [4480 9327] and at the Scar [4497 9355] contain a high concentration of ironstone clasts and plant stems within the basal beds, which may represent the base of the Middle Jurassic in this area.

Fox-Strangways et al. (1886) recorded as Dogger a ferruginous limestone some 0.45 m thick in the old Alum works [4640 9626] near Thimbleby Lodge.

A disused quarry [4689 9644] on the north side of Oakdale was probably worked for limestone, which lies at the horizon of the Dogger Formation.

No exposures of the Dogger were seen between the Osmotherly area northwards past Mount Grace Priory and the

Table 6   Classification of Middle and Upper Jurassic strata.

Chronostratigraphy		Yorkshire coast (typical sections)	Wright (1983), Hemingway and Knox (1973) and Hemingway (1974)	Cleveland and Northallerton	Hemingway and Knox (1973), Wright (1980), Powell and Rathbone (1983) and Powell et al. (1992)
Series	Stage	Fox-Strangways (1892) Fox-Strangways et al. (1886)		Parsons (Aalenian–Bathonian) and Wright (Callovian–Oxfordian) in Cope et al. (1980)	
UPPER JURASSIC	Oxfordian	Lower Limestone	Coralline Group: Coralline Oolite Formation / Hambleton Oolite Member	Coralline Oolite Formation / Hambleton Oolite Member	Coralline Group: Coralline Oolite Formation / Hambleton Oolite Member
		Lower Calcareous Grit	Lower Calcareous Grit	Lower Calcareous Grit; Oldstead Oolite	Lower Calcareous Grit Formation
		Oxford Clay	Oxford Clay	Upper Oxford Clay	Oxford Clay Formation
	Callovian	Kellaways Rock	Hackness Rock; Langdale Beds; Kellaways Rock	Hackness Rock; Osgodby Formation; Kellaways Rock	Osgodby Formation: Hackness Rock Member, Kellaways Rock Member
		Moor Grit; Cornbrash	Cornbrash		
	Bathonian / ?–?	Upper Estuarine (Deltaic) Series / Moor Grit	Scalby Formation / Moor Grit	Scalby Formation	Scalby Formation: Long Nab Member, Moor Grit Member
MIDDLE JURASSIC		Scarborough or Grey Limestone Series	Scarborough Formation: Crinoid Grit, Brandsby Roadstone	Scarborough Formation: Crinoid Grit, Brandsby Roadstone	Ravenscar Group: Scarborough Formation: Crinoid Grit Member, Brandsby Roadstone
	Bajocian	Millepore Bed and Whitwell Oolite; Middle Estuarine (Deltaic) Series; Lower Estuarine (Deltaic) Series	Ravenscar Group: Cloughton Formation: Gristhorpe Member, Lebberston Formation, Blowgill Mbr	Cloughton Formation: Gristhorpe Member, Cayton Bay Formation, Blowgill Mbr	Cloughton Formation: Lebberston Member
	?–?	Eller Beck Bed or Hydraulic Lst.	Eller Beck Formation	Eller Beck Formation	Eller Beck Formation / Ingleby Ironstone Member
	Aalenian	Lower Estuarine (Deltaic) Series	Saltwick Formation	Hayburn Formation	Saltwick Formation
		Dogger	Dogger	Dogger Formation	Dogger Formation

(Lias Group)

north-west prow of the Cleveland Hills escarpment into Scugdale. However, Fox-Strangways (1886, p.32) recorded a 1.22 m-thick calcareous ferruginous bed at Beacon Scar [459 998].

At Blue Scar [5129 9938] on the south side of Scugdale, the Dogger Formation comprises 3 m of massive, grey-brown, ferruginous limestone and calcareous ironstone. At the top, the formation is both conglomeratic and fossiliferous. It is overlain by 3.6 m of grey, silty, micaceous and ferruginous mudstone of the Saltwick Formation and underlain by at least 8 m of the Whitby Mudstone Formation.

The Dogger is well exposed at the head of Scugdale [5275 9882], where 0.80 m of massive, fossiliferous, ferruginous limestone crops out below a waterfall, formed by the sandstone at the base of the Saltwick Formation. A 0.7 m-thick ferruginous mudstone immediately overlies the limestone in this locality.

About half a kilometre farther north, near High House [5271 9944], the lithology of the Dogger is unchanged, but it is immediately overlain by a massive sandstone of the Saltwick Formation.

The Dogger Formation is exposed below a waterfall [5168 0116] in Snotterdale and some 20 m south-west of the falls [5165 0109], a similar section through the Dogger proved:

	Thickness m
Mudstone, grey	0.30
Ironstone	0.20
Mudstone grey	0.20
Limestone conglomeratic, ferruginous	0.60

WHITBY MUDSTONE FORMATION
Mudstone grey silty (Alum Shale Member)

At Carlton Bank, in the north of the district, a massive 10 m sandstone of the Saltwick Formation forms a sharp lithological break at the top of the old Alum Shale workings [5211 0271] on Carlton Moor. It rests on 0.23 m of ferruginous mudstone, which may be the lateral correlative of the Dogger. The under-lying mudstone is pale grey and leached for a depth of 1.20 m into the Alum Shale Member.

The best exposures of the Dogger Formation occur on the western flanks of Cold Moor [5495 0335] where an adit was driven eastwards to work the formation known in this area as the Cold Moor Ironstone (Plate 3). The 'ironstones' are described (Hemingway, 1974, p.186) as sideritic, chamositic, chamosite oolites with abundant echinoid and coral debris including *Montivaltia*, *Thecosmilia* and *Thamnasteria*, as well as fragmentary bivalves and gastropods. He considered the diagenetic changes which have taken place may be unique, suggesting deposition in a basin geochemically independent from the main Cleveland Basin. The 'Dogger' in the vicinity of the adit is some 8 m thick and overlain by sandstone of the Saltwick Formation. The fauna from this locality indicates the *murchisonae* Zone of the Aalenian Stage and includes *Dimorpharaea defranciana*?, *Dimorpharaea* sp., *Enallocoenia richardsoni*, an indeterminate montlivaltiid, *Thecosmilia*?, indeterminate coral, serpulid and bryozoan fragments, terebratulid and rhynchonellid fragments, *Trochotoma*?, *Astarte* sp., *Camptonectes laminatus*, *Camptonectes* sp., *Chlamys* sp., *Ctenostreon* sp., *Cucullaea* cf. *reticulata*, *Gervillella*?, *Liostrea* sp., *Lopha* sp., *Modiolus* sp., *Myophorella phillipsii*, *Myophorella* sp., *Opis* sp., indeterminate ostreids, indeterminate pectenids, *Pronoella* sp., *Propeamussium* sp., *Pseudolimea* sp., *Tancredia* sp., *Trigonia* sp., *Unicardium* sp., *Ludwigia* sp., crinoid columnals and echinoid spines.

Derived fossils include rolled nuculid, dactylioceratid and belemnite fragments.

Nearby at [5505 0345], the derived fossils included a *Hildoceras* sp. and dactylioceratid fragments.

In Bilsdale, the Dogger Formation underlies most of the Cold Moor spur and is exposed in many places along its eastern flank. Just south of the Lyke Wake Walk path [5536 0332], 3 m of massive ferruginous limestone are exposed. It is oolitic in texture in the top 0.30 m and overlain by 10 m of ferruginous mudstone. The Dogger rests upon mudstones of the Alum Shale Member, here over 5 m thick.

Just beyond the eastern edge of the district, the Dogger Formation is well exposed beneath the scarp known as the

Plate 3 An old adit [5495 0335] driven into the Dogger Formation which marks the conglomeratic base to the Middle Jurassic. The mine was worked largely for nodules and lumps of ironstone. Sandy, ferruginous and phosphatic limestone containing fossiliferous pockets rich in bivalves and corals is also present. (L2451)

Wainstones [5582 0357]. It consists of massive, oolitic, ferruginous limestone, 1.00 m thick; it rests on grey mudstone of the Whitby Mudstone Formation and is overlain by 10.60 m of ferruginous mudstone with distinct ironstone laminae.

A ferruginous limestone of similar thickness was worked from a small level on the opposite side of Garfit Gap [5546 0313]. South of this level, the Dogger Formation may be traced along the western side of Bilsdale by many small natural exposures. It ranges in thickness between 1 and 3 m and usually comprises a well-bedded ferruginous limestone. It is sporadically shelly, crinoidal and contains coral and bryozoan fragments. Ironstone clasts are also a typical feature. The most southern exposures on Cold Moor occur beneath a sandstone, which forms a waterfall [5510 0053] near Cock Flats and at Round Hill [5490 0020]. At the former locality, 3 m of well-bedded ferruginous limestone rest on over 7 m of olive-grey mudstones of the Alum Shale Member.

At Round Hill [5490 0020], the Dogger Formation is 7.50 m thick and comprises two beds of fine to coarse oolitic ironstone and calcareous sandstone separated by 1 m of dark grey laminated mudstone. The upper bed of 'Dogger' is 5 m thick and the lower bed 1.50 m. The formation was formerly worked from a quarry [5482 0025] north-west of Round Hill.

Sporadic exposures of the formation occur beneath the scarp feature formed by Middle Jurassic sandstones on the south side of Raisdale. The oolitic ironstone is usually only 0.70 m thick. At an exposure [5333 9950], west of Ewe Hill, the Dogger is directly overlain by massive sandstone. However, at the Clough [5480 9727], a massive sandstone at a comparable horizon is underlain by carbonaceous sandstone, coal traces and mudstone with nodular ironstone beds, and the Dogger Formation appears to have been cut out by erosion.

On Snilesworth Moor, the Dogger Formation dips south to south-east and is exposed as inliers in the deeply incised valleys of Arns Gill, Proddale Beck and Ryedale. In Arns Gill [5322 9653], the Dogger is 0.85 m thick. The top 0.15 m comprise a calcareous oolitic ironstone which overlies a massive conglomeratic bed. The base is sharp against grey fossiliferous mudstones of the Alum Shale Member. Bivalves and gastropods are fairly common. Downstream [5244 9568], the ironstone is up to 0.76 m thick.

In the River Rye [5146 9525], just above the confluence with Arns Gill, the Dogger Formation forms the stream bed for several hundred metres. Numerous old levels in the east bank sought a thin coal in the overlying Saltwick Formation. The Dogger here is an oolitic ironstone, 1.30 m thick, and passes downstream into a ferruginous sandstone. Both these lithologies are unusual in that they commonly contain rootlets.

RAVENSCAR GROUP

The Ravenscar Group (Hemingway and Knox, 1973), about 150 m thick, comprises four marine units, mostly fossiliferous mudstone and limestone, which separate clastic sediments of nonmarine, deltaic origin. The latter consist of thick sandstones together with thin conglomerates, ironstones, seatearths and coals. Classification of the group is shown in Table 6.

Saltwick Formation

The Saltwick Formation forms a series of dominant features in the escarpment of the Cleveland Hills. The lowest beds are commonly massive thick lenses of sandstone, which weather into near-vertical rock faces protecting the underlying Whitby Mudstone Formation.

The formation, 50 m thick, comprises sandstone, siltstone, mudstone, seatearth and coal. Sideritic nodules are common in the mudstones and are also present as clasts in the basal erosive units of the sandstones. The predominant lithology is a fine- to medium-grained micaceous sandstone, commonly containing carbonaceous and/or ferruginous plant fragments. Conglomerates with mudstone and ironstone clasts infilling erosive channels, are typical of the lower horizons. Cross-bedding is common and a northern provenance is indicated.

The base of the formation is taken, for practical mapping purposes, at the base of the lowest sandstone, which approximates to the top of the Dogger. However, in places the Saltwick Formation has infilled erosive channels cut down into the Whitby Mudstone Formation, and the Dogger Formation is absent, for example at Crookleth Crags [5570 9697]. Elsewhere grey mudstone lies between the Dogger and the lowest sandstone; this is generally thin but, towards the east, it is up to 10 m in thickness, for example on Cold Moor (see Details, p.41).

The top of the formation is defined by the base of the marine Eller Beck Formation throughout much of the district. Where this formation cannot be located, or where it is considered to be absent, the boundary is shown by a conjectural line or the formation is linked with the overlying Cloughton Formation.

Details

In the Kirby Sigston–Cotcliffe graben, the Middle Jurassic is capped, between Beacon Hill and Carrodell House, by a series of yellow-brown ferruginous sandstones and interbedded silty mudstones and siltstones. The sandstones form pronounced features and have been quarried in places, for example near Beacon Hill [4258 9385 and 4257 9400], at Landmoth [4255 9260], Cotcliffe Bank [4229 9095] and Leak House [4275 9092]. The maximum thickness exposed is some 4 m. Dips are variable in direction and amount, because of major faults traversing the area.

On the western escarpment, the formation crops out from north of Thimbleby Bank [456 945] to south of Atlay Bank [468 905]. The Eller Beck Formation is apparently absent over the southern part of this area, therefore it is not possible to distinguish the Saltwick Formation from the lithologically similar Cloughton Formation along much of the outcrop between Burton's Plantation [471 937] and south of Atlay Bank [468 905].

Sandstone, typically cambered, is sporadically exposed around the escarpment along Thimbleby Bank to Over Silton [4569 9477 to 4518 9352]. The sandstone is yellow-brown, dominantly fine- to medium-grained, micaceous, and commonly contains sparse plant fragments. It is almost invariably cross-bedded, with both trough and tabular sets. In places, channels occur at the base, infilled with intraformational mudstone-clast conglomerates. Excellent cambered exposures of up to about 11 m of these sandstones form the 'Hanging Stone' on Thimbleby Bank [4500 9426].

To the south, in a disused quarry [4513 9352] near Over Silton, about 6 m of buff to pale orange-brown sandstone displays an upward-fining sequence, from fine to medium grained at the base, passing up into fine-grained sandstone. Trough cross-bedded sets with erosive scour bases are well developed, but the topmost metre shows thin, planar bedding. Intraformational mudstone wisps and clasts occur at the base of most channels, and are commonly surrounded by a ferruginous cement.

In a disused quarry [4607 9267] near Skirt Bank, 3.3 m of sandstone is exposed, low in the formation. The sandstone is pale grey and orange-brown in colour, thinly bedded, fine grained, and contains carbonaceous and mudstone wisps; it is cross-bedded in part.

Small exposures of sandstone, in the forest on Nether Silton Moor [4669 9381], also contain coaly laminae. Exposure is poor both east and south of Over Silton.

Farther north, on Thimbleby Moor and in Oakdale, the sandstones of the Saltwick Formation form distinct topographical features and individual beds can be traced for several kilometres. Up to three sandstones, separated by mudstones, are mapped and the Eller Beck Formation is inferred to lie above the topmost sandstone feature. Quarries [4626 9596, 4675 9609 and 4723 9621] expose yellow-brown, fine-grained, massive, cross-bedded sandstone. A typical sandstone of the formation is exposed north of Osmotherly, in an 8 m-high quarry face [4580 9828]; ironstone nodules in the sandstone show evidence of distortion where they are aligned along joints.

At Beacon Scar [4599 9987], the basal sandstone is about 15 m thick. It is mostly massively bedded but the lowest 2 m are flaggy, ferruginous, and have numerous plant fragments and coal 'scares'.

Between Beacon Scar and the entrance to Scugdale, the Saltwick Formation comprises one main bed of sandstone up to 25 m thick. It was quarried along much of the escarpment, for example at Cop Loaf [4635 0026], Scarth Nick [4732 0018], below Whorlton Moor [4765 0021], and at Raindrip [4815 0037].

In Scugdale, the basal sandstone of the Saltwick Formation is exposed in old quarries and natural scars at Blue Scar [5129 9938] (6 m), Scugdale Head Waterfall [5278 9880] (4 m), Horse Hole [5280 9889] (5 m), Rance Crag [5280 9930] (6 m), and High House [5274 9942] (2 m).

The section beneath the sandstone at Blue Scar proved 25 m of strata, typical of deposits formed in deltaic conditions.

	Thickness m
SALTWICK FORMATION	
Sandstone, yellow-brown, fine-grained, massive	6.50
Mudstone, grey, silty and sandy, with plant fragments	1.00
Sandstone, fine-grained	0.20
Mudstone, grey, silty, laminated	1.50
Mudstone, dark grey, carbonaceous	0.10
Sandstone, grey-brown, fine-grained	0.20
Mudstone, grey, silty	1.20
Sandstone, grey-brown, fine-grained	0.20
Gap	c.1.70
Ganister, grey	0.60
Sandstone, off-white, fine-grained	1.00
Gap, with mudstone	2.00
Mudstone, dark grey, carbonaceous	0.40
Seatearth, siltstone, grey, passing down to sandstone at base	1.30
Coal	0.15
Seatearth; mudstone, grey	0.30
Mudstone, grey, micaceous, silty, ferruginous	3.65
DOGGER FORMATION (see p.38)	3.00

The section (15.95 m thick) at Horse Hole proves coal and is well exposed:

	Thickness m
Sandstone, massive, cross-bedded; top metre flaggy	6.00
Mudstone, pale grey, ?leached	0.10
Mudstone, grey, laminated	0.50
Mudstone, grey, ferruginous	0.50
Mudstone, grey, laminated	0.30
Mudstone, dark grey	0.03
Mudstone, purplish grey, laminated	0.07
Coal	0.05
Mudstone, carbonaceous, purple interlaminae	0.30
Seatearth; siltstone/sandstone, purplish dark grey	0.60
Siltstone and sandstone, pale grey	1.50
Gap	3.00
Sandstone, massive, ganisteroid top	3.00

Some 40 m to the north, at Rance Crags, cross-bedding in the sandstone indicates derivation from the north. The top of the foreset beds show slight overturning.

At the head of Thackdale, the waterfall [5169 0116] is formed by the basal sandstone of the Saltwick Formation. The complete sequence is 19.45 m thick and is as follows:

	Thickness m
SALTWICK FORMATION	
Sandstone, yellow, fine-grained massive; coal 'scares' and stigmarian roots in erosive basal zone	5.00
Mudstone, grey	3.00
Coal, shaly	thin
Gap	0.20
Sandstone (waterfall)	10.00
Mudstone, grey, silty	0.10
Ironstone, nodular	0.15
Mudstone, grey, silty	1.00
DOGGER FORMATION	

A landform feature can be traced from the waterfall westwards, skirting Pond Hole [512 012] and forming the steep edge of Whorlton Moor and Round Hill. A quarry on the north-west nose of the hill [4960 0110] showed 8 m of yellow-buff, massive, cross-bedded, fine- to medium-grained, micaceous sandstone overlying 4.5 m of well-bedded, fine-grained, ferruginous sandstone, resting on a further 2 m of massive sandstone. The topmost sandstone exhibits ferruginous patches and stains.

In the north of the district, the sandstones of the Saltwick Formation form impressive scarp features along the length of Faceby Bank, Carlton Moor, and the outliers of Cringle Moor and Cold Moor.

The crags at Gold Hill [5190 0160] coincide with a lens-shaped thickening of the beds. The crags expose some 9 m of massive, yellowish brown sandstone, showing isolated pockets of small-scale, cross-laminated, ferruginous sandstone and large-scale troughs emphasised by ironstone layers. Farther east, at the entrance to Raisdale, evidence of channelling is seen within the sandstone at Red Screes [5240 0215].

Excellent exposures are present on the northward facing prow of Howe Moor above Carlton Bank [5200 0270]. The 23.90 m-thick section, close to the Lyke Wake Walk path, is as follows:

	Thickness m
SALTWICK FORMATION	
Sandstone, massive, cross-bedded; coarse-grained at base, with ferruginous fragments; base irregular	9.00
Sandstone, brown, fine-grained, micaceous	1.20

	Thickness m
Sandstone and mudstone, interlaminated	0.20
Sandstone, massive, ferruginous	0.60
Coal, shaly	1.50
Coal	0.20
Seatearth; mudstone, grey-brown	0.05
Mudstone, dark grey, silty	0.30
Mudstone, purplish grey	0.40
Mudstone, pale grey	0.50
Sandstone, fine-grained	0.15
Mudstone, grey	0.40
Sandstone, yellow-brown	0.20
Mudstone, grey	0.20
Sandstone, yellow-brown	0.20
Mudstone, grey	0.20
Sandstone, yellow-brown, flaggy	0.40
Sandstone, yellow-brown, massive	10.00

DOGGER FORMATION

A mudstone parting, between 12 and 13 m above the Alum Shale Member, here yielded abundant *Equisetum columnare*.

The northern scarp of Cringle Moor, known as Kirkby Bank [538 032], forms an almost continuous exposure of the Saltwick and Cloughton formations, about 1 km long and 60 m high. To the west, on Cringle End, up to four distinct sandstone divisions are present. When traced eastwards, the lower two units merge into a 30 m-thick sequence composed almost entirely of sandstone. The Saltwick Formation is correlated with the lower 16 m of this sequence. Large quarries, half a kilometre to the south of Kirkby Bank, expose about 14 m of Saltwick Formation sandstone in the northernmost quarry face [5349 0288].

The most easterly outlier of the Saltwick Formation is formed by sandstones which crop out on Cold Moor. The basal sandstone, some 6 m thick, shows an erosive base which cuts down several metres into the underlying ferruginous mudstone. The mudstone is 10 m thick, and overlies the Dogger Formation near the Lyke Wake Walk path of the eastern side of the Moor [5536 0337].

On the western side of the Moor, in the vicinity of the old ironstone levels driven into the Dogger Formation [5495 0340], the following section, 25.60 m thick, was recorded:

	Thickness m
SALTWICK FORMATION	
Sandstone, yellow-brown, fine-grained, massive	10.60
Mudstone, grey, sandy, laminated	10.00
Sandstone, yellow-brown, fine-grained, massive, cross-bedded; top metre with shaly laminae	4.00
Sandstone, brown, ferruginous	1.00

DOGGER FORMATION

In Raisdale, the best exposures of the Saltwick Formation occur on the south and west sides of the valley where the lowest sandstones form natural scarps of bare rock or have been quarried sporadically along the crop; exposures up to 4 m are common. The beds consists of massive, cross-bedded yellow-brown sandstone; ironstone clasts occur towards the base, and commonly show parallel orientation along the foreset beds. Cross-bedding indicates derivation from the north and north-east. Ripple marks are also present with crests aligned east–west. Good exposures may be seen at The Clough [5275 0125], Clough Gill [5314 0071], west of Ewe Hill [5333 9950], Harten Gill [5438 9890], and Tennet Bank [5508 9955] at the entrance to Bilsdale.

The western edge of Bilsdale is marked by dominant crags of sandstone up to 9 m thick. In the north, near the Wain Stones, the basal sandstone of the Saltwick Formation is separated from the underlying Dogger Formation by some 10 m of ferruginous laminated mudstone. The mudstone increases in thickness to over 20 m southwards towards Chop Gate. The sandstone is variable and split in places into three units separated by mudstone, for example on the eastern flank of Cold Moor [557 010]. An exposure at Beacon Guest Crags [5590 9667], just beyond the eastern margin of the district, proved a coaly shale, up to 1 m thick, overlying the lowest sandstone unit.

In the central area of the Cleveland Hills, south of Snilesworth Moor, inliers of Middle Jurassic, totalling 10.67 m, are exposed in the banks of Arns Gill [5322 9653].

	Thickness m
SALTWICK FORMATION	
Sandstone, yellow, fine-grained, massive	2.00
Mudstone, grey, laminated	0.03
Coal and carbonaceous mudstone	0.16
Mudstone, grey, laminated	0.14
Ganister, pale grey to black	0.60
Sandstone, pale grey	0.20
Mudstone, grey, laminated	0.15
Coal and carbonaceous mudstone	0.20
Seatearth; mudstone, grey, silty	0.30
Mudstone, grey, silty	0.55
Coal and carbonaceous mudstone	0.25
Mudstone, pale grey	0.14
Coal and carbonaceous mudstone	0.45
Sandstone; ganisteroid, yellowish grey mudstone laminae; black rootlets in top 0.7 m	0.90
Mudstone, grey, laminated	2.00
Ironstone	0.10
Sandstone, grey-brown	0.70
Mudstone, grey, laminated	1.60

DOGGER FORMATION

An inlier at a similar stratigraphical position occurs in the River Rye between the confluence with Proddale Beck and the Arns Gill. The section, is about 1 km in length, and exposes the Dogger Formation in the river bed, overlain by up to 9 m of mudstones with variable sandstone beds. The mudstone contains large ironstone nodules beneath a sandstone, which forms a waterfall about 1 km north-east of Snilesworth Lodge.

At the southern end of the section [5141 9534], a sequence, 10.65 m thick, has been recorded.

	Thickness m
SALTWICK FORMATION	
Mudstone, grey-brown, silty, ferruginous, laminated	3.00
Sandstone, yellowish brown, fine-grained	5.00
Mudstone, coaly, pale grey to black	0.30
Seatearth; sandstone	0.40
Sandstone, yellow-brown, massive, fine-grained; grey and silty towards base	1.10
Mudstone, grey, laminated, coal 'scares'	0.45
Mudstone, dark grey, carbonaceous	0.05
Coal	0.05
Seatearth; siltstone	0.30
small gap	

DOGGER FORMATION

Cleveland Hills No. 1 Borehole proved the Middle Jurassic in the top 70 m (228 ft). The strata are recorded as weathered, yellow, micaceous sandstone with thin beds of shale and very thin coals in the uppermost 43 m. The lowest 27 m, tentatively correlated with the Saltwick Formation, were described as grey micaceous sandstone with grey sandy shale.

Eller Beck Formation

The Eller Beck Formation is lithologically heterogeneous and comprises oolitic, chamositic and sideritic ironstone, mudstone, and siltstone with sandstone lenses. It records the first marine transgression in the Ravenscar Group of the Cleveland Basin, when the low-lying delta swamps of the Saltwick Formation were inundated from the east or south-east (Kent, 1980b).

In coastal sections in East Yorkshire, a characteristic sandstone forms a prominent marker horizon at the top of the formation, but the equivalent sandstone in the Cleveland Hills is not well developed, and the upper boundary of the formation is not easily defined. In this district, the formation ranges in thickness from 4 to 6 m, but shows a lithofacies transition from an ironstone–shale–sandstone sequence in the north, to a limestone–shale–sandstone sequence to the south of the district (Powell and Rathbone, 1983). The formation is not well exposed, and may be absent locally due to facies changes at the north-western limit of the marine transgression, for example in the Kirby Sigston–Cotcliffe graben area, or to penecontemporaneous erosion.

Hemingway and Knox (1973) suggested the presence of a second marine transgression above the Eller Beck Formation; they named these beds the Blowgill Member. However, Powell and Rathbone (1983) demonstrated that there was only one transgression and the term Blowgill Member was rejected. The basal ironstone is named the Ingleby Ironstone.

Details

A section on Thimbleby Bank [4560 9460], poorly exposed at the time of this survey, was recorded by R W O'B Knox (personal communication, 1980) as follows:

	Thickness m
CLOUGHTON FORMATION	
Sandstone, medium-grained, cross-bedded, with channelled base	c.4.7
ELLER BECK FORMATION	
Mudstone, silty, micaceous, poorly bedded	c.0.6
Mudstone, laminated	c.1.07
Ironstone, hard, non-oolitic, silty, sideritic mudstone	0.23
Mudstone, brown and green-grey, shelly, passes down into grey silty shale	0.13
Ironstone (sideritic mudstone), shelly, with abundant oysters; burrows at base	0.16
SALTWICK FORMATION	
Siltstone, yellow-brown, soft	0.09
Mudstone, grey, silty, soft	0.10
Mudstone, grey, silty, with rootlets	c.0.01

Farther north, at Beacon Scar [4595 9980], 1.5 m of grey silty mudstone with siltstone and sandstone laminae at the top, and with bivalves towards the base, overlies a very thin weathered ironstone which is correlated with the Ingleby Ironstone.

In Scugdale, [5170 9915] near Holiday House, R W O'B Knox (personal communication, 1980) recorded a 2.7 m mudstone overlying a 0.20 m ironstone containing a few burrows at the base, on the south side of Scugdale; he considered these beds to represent the Eller Beck Formation.

In the north, sporadic exposures of the formation were noted on Carlton Bank [518 024], Cringle Moor [538 032], and Cold Moor [5455 0080]. At Cold Moor, the Ingleby Ironstone was recorded as 0.30 m in thickness and partially oolitic in the upper section.

On Snilesworth Moor, some 0.30 m of sandstone, overlying ferruginous shales, are exposed in Parci Gill [5380 9550]. An oolitic ironstone, 0.50 m thick, probably marks the base of the Eller Beck Formation within this inlier.

To the south-east, in Wheat Beck [5018 9476 to 5080 9457] the following composite section was recorded:

	Thickness m
CLOUGHTON FORMATION	
Mudstone and silty mudstone, grey, with plant fragments	c.1.1
Sandstone, buff, fine-grained, cross-laminated; plant fragments and rootlets at base	c.0.7
ELLER BECK FORMATION	
Siltstone, grey, micaceous, with buff-grey, fine-grained sandstone laminae and thin beds; coarsens upwards, with sandstone common in upper 0.5 m; sideritic ironstone nodules throughout and plant fragments in upper 1 m	c.2.1
Sandstone, buff-khaki, micaceous, thin-bedded, cross-laminated, fine-grained, with plant fragments	c.0.3
Siltstone, grey, micaceous, laminated	c.0.75
Siderite band, grey, soft, with hard sideritic nodules and disseminated pyrite	0.06
Siltstone, grey, micaceous, with small thin shelled bivalves in lower 0.9 m	1.0
Mudstone, dark grey, silty, with bivalves	0.08
Ironstone, pale grey, chamositic, sideritic and oolitic, with poorly preserved gastropods, thin-shelled bivalves including *Astarte*, *Corbula*, *Meleagrinella*, ostreids, *Nuculana* and *Protocardia*	0.46
Siltstone, dark grey, micaceous, sparse ooliths and grey siderite nodules containing small bivalves; abundant poorly preserved gastropods and small bivalves including *Astarte*, *Camponectes*, *Eotrapezium?*, *Meleagrinella* sp., *Modiolus* sp., ostreids and *Pseudolimea*. Lenses of pale grey iron-stained calcilutite yield *Astarte*, *Cucullaea*, *Grammatodon?*, *Liostrea*, *Mactromya?*, *Meleagrinella* and *Pleuromya*.	0.33
SALTWICK FORMATION	
Siltstone, pale grey, micaceous, with laterally impersistent buff-grey, micaceous, cross-bedded, fine-grained sandstone containing abundant plant remains and rootlets	c.1

Micropalaeontological samples from the basal siltstone of the formation in Wheat Beck [5074 9458] yield the arenaceous foraminifer *Trochammina sablei*.

Towards the south-east, the Ingleby Ironstone Member (Knox, 1973; Powell and Rathbone, 1983) is exposed on the banks of the Rye [5252 9310]. Here, a 0.7 m-thick pale green-grey, chamositic, oolitic, sideritic ironstone with abundant bivalves is overlain by at least 2.8 m of poorly exposed grey, silty mudstone with siderite nodules, passing up into grey, silty mudstone and siltstone with thin, cross-laminated, fine-grained sandstone lenses and siderite nodules.

From the many exposures in Blow Gill, towards the east and north-east, two detailed composite sections are described below.

Blow Gill (north), composite section [5295 9381 to 5335 9455]:

	Thickness m
CLOUGHTON FORMATION	
Sandstone, yellow-buff, micaceous, thin-bedded, cross-bedded, with carbonaceous laminae	c.1
ELLER BECK FORMATION	
Siltstone, grey-buff, with carbonaceous laminae and pale grey siderite nodules	0.95
Mudstone, pale grey, micaceous	0.68
Sandstone, buff-grey, micaceous, cross-laminated, fine-grained, with oscillatory ripples, mudstone partings, burrows and a channelled base	0.65–1.05
Siltstone, grey, micaceous, and subordinate mudstone, with siderite nodules in upper part	0.10–0.5
Sandstone, grey, fine-grained	0.15
Siltstone and mudstone, grey, micaceous, with siderite nodules	0.58
Mudstone, grey, silty, passing up into siltstone with subordinate thin beds of fine-grained sandstone; abundant siderite nodules with sparse bivalves at base	0.60
Mudstone, pale grey, slightly micaceous, silty, with sporadic siderite nodules and thin shelled bivalves in lower 0.8 m	1.68
Ingleby Ironstone Member: ironstone, grey, chamositic, oolitic sideritic, with abundant bivalves, many preserved in life position; burrows at base	0.71
Mudstone, grey, soft, with abundant bivalves	0.05
Siltstone, dark grey, micaceous, laminated, with abundant bivalves, many in life position, and sporadic rounded chert and sandstone pebbles; oolitic in lowest 0.15 m	0.31
SALTWICK FORMATION	
Siltstone, pale grey, micaceous, with plant fragments and rootlets	0.0–0.55
Sandstone, white, pale grey and brown, cross-bedded, fine-grained	1.15–1.7

Blow Gill (south) [5280 9303]:

	Thickness m
CLOUGHTON FORMATION	
Sandstone, brown, micaceous, cross-bedded, fine-grained	c.1.8
ELLER BECK FORMATION	
Sandstone, buff to green-brown, micaceous, thin-bedded, fine-grained, with oscillatory ripples and burrows	0.36
Siltstone, pale grey, micaceous	0.33
Mudstone, pale grey, silty, with sporadic siderite nodules and small bivalves	1.37
Ironstone, pale grey, sideritic, with pyrite	0.11
Mudstone, grey, silty, with abundant small bivalves; pyritised in upper 0.15 m	0.30
Mudstone, pale grey, soft, with small bivalves	0.20
Ironstone, pale grey, calcareous, sideritic	0.11
Mudstone, grey, slightly micaceous, calcareous, silty, sporadic siderite nodules, plant fragments; small thin-shelled bivalves include *Meleagrinella?*, *Modiolus*, ostreids and *Pleuromya*	0.82
Ironstone, grey, calcareous, sideritic	0.12
Mudstone, pale grey, silty; calcareous in upper 0.15 m	0.30

Stream bed (at time of survey)

Micropalaeontological samples taken from the mudstones described above yield a sparse foraminifer fauna including *Trochammina topogorukensis*, *Reophax helvetica*, *Spirillina infima*, and *Ammodiscus* sp., which indicate near-marine conditions.

Cloughton Formation

The term Cloughton Formation was introduced by Hemingway and Knox (1973), and replaces the Middle Deltaic Series (Hemingway, 1949). The formation averages 40 m in thickness and consists of laterally variable, channel-fill sandstone, siltstone and mudstone of fluviodeltaic origin. Sandstone dominates the sequence and thin, laterally impersistent coals are present. To the south, over much of the Cleveland Basin, the formation is divided by the marine Lebberston Member (formerly the Whitwell Oolite or Millepore Bed), which marks a marine transgression from the south and east. It comprises a wedge of shallow-marine calcareous sandstone and oolitic limestone, becoming more sandy and ferruginous to the north. However, the district probably lies close to the north-west limit of the transgression (Rathbone, 1987 a and b), and the member has been recognised only in the south-east, at one poorly exposed locality (see Details). It has not been mapped in this district.

The sandstones of the Cloughton Formation are usually orange-brown to buff and grey, commonly cross-bedded and fine to medium grained. Both trough and planar cross-bedding are evident. In places, up to five distinct, feature-forming sandstones can be distinguished, but they die out laterally so that correlation of individual beds over wide areas is not possible. These deposits represent fluvial or delta-top channels. Other sediment types, such as interdistributary siltstone and mudstone, or coal, are exposed rarely.

Details

The highest beds within the Kirby Sigston–Cotcliffe graben area are assigned to the Cloughton Formation, but, in the absence of the Eller Beck Formation, the age of these beds is uncertain, and the boundary between the Saltwick and Cloughton formations is speculative (p.39, Details: Saltwick Formation).

Over 7 m of grey and orange-brown, thick-bedded, medium-grained sandstone, with plant debris and discontinuous horizons of ferruginous nodules, have been recorded in both natural exposures and disused quarries west of Hood Howe Stone [4586 9483 and 4575 9469].

Towards the south-east, along Thimbleby Bank, there are several natural and quarry exposures immediately above the Eller Beck Formation. In Windy Pen Plantation [4505 9400], 8.5 m of sandstone is exposed; it is orange-brown, slightly micaceous, thick bedded, fine to medium grained and, in part, displays erosive surfaces with channel bases floored by intraformational mudstone-clast conglomerates. The same sandstone unit is well exposed in several disused quarries above Over Silton [4509 9369 to 4529 9382]. It can be traced around Knipes Hill [4605 9325], and is particularly well exposed in four disused quarries [4594 9363, 4618 9329, 4622 9339 and 4636 9368]. Many small exposures of the same unit occur around the escarpment from these quarries to Mother Gill [4665 9443] and Red Way Gill [4704 9457]; it is concealed beneath a landslip at Cockle Beck [4719 9395].

Numerous exposures of sandstone above this basal unit also occur around Knipes Hill. The exposures are commonly cambered, but up to 4 m of orange-brown, cross-bedded, fine- to medium-grained sandstone are present adjacent to a forestry track [4597 9357], and around Knipes End [4597 9305 to 4605 9448], and form a prominent feature around the escarpment from Knipes End to Cockle Beck.

About 3 m of sandstone above the basal two units form mappable landform features with springs at their bases and are exposed near Red Way [4710 9447]. The sandstone is pale grey to buff and cross-bedded towards the base, but passes upwards into thinly bedded units. Coal laminae occur sporadically throughout.

Several disused adits for coal have been reported below Swinestone Cliff (Fox-Strangways et al., 1886, p.37). The area is now densely afforested with conifers, and these adits were not seen. A coal has been mapped below Swinestone Cliff [4702 9437 to 4722 9407] using stratigraphical data obtained from the adjacent sheet (Rathbone, 1987a). It is not exposed.

The upper 15.5 m of the formation were penetrated in the Silton Borehole (SE49SE/2) [4724 9471] where the strata display an upward-fining sequence dominated by pale buff, medium- to coarse-grained massive sandstone, which is overlain by 2 m of dark grey carbonaceous mudstone and siltstone.

The Cloughton Formation is not well exposed between Cockle Beck [4730 9398] and Kepwick [472 906]. The best exposure occurs in a disused quarry [4725 9184] and below The Nab, where nearly 16 m of orange-brown, fine- to medium-grained sandstone is patchily exposed. It is commonly cross-bedded, with planar bedding in part, and contains some plant debris, mudflakes, and ferruginous nodules.

In an overgrown quarry [4782 9155] to the south, some 2 m of grey shale were recorded resting on a thin sandstone.

About 2.5 m of orange-brown, cross-bedded, fine- to medium-grained sandstone is exposed in a small stream in Butcher's Wood [4809 9038]. Fox-Strangways et al. (1886, p.37) record old coal pits nearby in Butcher's Wood and collapsed bell-pits can still be seen. No exposure of coal was found.

Extensive man-made and natural exposures provide excellent sections of sandstone in a disused quarry south of Kepwick [4712 9021], to Atlay Bank [4679 9053] and finally around to Cowesby Quarry [4712 9021]. The best section, at Atlay Bank [4678 9059], shows about 9.5 m of orange-brown, fine- to medium-grained, trough cross-bedded sandstone. Abundant scour bases are infilled with sandstones containing intraformational mudstone clasts, and in places a ferruginous cement, results in a ribbed appearance along bedding planes, foreset laminae, and fissures within the sandstone. Over 7 m of this sandstone, with some subordinate thin-bedded sandstone, is exposed in Kepwick and Cowesby quarries.

In the Thimbleby Moor–Middlesbrough area, near Osmotherley, exposures are rare, but numerous irregular and discontinuous features suggest laterally variable sandstones of a lensoid nature.

Some 3 m of massive, ferruginous, fine-grained sandstone are exposed in Priests Spa Quarry [4645 9905]. Nearby, in Crabdale [4752 9937], the following 5 m or so of measures are exposed in Crabdale Beck beneath a massive fine-grained sandstone.

	Thickness m
Mudstone, grey, silty	1.00
Sandstone, yellow-brown, fine-grained	0.80
Mudstone, grey, laminated, with yellow ferruginous bed near base	0.35
Mudstone, carbonaceous	0.02
Mudstone, grey	0.80
Coal, dirty	0.14
Mudstone, grey	0.80
Sandstone, ferruginous	1.00
Mudstone, grey, carbonaceous	0.30

On the highest part of Carlton Bank [5194 0258], a series of sandstone beds, separated by mudstones and flaggy sandstone partings, are the uppermost beds of the Cloughton Formation. The general succession measured along the Lyke Wake Walk path is as follows:

	Thickness m
Sandstone, brown, fine-grained (Trig Point)	1.00
Gap	5.00
Sandstone, brown, massive	0.30
Gap, with mudstone and sandstone	3.00
Sandstone, massive, ganisteroid top 1 m thick	1.80
Gap	4.60
Sandstone and mudstone	c.21.80
Sandstone, massive, fine-grained, cross-bedded; erosional base with coarse-grained sandstone containing ferruginous plant fragments	9.00
Sandstone, brown, fine-grained, micaceous	1.20
Sandstone, with mudstone partings	0.20
Sandstone, massive, very ferruginous	0.60

The higher scarps of Kirkby Bank [5375 0315] comprise sandstones and mudstones of the Cloughton Formation. The top 11 m, capped by Drake Howe, are massively bedded, micaceous and particularly ferruginous.

Underlying these sandstones, other feature-forming beds are not so well exposed. An estimated gap of some 14 m presumably contains less resistant mudstones and shaly sandstones. Beneath this gap, a distinctive double landform feature is produced by well-exposed sandstones and mudstones some 6 m in thickness. The topmost sandstone is 3.35 m thick with a ganisteroid top, and rests on a more thinly bedded, ripple-marked sandstone; the ripples have a wavelength of 0.8 m and their axes are aligned east–west. Finely comminuted plant fragments and large-diameter boring and burrowing structures further emphasise this distinctive horizon. This sandstone passes downwards into a mainly mudstone sequence, some 9 m thick, but with a 0.50 m-thick sandstone 3.35 m from the base. The mudstone rests on 12 m of sandstone with pale grey micaceous partings, and with a basal bed which contains many ferruginous inclusions.

Interbanded sandstones and mudstones of the Cloughton Formation form the high ground of Cold Moor [550 020], Black Moor [520 980] and Bilsdale West Moor [555 965], and also crop out on the sides of Ryedale, Arns Gill and Parci Gill in the Snilesworth Moor area [520 970].

The topmost 45 m of strata in the Cleveland Hills Borehole are correlated with the Cloughton Formation and were described as 'weathered yellow micaceous sandstones with thin beds of shale and very thin coal traces'.

On the north side of Wheat Beck [5046 9495] a thin coal is exposed:

	Thickness m
Mudstone, silty, and siltstone, dark grey, with plant fragments	c.0.9
Coal, poor quality	0.15
Siltstone, micaceous, with abundant plant debris and rootlets; passing down into grey, silty mudstone with thin sandstone lenses containing plant debris	c.0.9

There are many disused bell-pits for coal extraction on both sides of Ladhill Gill [5450 9300 and 5507 9270]. They have a stratigraphical level from close below the Brandsby Roadstone to some 20 m below the top of the Cloughton Formation when traced northwards [5460 9350].

The Lebberston Member was deposited during a marine transgression which advanced northwards from the East Midlands Shelf into the Cleveland Basin, but the member has been recognised only at one poorly exposed locality, in Ladhill Gill [5464 9166]. It was not possible to map the member elsewhere, and it may be absent over much of the district.

	Thickness m
Sandstone, fine-grained	c.0.5
LEBBERSTON MEMBER	
Siltstone, and silty mudstone, grey, micaceous, with plant debris, and nodules and a 0.18 m bed of sideritic ironstone; sandy, and with bivalves towards the base; passing down into pebbly, ferruginous sandstone with a poorly preserved macrofauna including pectinid bivalves, *Gervillella*?, crinoid columnals, and woody debris	c.2.7
Mudstone, grey, silty	c.0.3

Scarborough Formation

The Scarborough Formation, formerly the Grey Limestone Series (Fox-Strangways et al., 1886), represents a major marine transgression within the Ravenscar Group. It can be traced throughout the Cleveland Basin. In coastal exposures, it is 20 m thick and has yielded ammonites of late Bajocian age (*humphriesianum* Zone) (Parsons, 1977). Within the district, the formation ranges from 14 m to 17 m in thickness. Over much of the outcrop it comprises limestone, mudstone, siltstone and calcareous sandstone. Fox-Strangways (1892, p.236) noted that the succession is dominated successively, from base to top, by calcareous, siliceous and argillaceous beds.

The calcareous beds, now named the **Brandsby Roadstone** (Phillips, 1829, p.152), are predominantly limestone with subordinate mudstone and calcareous sandstone. The siliceous beds (equivalent to the Fossiliferous Grit of Fox-Strangways) are now termed the **Crinoid Grit Member** (Richardson, 1912; Parsons, 1977), and comprise sandstone with subordinate siltstone and mudstone, and sporadic limestone. At outcrop, the sandstone is commonly decalcified and highly porous, and is characterised by moulds of pentacrinoids and scattered bivalves. The argillaceous beds are represented by a wet 'slack' which marks their outcrop between the top of the Crinoid Grit and the base of the Moor Grit.

The Brandsby Roadstone and Crinoid Grit form positive topographical features, and can be traced throughout the district, encircling the Cleveland and Hambleton hills. They also form outliers north of Osmotherley and Scugdale, and on Snilesworth Moor and Bilsdale West Moor.

Details

In the western part of the outcrop, exposure is poor around Over Silton Moor. Small sections of blue-grey, siliceous, micritic limestone occur patchily along a forestry track [4615 9498 to 4608 9492], and there are many fragments of limestone and sandstone along the outcrop. The Silton Borehole (SE49SE/2) [47249471] penetrated the upper part of the formation; the relevant part is summarised below.

	Thickness m
CRINOID GRIT MEMBER	
Siltstone, yellow-brown	0.15
Mudstone, ferruginous	0.15
Sandstone, coarse-grained, ferruginous	0.04
Sandstone, yellow, finely shelly	0.02
Mudstone, yellow, ferruginous	0.04
Sandstone, yellow-brown, fine- to medium-grained, massive	7.6
Sandstone, pale grey, fine-grained, bioturbated	1.0
BRANDSBY ROADSTONE	
Mudstone, grey, silty, and siltstone with fine-grained sandstone	0.3
Sandstone, pale grey, massive, calcareous, bioturbated	0.3
Limestone, pale blue-grey, argillaceous, bioclastic	0.7
Mudstone, dark grey, calcareous, rich in ostracods and holothurians	0.1
Mudstone, dark grey, silty, pyritic, sporadically shelly	0.2
Limestone, grey, massive, bioclastic	0.1
Mudstone, grey	0.05
Limestone, grey, bioclastic	0.69
CLOUGHTON FORMATION	
Mudstone, dark grey, carbonaceous, sporadic plant debris	0.46

Patchy exposure of the Crinoid Grit, with bivalve casts and mudflakes, is evident in the forestry tracks to the south and south-west [4721 9468 and 4746 9405]. At Swinestone Cliff [4728 9412], within a dense coniferous forest, about 3.5 m of cambered, cross-bedded, fine- to medium-grained sandstone is exposed. It is pale grey near the base but is very ferruginous in the upper part, resulting in an intense red-brown colouration. The sandstone is decalcified, porous, and contains abundant bivalve moulds in some places. Powerful springs flow from the base, and the ground beneath the cliff is strewn with boulders of sandstone.

South of a landslip above Burton's Plantation [4728 9346], the following section was noted:

	Thickness m
CRINOID GRIT MEMBER	
Sandstone, ferruginous, fine-grained, with lenses of sandy limestone and calcareous sandstone	0.5
BRANDSBY ROADSTONE	
Limestone, grey, sandy, bioclastic, with crinoid debris	0.8

On the bank of White Gill [4810 9243], 4 m of cambered, very porous and ferruginous, cross-bedded, medium- to coarse-grained sandstone is exposed at the base of the Crinoid Grit. Towards the north-west and stratigraphically above these beds, several exposures [4800 9258 to 4811 9249] show up to 3.5 m of white to pale grey, porous, cross-bedded, medium-grained sandstone with decalcified bivalve casts mostly represented by voids.

The only recorded exposure of the argillaceous beds above the Crinoid Grit occurs east of Kepwick Hall [4775 9085] in a disused quarry in Hall Plantation [4793 9094], and is as follows:

	Thickness m
Siltstone, sandy, buff, with abundant poorly preserved, mainly indeterminate small bivalves, including *Nicaniella* sp. and a ?limid fragment	c.0.3
Gap	c.0.5
CRINOID GRIT MEMBER	
Sandstone, pale grey, with slight ferruginous weathering, cross-bedded, porous, decalcified, with bivalve moulds; mainly inaccessible due to quarry being flooded	c.3.5

A poorly exposed section in Tinkler's Grain [4813 9084], east of Kepwick Hall, shows some 0.9 m of the Crinoid Grit Member overlying a similar thickness of the Brandsby Roadstone but a better section occurs nearby, in a stream to the south [4816 9076], as follows:

	Thickness m
CRINOID GRIT MEMBER	
Limestone, pale grey, bioclastic, well cemented	c.0.6
Gap	c.0.1
Sandstone, slightly ferruginous, medium-grained, cross-bedded in part, commonly decalcified; sporadic bivalve casts represented by voids	c.2.8
BRANDSBY ROADSTONE	
Limestone, blue-grey, hard, micritic, with wavy bedding, passing up into siliceous limestone and bioclastic limestone, with subordinate calcareous sandstone in the upper 1.2 m; patchy exposure	c.2.8
Gap	c.1.2
CLOUGHTON FORMATION	
Sandstone, buff, weathering orange-brown, thin-bedded, cross-bedded, fine-grained	c.1.1

A further stream section to the south, in Butcher's Wood [4820 9028 to 4823 9026] shows:

	Thickness m
CRINOID GRIT MEMBER	
Sandstone, pale grey, commonly decalcified, porous, cross-bedded, fine- to medium-grained; bivalve moulds particularly common towards the top; many small gaps in the section	c.8.5
Gap	c.0.8
BRANDSBY ROADSTONE	
Limestone, grey, siliceous, hard, poorly exposed	c.1.1

The following composite section was compiled from exposures immediately to the west, in Butcher's Wood [4794 9027 to 4820 9029].

	Thickness m
CRINOID GRIT MEMBER	
Sandstone, dominantly pale grey but ferruginous in part, commonly decalcified and porous, fine- to medium-grained, medium-bedded, cross-bedded; some very fossiliferous horizons with bivalve casts. Sandy limestone lenses and nodules, up to 0.9 m wide and 1.3 m long, concentrated at 0.4–1.5 m above the base	c.9.5
BRANDSBY ROADSTONE	
Limestone, blue-grey, with subordinate pale grey towards base, siliceous in part	c.1.8

At the side of Jenny Brewsters Gill [4770 9635], the formation has been quarried and partly mined for road metal. A drift was driven into the limestone which was reported to be very hard and some 2 m thick (Fox-Strangways et al., 1886, p.40). An old limekiln was marked on the 1854 version of the topographic map close to the junction of the Gill and Hambleton Street. The section now exposed in the old quarry is as follows:

	Thickness m
CRINOID GRIT MEMBER	
Sandstone, brown, ferruginous, shelly at top	2.50
Mudstone, dark grey, finely laminated	0.50
Sandstone, yellow, fine-grained	0.07
BRANDSBY ROADSTONE	
Limestone, pale grey, sandy, bioclastic	0.50 to 0.80
CLOUGHTON FORMATION	
Mudstone and ganisteroid sandstone	

A small quarry [4720 9732] at the side of the Osmotherley Road exposes 1.50 m of brown, massive, fine-grained, ferruginous sandstone; shelly pockets are common together with sporadic coarse quartz grains, suggesting a correlation with the Crinoid Grit.

The Brandsby Roadstone is well exposed in the extreme north-west of the Cleveland escarpment. An old quarry [4642 9907] on the west of Osmotherley Reservoir proved 0.40 m of dark grey, argillaceous, shelly and finely bioclastic limestone. A similar thickness of limestone crops out in the path [4717 9936] on Sheep Wash Bank. The distinctive Crinoid Grit, which closely overlies the Brandsby Roadstone, is sporadically exposed on Pamperdale Moor [4770 9870] and on Stony Ridge [4895 9930].

An outlier of Crinoid Grit forms a faulted area of ground south of Whorlton Moor. Crags up to 3 m high comprising fine- to medium-grained, cross-bedded sandstone with ferruginous inclusions, and numerous trace-fossil 'tracks' and impressions. The best exposures are at Scot Crags [5170 0044], Barkers Crags [5200 0035] and Stony Wicks [5270 0025].

On Snilesworth Moor, there are three outliers of the Scarborough Formation, namely at Stony Moor [5130 9730], Scotgrave Ridge [5220 9650], and Iron Howe [5270 9500]. The Brandsby Roadstone is poorly exposed, though once quarried on the western side of Scotgrave Ridge [5193 9630], its proximity and past importance is emphasised by old lime kilns on Stony Moor [5095 9700] and south of Iron Howe [5150 9419] and [5267 9392].

The overlying Crinoid Grit forms bold topographical features up to 9 m in height in these inliers; sporadic exposures show white, medium-grained, porous sandstone with bivalve impressions.

Hawnby Moor and Bilsdale West Moor are relatively free superficial deposits, allowing detailed mapping of the Brandsby Roadstone and Crinoid Grit in these areas. The outcrop of the Brandsby Roadstone limestone is between 30 and 40 m wide in the Round Hill area [5560 9435]. The limestone has been extensively dug on Wetherhouse Moor [5510 9490] in a series of pits up to 3 m deep. Numerous shelly limestone fragments are present in a distinctive yellow-brown ferruginous soil, and local stone walls are built largely of the limestone. An exposure [5468 9502] near an old limekiln reveals 0.20 m of grey shelly limestone. The boundary between the limestone and the overlying Crinoid Grit is commonly marked by potholes as well as a small feature and distinctive change in vegetation.

The Crinoid Grit forms much of the high ground of Hawnby Moor [540 940] which is strewn with fragments of white, medium-grained, porous, fossiliferous sandstone. Exposures are rare, but a small quarry [5425 9483], north west of High Twaites Farm, proved the basal 0.50 m of the member to be ferruginous, and with common planar cross-bedding. Other depressions marked as Hell Holes [5360 9330] are natural collapses or sink holes due to the solution of the underlying limestone of the Crinoid Grit.

An exposure of the Scarborough Formation occurs in a small stream [5609 9077] flowing into the River Seph just beyond the eastern margin of the district.

	Thickness m
CRINOID GRIT MEMBER	
Sandstone, yellow-brown, massive, shell casts at base	3.00
Sandstone, yellow-brown, flaggy	1.00
Sandstone, ganisteroid	0.30
Gap	2.00
BRANDSBY ROADSTONE	
Limestone, grey, shelly, cross-bedded	1.00
Siltstone, calcareous, irregularly bedded	1.00
Limestone, blue-grey, massive	0.30

The Brandsby Roadstone, some 3 m thick, is exposed in the banks of the River Rye [5330 9135] north-east of Arden Hall.

	Thickness m
CRINOID GRIT MEMBER	
Sandstone, brown, ferruginous	0.70
Limestone, grey, silty, white-weathering	0.20
Mudstone, grey, silty, calcareous	1.00
Limestone, grey, rubbly bedded	0.20
Limestone, grey, massive	0.15
Limestone, grey, cross-bedded; small brachiopods towards base	1.55
CLOUGHTON FORMATION	
Mudstone, grey, ironstone nodules	

A few exposures of the Crinoid Grit and, less commonly, the Brandsby Roadstone occur to the west of Ladhill Gill [5463 9252 to 5452 9120]. The best section is near Nova Scotia Farm [5452 9133], as follows:

	Thickness m
BRANDSBY ROADSTONE	
Limestone, blue-hearted, hard, siliceous cross-bedded, micritic, with sporadic shelly horizons and stylolitic bedding surfaces	c.1.75
Limestone blue-grey, hard, siliceous, micritic limestone, interbedded with rubbly, calcareous siltstone and silty limestone; abundant trace fossils, including *Diplocraterion* and *Thalassinoides* burrows	c.2.3
CLOUGHTON FORMATION	
Sandstone, fine-grained, and siltstone, laminated, passing up into silty mudstone with siltstone laminae; abundant plant debris	c.3.2
Sandstone, fine-grained	c.0.2

The above section was obviously better exposed in the past; Fox-Strangways et al. (1886, pp.39–40) reported that, 'above this comes a considerable thickness of porous grit containing casts of *Avicula* [*Meleagrinella*] *braamburiensis* and other fossils in great abundance'. Lastly, above the grit is a bed of shale forming a bank of wet ground beneath the Moor Grit above. The total thickness of these beds is about 70 feet [c.21 m]', but they are no longer exposed.

Scalby Formation

The Scalby Formation forms the uppermost subdivision of the Ravenscar Group. It is up 40 m thick, and comprises sandstone, siltstone, mudstone and a thin coal. The formation crops out extensively along the western escarpment, on Osmotherley Moor, Hawnby Moor and on the lower slopes of Black Hambleton. It occurs as inliers on Stony Moor and Iron Howe. The Moor Grit Member forms a prominent sandstone at the base of the formation. The overlying beds, the Long Nab Member of previous authors (Table 6), is poorly exposed, and it is likely that there is a much higher ratio of siltstone and mudstone to sandstone than occurs in the underlying formations of the Ravenscar Group.

Black (1929) suggested a deltaic environment for the deposition of these beds, and Hemingway (1949) proposed the replacement of the name 'Estuarine Series' (Fox-Strangways, 1880) by 'Deltaic Series'. This was subsequently renamed the Scalby Formation by Hemingway and Knox (1973). Later research (Nami, 1976; Nami and Leeder, 1978; Leeder and Nami, 1979) led to the proposal of a wholly alluvial depositional model for the Scalby Formation. However, the occurrence of *Ophiomorpha* burrows, together with bioturbation, and the argillaceous nature of certain channel deposits led Livera and Leeder (1981) to suspect some marine influence. Confirmation of marine influence at particular stratigraphical levels comes from palynological evidence (Hancock and Fisher, 1981; Fisher and Hancock, 1985; Riding and Wright, 1989). Fisher and Hancock suggested that the upper part of the Scalby Formation was deposited in a delta-plain setting with saline interdistributary environments. Leeder and Alexander (1985) disagreed, suggesting a coastal plain, alluvial environment for the deposition of the Scalby Formation. They proposed that tidal prism back-up effects produced temporary marine-influenced floods in an otherwise alluvial levee, backswamp, and lake environment.

Moor Grit Member

The Moor Grit Member is a white to grey, fine- to medium-grained, orthoquartzitic sandstone. It is commonly cross-bedded, with planar and trough-shaped cosets, but, in places, it is parallel-bedded or massive. Studies elsewhere have indicated that the Moor Grit was deposited in a braided-river environment (Nami and Leeder, 1978; Leeder and Nami, 1979). However, on the Yorkshire coast, Fisher and Hancock (1985) have shown that saline water penetrated between the active channels in the high part of the member. To the south of this district, Powell et al. (1992) cite evidence of sheet-flood or crevasse-splay processes within the member.

The lateral persistence, distinctive lithology and stratigraphical position of the Moor Grit clearly distinguish it from the unnamed sandstones within the Scalby Formation. It represents, along with the Scarborough Formation, one of the most mappable units of the Ravenscar Group. The outcrop is commonly strewn with fragments of sandstone, particularly along dip-slopes, and is marked by a pronounced step-like feature, occurring immediately above the Scarborough Formation.

Details

Exposure is extremely poor in the south-west, near Kepwick, but the outcrop is marked by abundant brash. A small exposure, above Old Gill [4797 9278], comprises white, fine-grained, cross-bedded sandstone with sporadic mudflakes.

Farther north, on Thimbleby Moor, the member forms an excellent feature, but only weathered fragments of off-white, fine-grained, massive, siliceous sandstone lie over the outcrop. In Jenny Brewsters Gill [4784 9640], south-east of Osmotherley, some 7 m of yellow fine-grained sandstone are exposed in the bed and banks of the stream. The sandstone contains many carbonaceous, micaceous partings, which locally reveal Liesegang rings in a 0.80 m-thick bed. Above this bed the lamination is horizontal, but below it, flaggy beds are cross-bedded on a small scale. Farther upstream, above the road, and stratigraphically at a higher level, a further 2 m of sandstone with carbonaceous partings are overlain by fine-grained ganisteroid sandstone.

A similar sequence is exposed in the stream [4750 9697] near Chequers Inn. The succession is as follows:

	Thickness m
MOOR GRIT MEMBER	
Sandstone, brown, fine-grained, massive	0.40
Gap	
Sandstone, off-white, fine-grained, micaceous, many carbonaceous partings in beds 0.10 m thick	1.00
Sandstone, yellow, fine-grained, ferruginous massive, strongly jointed (waterfall)	1.50
Sandstone, yellow, fine-grained, laminated, soft at top	3.40
Gap	c.5.00
CRINOID GRIT MEMBER	

On Snilesworth Moor, the Moor Grit forms large areas of outcrop strewn with off-white, siliceous and pale greenish grey ganisteroid fragments. A small quarry near Douglas Ridge [5045 9655] exposes 2 m of flaggy, ferruginous, fine-grained sandstone. At Crying Ings Slack [4960 9610], the features suggest that the Moor Grit is divided into an upper and lower bed, 6 m and 3 m thick respectively, separated by a 3 m parting. A further 3 m of beds separates the Moor Grit from the Crinoid Grit.

In the extreme east of the district, the Moor Grit is 7 m thick [5550 9180].

On Hawnby Moor, exposures are rare in the interfluve between Ryedale and Bilsdale; the outcrop is 50 m wide and is strewn with boulders of white fine-grained porous sandstone with plant fragments and sporadic mudstone clasts.

Scalby Formation, undivided

This part of the sequence is poorly exposed in the district and large tracts of the outcrop are obscured by landslip and head. It is likely that these beds are more argillaceous than the underlying part of the Ravenscar Group. Pale greenish grey and grey mudstone is exposed on Osmotherly Moor where springs erode sandstone at the base of the Osgodby Formation. Elsewhere, only very sparse exposures of calcareous and ferruginous sandstone occur.

Laterally impersistent features, assumed to be channel-fill sandstones, have been mapped in many places along the western escarpment. They vary from less than 1 m up to some 7 m in thickness. The thickest sandstone occurs immediately below the Osgodby Formation and has been mapped in three places along the main escarpment [4825 9230, 4827 9153 to 4817 9108 and 4822 9002].

Details

An exposure [4806 9738] on Osmotherley Moor shows about 1 m of shelly, calcareous and ferruginous sandstone with ganisteroid rootlets in the top of the bed.

Laterally impersistent sandstones have been inferred west of Lower Locker Farm [504 941] and at the southern end of Hawnby Moor [538 920]. They vary between 0.5 and 5 m in thickness. Springs commonly mark the base of the sandstones on Hawnby Moor.

In Thorodale [5052 9129], a very small exposure of grey silty mudstone occurs near the top of the formation.

CORNBRASH FORMATION

The Cornbrash Formation marks the base of the Callovian succession on the Yorkshire coast and in north Cleveland, but it has not been found in this district Table 6. It represents a major transgression across the delta-marsh of the Scalby Formation (Wright, 1977).

Versey (1928) reported traces of the Cornbrash Limestone at Kepwick, but the observation was based on loose blocks of uncertain origin. Wright (1977) suggested that the Cornbrash Limestone may possibly merge into a sandstone in the Hambleton Hills.

OSGODBY FORMATION

The name Osgodby Formation was introduced by Wright (1978) to include all the dominantly sandstone units of

Callovian age in the Cleveland Basin. It includes, in ascending order, the Kellaways Rock, Langdale Beds, and Hackness Rock of the coastal succession (Wright, 1968). The Kellaways and Hackness rocks have been identified in the Arden Hall Borehole [5037 9157] (Rathbone, 1987b), but individual members of the formation have not been mapped during this survey, which predates the lithostratigraphical revision of Page (1989).

The formation is about 30 m thick and consists mainly of brown, ferruginous, fine- to medium-grained sandstone, which is decalcified in places and is commonly fossiliferous. It forms an outlier on Osmotherley Moor below Miley Pike, and crops out around Arden Great Moor and the Hambleton Hills, and around Hawnby Hill and Easterside Hill in the south-east of the district. A large area of the outcrop is covered by landslip, scree and head.

In the western part of the outcrops, south of Shaw Corner, there are two small, cambered exposures [4776 9312 and 4794 9327] of brown, porous, fine- to medium-grained sandstone with *Meleagrinella* and other bivalves. A small exposure of the same lithology occurs in White Gill [4884 9272]. The same lithology is again exposed in a small section, north-west of Dunsforth's Hill [4867 9196]. This section is so extensively cambered that it dips at about 50° to the west.

A disused quarry [4828 9137], high in the formation, exposes some 0.9 m of brown, fine- to medium-grained sandstone, with sporadic very fossiliferous horizons; these are typically less than 0.05 m thick, and contain many small *Gryphaea* and less abundant belemnite guards. Many similar, cambered, small exposures of the same lithology occur in the immediate vicinity.

The best exposures are in the south of the outcrop [4846 9010 to 4840 9005], where up to 3 m of cambered, brown and grey-brown, medium-grained, fossiliferous sandstone occurs high in the formation. It is typically very fossiliferous in the upper 1.5 m, with belemnite guards and abundant bivalves, including *Gryphaea dilobotes*, *Chlamys* sp., *Liostrea* sp., and *Meleagrinella braamburiensis*.

On Osmotherley Moor, the Kellaways Rock forms the highest ground east of Chequers, rising to nearly 320 m near the Fabers Stone. The member weathers into a series of upstanding features depending on the cementing material of the sandstone. Exposures are rare, but brown, ferruginous, sporadically fossiliferous sandstone protrudes from beneath the heather. The base is marked by a line of springs where the sandstones overlie mudstones of the Scalby Formation.

In the east of the main outcrop, brown, fine- to medium-grained sandstone with bivalves and belemnite guards is exposed in Limekiln House Gill [4999 9160]. The outcrop is partially encrusted by calcareous tufa.

In Arden Hall Borehole [5037 9157] (Rathbone 1987b), the Hackness Rock occurs between 32.5 to 47.3 m depth. It consists of 3.1 m of siltstone resting on 11.7 m of sandstone. Both lithologies are pale grey, laminated and bioturbated. The siltstone yields *Quenstedtoceras* sp., *Peltoceras* sp., and *Aspidoceras*. The sandstone yields a sporadic fauna including *Procerithium* sp., *Entolium* sp., *Pinna* sp., *Thracia* sp., *Kosmoceras* sp.

Characteristic Kellaways Rock occurs between depths of 47.30 m and 60.42 m. It comprises a ferruginous brown, fine-grained, massive, sandstone. Clasts of ironstone, and shell and wood fragments are common. A calcareous shelly dogger with *Meleagrinella* and a macroconch *Proplanulites* was proved between depths of 49.70 m and 49.92 m. Decalcified or partially decalcified shell beds are common in the top 5 m yielding, in particular, *Gryphaea* and belemnites. Between the shell beds, other recorded bivalves included *Chlamys*, *Entolium*, *Liostrea*, *Meleagrinella*, *Myophorella*, and *Nicaniella*. Plant fragments are common below 53.90 m, and the sandstone showed evidence of bioturbation with mudstone filling the burrows.

Between 60.42 m and 61.28 m, soft sandstone and siltstone with a burrowed top surface contains *Meleagrinella*, burrow structures and traces including *Chondrites*, and wood fragments. Below this, a 0.07 m-thick calcareous shell bed yielded *Entolium*, *Meleagrinella*, ?*Modiolus bipartitus*, ?'myids', *Pinna*?, belemnite voids and wood fragments.

Between 61.35 m and the final depth at 67.80 m, grey to pale grey sandstone, with black carbonaceous, micaceous partings and inclusions, showed bioturbation and a well-scattered bivalve fauna of *Meleagrinella* and rarer *Nicaniella* and *Oxytoma*, together with wood fragments. Palynological samples yielded dinoflagellate cysts. A re-appraisal of the evidence indicates that the borehole sequence lies entirely within Kellaways Rock Member, and thus the beds between 60.42 and 61.35 m depth are not Cornbrash as suggested by Rathbone (1987b).

Upper Jurassic

Oxford Clay Formation

The Oxford Clay of the Cleveland Basin is equivalent to the Weymouth Member (Upper Oxford Clay) of southern England. It has yielded a fauna dominated by bivalves, including species of *Gryphaea*, nuculoids, pectinids, *Pholadomya* and *Pinna*, together with sporadic ammonites sufficient to fix its stratigraphical position in the Lower Oxfordian.

The Oxford Clay Formation is 21–25 m thick, and 23 m was proved in the Arden Hall Borehole (Rathbone, 1987b). It consists of grey-green mudstone and siltstone. The formation crops out on the escarpment around the margins of the Hambleton Hills, in the valley sides above Limekiln House Gill [497 918], and on Hawnby and Easterside hills in the south-east. It forms a broad 'slack' between the Osgodby and Lower Calcareous Grit formations, and the outcrop is covered in extensive landslips, head and scree.

Small exposures are recorded on the steep banks of White Gill [4901 9298] where grey-green silty mudstone and siltstone yielded abundant *Cardioceras*, *Peltoceras* and many bivalves including *Entolium* and *Pinna*.

CORALLIAN GROUP

The total thickness of the Corallian Group in the Yorkshire coastal area is about 100 m, but only half that thickness is preserved in this district. It comprises a succession of limestone and fine-grained calcareous sandstone formed in warm shallow water. The lower 30 m are attributed to the Lower Calcareous Grit Formation, and the upper beds are classified as the Hambleton Oolite Member of the Coralline Oolite Formation. Together, they form the highest ground between Black Hambleton and the Hambleton Hills, and the outliers on the top of Hawnby and Easterside hills (Plate 4).

Lower Calcareous Grit Formation

The formation consists of calcareous and siliceous sandstone with subordinate limestone beds and concretions; near the top, the lithologies are commonly oolitic. Siliceous spicules of the sponge *Rhaxella* form a high proportion of some sandstones, and diagenetic changes have produced thin beds and nodules of chert. *Thalassinoides* burrows are abundant at some horizons. They are infilled with material which has a high spicule content and is more resistant to erosion, giving an irregular, nodular appearance to the rock (Plate 5).

The Lower Calcareous Grit forms a prominent feature above the Oxford Clay. It crops out along the main escarpment, around the slopes of Black Hambleton [485 940], on the steep valley sides above Limekiln House [4965 9215] and Arden Hall [520 905], and on Hawnby Hill and Easterside Hill. The formation is estimated at 28 to 37 m thick, but the almost ubiquitous cambering, and many landslips, make thickness estimates very uncertain.

Details

There are many exposures in the western part of the outcrop, between Hambleton Street [4782 9463] and Whitestone Scar [4870 9295] and above Bawderis Wood [487 942]. They show interbedded calcareous and siliceous sandstones and many have subordinate grey limestone beds, typically less than 0.4 m thick. A good section occurs at Whitestone Scar [4870 9295].

	Thickness m
HAMBLETON OOLITE MEMBER Limestone, white to pale grey, oolitic, bioclastic, thin- to medium-bedded, with *Rhaxella* spicules, *Gervillella*, and '*Lucina*'	c.2.0
LOWER CALCAREOUS GRIT FORMATION Sandstone, buff, fine-grained, calcareous, sporadically oolitic, medium-bedded, with *Rhaxella* and a few bivalves; interbedded with white, hard, siliceous, spiculitic, sporadically oolitic sandstone, with sparse shell fragments; bedding surfaces are sharp but irregular; the calcareous beds are burrowed by *Thalassinoides* (Plate 6)	c.2.8
Sandstone, buff, fine-grained, calcareous, with *Rhaxella* spicules, interbedded with white to pale grey, hard, siliceous, spiculitic sandstone and very subordinate sandy limestone; sparse shells throughout including indeterminate pectinid bivalves, *Nanogyra*, *Gryphaea* and *Myophorella*; bedding surfaces are sharp but irregular, with a topography of up to 0.3 m, resulting in a pseudo-nodular appearance in places; common *Thalassinoides* burrows	c.5.5
Sandstone, buff, calcareous, massive, with very abundant *Thalassinoides* burrows infilled with a more siliceous cement	c.3

No exposures occur on the high moorland of Black Hambleton as much of the outcrop is covered by peat.

Plate 4 General view from Arden Great Moor [500 930] towards North Moor (foreground), Hawnby Hill, with Easterside and Rievaulx Moor and beyond. The features seen comprise a series of north-facing scarps of mostly Upper Jurassic rocks (Lower Calcareous Grit Formation and Hambleton Oolite Member) overlying the Oxford Clay Formation (L2670).

Plate 5 Irregular concretionary limestone structures and chert beds in the Lower Calcareous Grit Formation (Upper Jurassic) at Whitestone Scar [4870 9295]. (L2457)

Plate 6 Silicified *Thalassinoides* burrows in the Lower Calcareous Grit Formation (Upper Jurassic) at Whitestone Scar [4873 9294]. (L2460)

On the western scarp face of Easterside Hill, the Lower Calcareous Grit Formation is well exposed and is seen in quarries towards the southern end of the feature [5530 9041]. The beds are highly cambered, with dips up to 70° to the west, and over half the total thickness is exposed. They comprise buff, calcareous, finely oolitic sandstone containing quartz banding and nodules. The top surfaces of some beds are bioturbated and rich in *Rhizocorallium* and *Thalassinoides* burrows.

Coralline Oolite Formation

The Coralline Oolite Formation consists of an interfingering sequence of limestones and calcareous sandstones of Oxfordian age. Only the Hambleton Oolite Member crops out in this district.

The Hambleton Oolite forms outliers, capping Hawnby Hill and Easterside Hill in the south-east of the district. It is lithologically uniform throughout most of the district, and consists predominantly of white to pale grey, shelly, oolitic limestone with variable proportions of sand. Chert nodules are common in part, and subordinate, thin, shaley micritic beds occur throughout. Thin beds of calcareous sandstone containing spicules of the sponge *Rhaxella* occur towards the base.

The top of this member is not present within the district, and the maximum mapped thickness is about 25 m. The member caps the main escarpment south of Black Hambleton [483 938]. The outcrop covers a large area of moorland, mainly as dip slopes, and is partially obscured by peat in the north; it is characterised by many small, shallow swallow holes.

The Corallian was deposited in a warm shallow-water environment (Hemingway, 1974, p.217) with a rich fauna dominated by bivalves, crinoids, echinoids and gastropods. Carbonaceous debris is also present. Fine-grained micritic limestone accumulated in back-reef lagoons and bioclastic screes banked up against their seaward faces. The reefs and shell beds were destroyed by erosion and the fauna reduced to debris by bioturbation. This debris was mixed with abundant *Rhaxella* spicules which played a major rock-forming role. Ooliths were ubiquitous amongst the clastic debris but are quantitatively variable.

Nodular and tabular chert occur in both limestones and sandstones, and are commonly concentrated in the middle of individual beds, replacing all the original carbonate constituents (Plate 5). The chert was probably derived from the opaline spicules of the sponge *Rhaxella perforata*.

Details

Numerous disused limestone quarries line both sides of Hambleton Street, south of White Gill Head [4910 9293 to 4962 9000]. Many contain exposures of up to 2 m of shelly oolitic limestone with common bivalve debris, including *Nanogyra* sp., *Chlamys fibrosus*, *Meleagrinella* sp., *Gervillella* sp., '*Lucina*' sp. and *Lopha* sp.. Echinoid fragments are present throughout; *Nucleolites* is particularly common in places, for example near Limekiln House [4899 9194].

An excellent section at Kepwick Quarry displays 17.5 m of white to pale grey, shelly oolitic limestone with subordinate shaley partings. *Rhaxella* spicules are present towards the base and some detrital quartz occurs throughout. The oolite is commonly medium- to thick-bedded. Cross-bedding is common between 2.8 and 5.8 m above the base of the section. Chert nodules occur sporadically throughout, but are most abundant in the lowest 6 m and at 9.5 to 10.5 m above the base.

The transitional nature of the contact with the underlying Lower Calcareous Grit is well displayed in many exposures along Clarke Scar [4870 9069 to 4857 9098]. Some 5 m of siliceous and calcareous sandstone with *Thalassinoides* burrows and subordinate sandy limestones pass up through 3 m of calcareous sandstone with ooliths and *Thalassinoides* burrows, and finally into 4 m of shelly oolitic limestone of the Hambleton Oolite. *Rhaxella* spicules occur throughout, but are particularly common below the Hambleton Oolite. Many of the sections form the back scars of landslips and are extensively cambered.

SIX

Structure

The resurvey of the Northallerton district has shown a relatively uncomplicated geological structure, despite the number of tectonic episodes which are known to have affected this and adjacent areas since Devonian times.

The district lies within the Stainmore Trough, north-east of the Askrigg Block, about 20 km south of the Butterknowle Fault System which marks the southern margin of the Alston Block and some 30 km north of the Craven Fault System (Figure 10a). At outcrop, Permo-Triassic and Jurassic strata dip gently to the east and are cut by scattered small faults. The Permian and Mesozoic cover rocks overlie, with angular unconformity, a very thick Carboniferous sequence (Figures 10b and 11) which in turn rests unconformably upon strongly folded and faulted Lower Palaeozoic rocks of the Caledonian basement. The nature of the Caledonian basement hereabouts is poorly understood because it is not penetrated by boreholes within the district. Farther to the west, it was intruded by granite of Silurian age (400±10 million years) beneath the Askrigg Block in Wensleydale (Dunham, 1974).

STRUCTURE IN THE CARBONIFEROUS STRATA

The broad structure of the Carboniferous strata is relatively well constrained by surface exposures from adjacent areas (Rayner, 1953; George, 1958; Dunham, 1959; Kent, 1966; Bott, 1967; Bott et al., 1985; Dunham and Wilson, 1985) and, more particularly, from recently acquired subsurface information, including seismic reflection data and the Harlsey Borehole. Seismic reflection coverage is by no means uniform; lack of data in the east of the district means that the structure thereabouts has to be extrapolated from the better constrained central and western parts.

A very thick basinal Carboniferous sequence is present beneath the district, composed principally of Dinantian and Namurian strata (Figure 11). The base of the Carboniferous succession, nowhere penetrated by boreholes, is taken at the base of a thick sequence of well-developed, subhorizontal seismic reflections (Figure 12). The full Dinantian succession is nowhere proved by boreholes and Devonian strata may also be present within this seismic sequence; however for the purposes of this account they are assumed to be absent, the top of Caledonian Basement being taken as synonymous with the base of the Carboniferous.

The Carboniferous basin fill has a regional gentle eastward dip. Structure contours on the top of Caledonian basement and the base of the Stainmore Group (Namurian) are given in Figure 13a, b. Caledonian basement is shallowest (less than 4000 m deep) in the south-west of the district, closest to the flank of the Askrigg Block. The Caledonian basement surface deepens eastwards into the Stainmore Trough, and may lie at depths greater than 6000 m in the southeast of the district (Figure 13a). From seismic reflection evidence (Figure 12), its thickness is interpreted to increase from less than 4500 m in the south of the district, to nearly 5500 m in the north (Figure 11), as part of a regional northwards thickening towards the Butterknowle Fault System at the northern margin of the Stainmore Trough (Figure 10b). Minor thickness variations also occur across small normal faults which cut the unit (Figures 11 and 12).

The base of the Namurian succession (the Stainmore Group) dips generally eastwards from about 200 m in the west of the district to perhaps more than 1800 m in the south-east (Figures 13b and 14). The thickness of the Stainmore Group varies considerably, depending upon how much is preserved beneath the angular unconformity at the base of the Permo-Triassic succession (Figure 14). In much of the central and western parts of the district only the lower part of the unit is preserved (Figure 12). For example along Section A–B, the Stainmore Group is in places only about 100 m thick (Figure 11), elsewhere, it may even be locally absent (Figure 14). The marked angular unconformity at the base of the Permian allows progressively younger Namurian strata to come to subcrop farther east (Figure 14), such that the Stainmore Group thickens to more than 750 m in the east of the district. These thickness changes are principally a preservation effect; the seismic data indicate that stratigraphical (i.e. depositional) thickness variations in the Stainmore Group hereabouts are minimal. It is possible that pockets of Westphalian strata (Coal Measures) are preserved beneath the unconformity in the south-east of the district, but this cannot be confirmed without more borehole information. To the east of the district, Coal Measures have been proved at Eskdale, near the Yorkshire coast (Calver, 1958, p.47).

The Dinantian and Namurian rocks of the district are relatively undeformed being cut by only a few, rather small faults (Figure 13a, b). Most of these faults do not penetrate the base Permo-Triassic unconformity (Figure 12), their displacements therefore predating deposition of the basal Permian deposits. The faults in general trend roughly east–west, are subplanar with moderate to steep dips, and have normal, dominantly down-south, displacements. Smaller, down-north, antithetic normal faults are also present (Figure 11). One of the faults has a throw of about 600 m but the others all have throws considerably less than 500 m at the base of the Carboniferous sequence (Figure 11). On most of the faults the throw decreases upwards through the Carboniferous sequence, signifying syndepositional (i.e. early Carboniferous) movement as well as post-

Figure 10a   Regional setting of the Northallerton district with location of cross-sections N–S and A–B.

Figure 10b   Regional simplified cross-section N–S through the Stainmore Trough, showing the location of the Northallerton district.

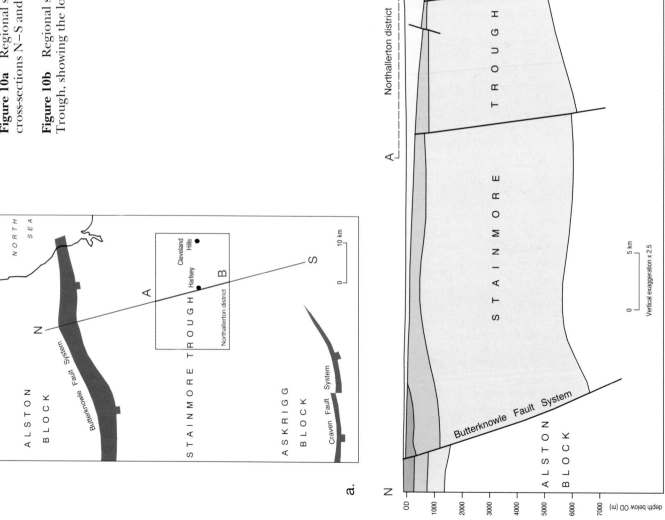

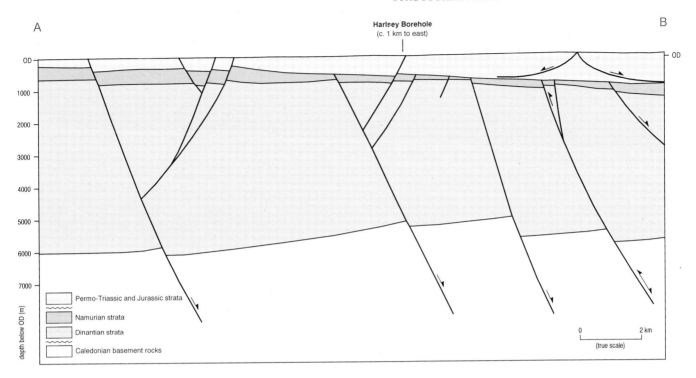

Figure 11   Cross-section A–B through the Northallerton district (location of section in Figure 10a).

early Carboniferous) movement as well as post-Namurian displacement. Locally, the base of the Stainmore Group is cut by minor reverse faulting (e.g. Figure 12). These small reverse faults appear to pass downwards into normal displacements in the Dinantian succession, indicative of minor reversal of an earlier, syn-depositional normal fault. These reverse faults do not penetrate the basal Permian unconformity and presumably occurred in Variscan (end-Carboniferous) times. Minor folding associated with Variscan events is also locally present. Just north of the district, in the Teesside area, a series of approximately east–west-trending Variscan folds occur in the Carboniferous strata south of the Butterknowle Fault (Chadwick et al., 1995). The most southerly of these structures, the Wolviston Anticline, is sufficiently close to the Northallerton district to extrapolate the southerly dip in the Namurian strata into the district from its southern limb.

STRUCTURE IN THE PERMIAN AND TRIASSIC STRATA

Permo-Triassic strata rest unconformably on the Carboniferous succession. They have a regional south-east dip (Figure 13c) whose easterly component is less steep than that of the underlying Carboniferous succession, giving the above-mentioned angular unconformity (Figure 14).

Most of the structures in the Permian and Triassic rocks of the district were the consequence of three main influences:

1   Regional tilting.
2   Post-Triassic faulting.
3   Dissolution and movement of soluble strata.

The Permo-Triassic sequence crops out in the west and north of the district and is here only partly preserved. Farther east a full stratigraphical sequence was proved in the Harlsey Borehole with a thickness of 633 m. The unit thickens stratigraphically to the south and east, for example to 680 m in the Cleveland Hills Borehole. This indicates that south-eastward tilting was already occurring during deposition. The general eastward thickening of most of the Permian and Triassic formations across north Yorkshire shows that tilting continued until the Late Triassic, and episodically through the Jurassic and Cretaceous as well.

Normal faulting within the Permo-Triassic sequence falls into two main categories:

Sub-planar normal faults

One set of faults trends dominantly east–west (Figure 13c), parallel to the structures in the underlying Carboniferous sequence. These faults have small normal displacements, are subplanar with moderate to steep dips, and affect also the underlying Carboniferous rocks (Figure 12). Some of the faults appear to be Carboniferous structures reactivated in post-Triassic times. Other faults displace both Permo-Triassic and Carboniferous beds by the same amount, implying an entirely post-Triassic age (see p.59).

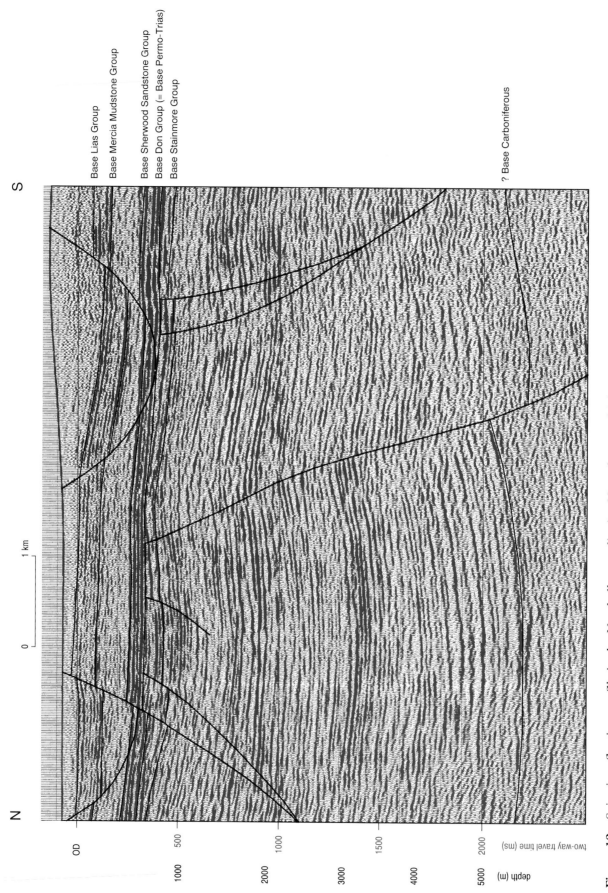

Figure 12 Seismic reflection profile in the Northallerton district. Note the very thick Dinantian sequence and the thin, partly eroded Namurian sequence; also the pre-late Permian normal and reverse faulting and post-Triassic planar and detached normal faulting. (Data courtesy of British Gas).

Figure 13   Northallerton district: depth contours, in metres, on (a) the top of the Caledonian basement, (b) the base of the Stainmore Group and (c) base Permo-Triassic strata.

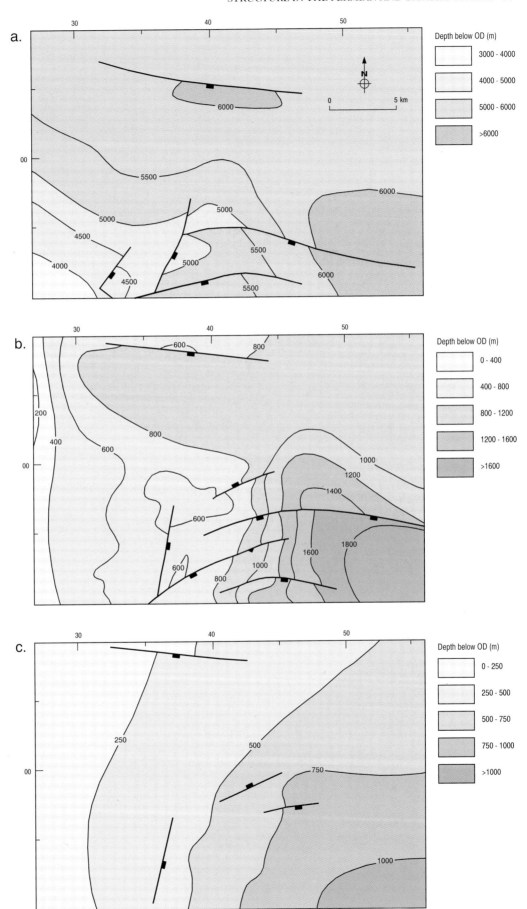

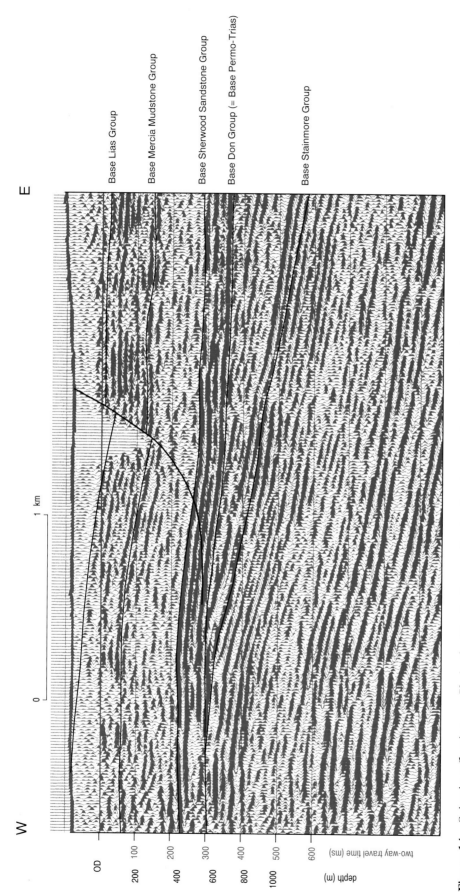

Figure 14 Seismic reflection profile in the Northallerton district showing angular unconformity at the base of the Permo-Triassic sequence, possible subcrop of Dinantian strata and eastwards thickening of the Stainmore Group. Note also listric normal fault cutting Permo-Triassic sequence. (Data courtesy of British Gas).

Curved detached normal faults

These faults commonly trend north–south (Figure 15). They are low angle and markedly curved ('listric') in profile, flattening at depth on to subhorizontal *décollement* surfaces within the Permian sequence (e.g. Figure 12). The faults appear to be effectively detached from the underlying Carboniferous rocks as they do not penetrate into them (consequently they do not appear on the Base Permo-Triassic structure contour map, Figure 13c). It is likely that beds of soluble anhydrite and halite present within the Permian sequence provided the weak layers necessary for this type of faulting to develop. It may be that gravity-sliding down the south-easterly dipping palaeoslope was a prime factor in the development of detached normal faulting hereabouts. A side effect of this detached normal faulting was severe localised structural attenuation of the Permo-Triassic sequence (Figure 16). The age of this faulting is uncertain, save to say that it was at least in part, post-middle Jurassic (see below).

In addition to the development of listric normal faulting, dissolution of evaporites by percolating ground-water can cause foundering of overlying strata and the development of many and varied accommodation structures. Such features are present in the Leeming Bar–Catterick area (p.13).

As well as the above-mentioned extension-related structures, localised minor folds are visible on the seismic reflection data. These appear to be associated with the reversal of underlying faults and may be indicative of post-Triassic compressional stresses associated with basin inversion (see below). A much larger Cainozoic inversion structure, the Cleveland Anticline (Kent, 1980a, Kirby et al., 1987), lies to the east. Its western end may just impinge on the north-east corner of the district, deflecting outcrop trends from north-east–south-west to north–south (Figure 15).

STRUCTURE IN THE JURASSIC STRATA

The Jurassic rocks of the district rest conformably upon the Permo-Triassic succession and have the same regional gentle south-easterly dip. Most, if not all of the faults which cut the Permo-Triassic rocks, also cut the Jurassic sequence. As with those of the Permo-Triassic,

Figure 15 Surface faults mapped in the Jurassic and uppermost Triassic strata of the district.

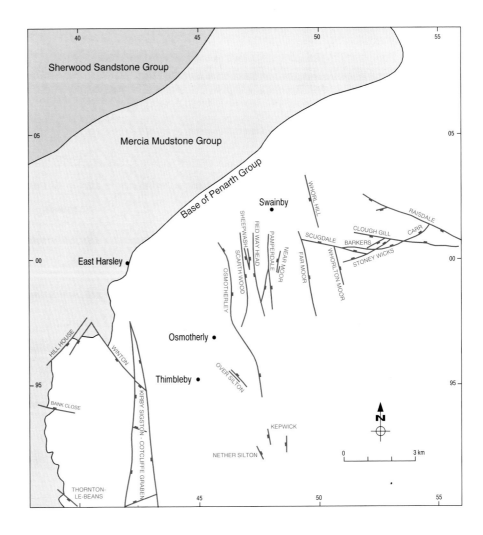

faults affecting the Jurassic fall into two main categories: dominantly north–south-trending faults which are probably predominantly listric in profile, detaching on to the Permian evaporites, and dominantly east–west-trending faults which are probably predominantly subplanar, penetrating up from the Carboniferous sequence. Faults which cut the lithologically variable Jurassic sequence can be readily mapped at the surface (Figure 15). Details of these faults are given below.

Kirby Sigston–Cotcliffe Graben

This important northerly trending, downfaulted block (Figure 15) forms a continuation of the Borrowby–Knayton Graben of the Thirsk district (Powell et al., 1992). It is well imaged by the seismic reflection data as a roughly symmetrical graben bounded by two opposed listric normal faults with similar throws (Figure 16). The master fault forms the western margin of the graben and dips eastwards to detach within the Permian evaporites. The eastern fault is antithetic to the western fault. The base of the Jurassic is downfaulted, in the central graben, by about 150 m. Because of the detached nature of the structure, the base of the Permo-Triassic sequence is virtually undisturbed.

At outcrop, to the south of the district and south of Beacon Hill [4255 9382] the more resistant sandstones of the Ravenscar Group (Saltwick and Cloughton formations) within the graben rise some 30 m above the softer strata of the Lias Group (Redcar Mudstone Formation) on either side. The eastern margin of the graben can be only inferred from the marked feature which parallels the main A19 highway in the vicinity of Leake [432 903]. To the west, however, exposures are common and despite large areas of landslip obscuring the north-west prow of the feature it is possible to calculate the amount of throw. Near Landmoth [4218 9250] old Jet Rock workings are present adjacent to the fault. A few metres on the west side of the implied fault-line an old quarry [4205 9790] was recorded by Fox-Strangways et al. (1886, p.60) in the 'Bucklandi limestones' of the Lower Lias (Redcar Mudstone Formation). The dislocation is therefore in the order of 120 m and a similar figure must apply to the easterly side of the graben. These estimated surface throws, are, within the limits of uncertainty, essentially the same as the throw at the base of the Jurassic estimated from the seismic data. This suggests that fault movement postdated deposition of the strata hereabouts. The throws decrease northwards and either die out or the fault lines converge and cancel each other out beneath the drift-covered featureless ground towards Foxton [422 960].

Small accommodation faults, trending north-east to south-west and north-west to south-east, cross the graben in the Landmoth Little House [4253 9305] and Carrodell House [4255 9025] areas. They have been inferred from the mapping of features corresponding to sandstones in the Ravenscar Group.

Bank Close Fault

The Bank Close Fault (Figure 15) trends west-north-west and downthrows about 12 m to the north. This fault displaces the Blue Anchor Formation (Mercia Mudstone Group) near Bank Close [3875 9368] and [3859 9402].

Thorton-le-Beans Fault

The close juxtaposition of grey Lias Group shales, containing limestone fragments [3971 9027], to the north and grey, finely laminated, mudstones of the Penarth Group [3955 9027] to the south fix the approximate north-west alignment of the Thorton-le-Beans Fault along the alluvial flats of a 'drain' between Northallerton and Thorton-le-Beans.

Hill House Faults

Two parallel north-east-trending faults throw down to the south-east (Figure 15). The westerly fault [3945 9645] displaces the base of the Penarth Group by about 14 m; the easterly fault [3985 9645] has a displacement of some 17 m.

Winton Fault

Blue Anchor Formation beds were formerly recorded (Fox-Strangways et al., 1886) on Rabbit Hill [4131 9700] at an elevation of about 260 m. This compares with an elevation of about 225 m approximately along strike [4075 9682]. A fault is therefore interpreted to lie near Winton House [4100 9662], trending north-north-west, and displacing the Penarth Group down to the south-west by about 35 m.

Osmotherley Fault

Some 3 to 4 km east of the Kirby Sigston–Cotcliffe Graben (Figure 15) another roughly parallel fault with downthrow of some 100 m to the east can be traced for some 7 km, from Ingleby Arncliffe [4570 0055] in the north towards Kepwick [4748 9431] in the south.

The fault surface is nowhere exposed but brings the Brandsby Roadstone into juxtaposition with the basal beds of the Middle Jurassic in Priests Spa Quarry [4624 9888] near Osmotherley. Displacement of the Brandsby Roadstone on Thimbleby Moor [4728 9558] suggests the throw here is reduced to some 30 m. The fault cannot be traced through the vast areas of landslip on the west side of Black Hambleton but a small displacement of topographic features was proved on Kepwick Moor [4780 9240] which appears to be the southern limit of the dislocation. A small fault, 1 km to the east, with a displacement down to the west [4848 9234] cuts the Oxford Clay outcrop.

Small offshoots to the main Osmotherley Fault trending north-westwards were mapped near Over Silton [4680 9474] and Nether Silton [4736 9205].

Scarth Wood Fault

The Scarth Wood Fault parallels the Osmotherley Fault for 4 km in its northern section and again downthrows east. On the north face of the escarpment shales of the

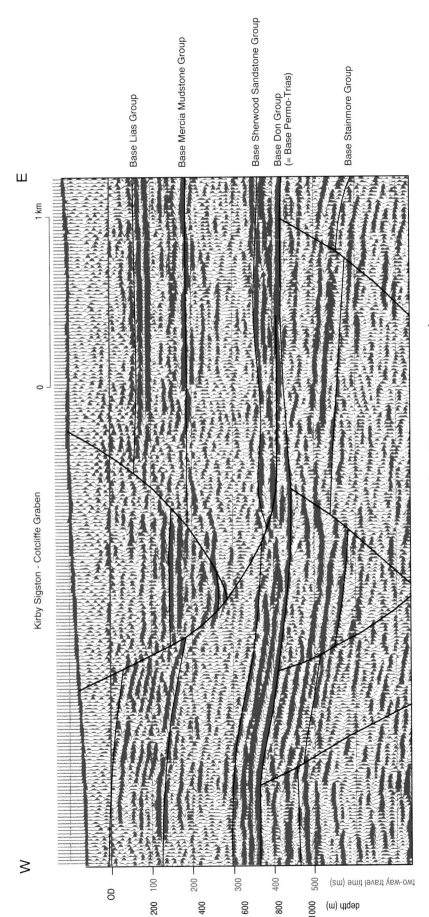

Figure 16 Seismic reflection profile across the Kirby Sigston–Cotcliffe graben. Note severe structural attenuation of the Permo–Triassic sequence by detached normal faulting, also pre-late Permian normal faults cutting the Carboniferous succession. (Data courtesy of British Gas).

Jet Rock Member are displaced [4674 0040] by some 20 m, an amount equivalent to their thickness.

The fault decreases in prominence southwards. Its position is well marked on Scarth Wood Moor [4677 9960] where the Bransby Roadstone and overlying grit are terminated against sandstones of the Cloughton Formation, and farther south near Trenholm House [4672 9729] where the Brandsby Roadstone is displaced vertically by some 7 m.

Red Way Head Fault

The Scarth Wood Fault is matched by a dislocation of similar length and alignment 0.5 km to the east forming a small graben, which also contains further minor faults near the Sheep Wash [4705 9942].

The main Red Way Head Fault is aligned with and passes through the deep gulley and glacial overflow channel of Scarth Nick [4722 0004]. The lowest sandstone of the Saltwick Formation crops out in a quarry [4746 0016] on the east side of Scarth Nick and shows a dip to the south-west of some 20°. This steep dip (for this area) is interpreted as a steepening of the beds into the fault line. The sandstone is strongly jointed with directions varying between 0° and 030°. The joints are mostly vertical but some are inclined at 60° and vary in width from 10 mm to 70 mm. One ferruginous and siliceous joint infill is listric and polished.

Pamperdale Fault

Another fault of north–south alignment with a downthrow to the east of about 15 m also cuts the northern scarp of the Cleveland Hills and its position is betrayed by the offset of the Crinoid Grit on Pamperdale Moor [4788 9872]. It is linked to the Red Way Head Fault by a cross fault [4765 9874] trending north-eastwards with a small downthrow to the south-east.

Two small faults (Near Moor Faults), of similar trend but with downthrow west, form slight breaks in the continuity of the Crinoid Grit outcrop on Near Moor [4820 9940].

Far Moor Fault

The Crinoid Grit again forms a useful marker to show the presence of the Far Moor Fault, trending north-south and having a downthrow to the east of about 15 m. The marked feature known as Stony Ridge is abruptly truncated by the fault [4948 9875].

Whorl Hill Fault

Fox-Strangways et al. (1886, p.59) recorded an outcrop of the Lower Lias on the north-east face of Whorl Hill [4940 0275] adjacent to the Jet Rock Member and cutting out the whole of the Middle Lias. A small parallel fault, with a downthrow of 4 m to the west, was recorded in the Jet Rock workings a little to the west.

The main Whorl Hill Fault trends north-west and displaces the outcrop of the Jet Rock Member on the north face of Whorlton Moor [4972 0151] vertically by about 20 m.

Whorlton Moor

A fault parallel to the Whorl Hill Fault, but about 0.5 km to the west, has a downthrow of nearly 40 m to the east judging by the displacement of the crop of the Jet Rock Member [5070 9960]. The fault is terminated to the north by the Scugdale Fault and cannot be traced far to the south over Whorlton Moor.

Scugdale Fault

The Scugdale Fault trends west-north-west and forms the first of three important dislocations of this trend — a typical fault direction in the Cleveland Ironstone mines (Fox-Strangways et al., 1886, p.58). The fault, which parallels the Scugdale valley, has markedly influenced the development of the local topography. The downthrow to the north is some 30 m, as evidenced by the difference in levels of the Staithes Sandstone Formation on either side of the valley. A smaller fault (not at surface), parallel to the Scugdale Fault but 200 m north of the main fault, was proved in Swainby Mine to pass through Huthwaite Green [49100 0082] and downthrow north, about 9 m. A similarly oriented fault farther east, passing through Raikes Farm [5118 0022], separates the lowest sandstones of the Ravenscar Group from the Jet Rock Member with only a very thin (25 m) representative of the intervening Whitby Mudstone Formation. This thin sequence may be due in part to erosive downcutting (see p.36) at the beginning of the Middle Jurassic.

Two north-east-trending dislocations of Barker's Crags mark faults which form a small graben on the north side of the Scugdale Fault. The maximum throw is about 7 m. To the west, the sandstone scarp of Scot Crags [5170 0040] is continuous with Barker's Crags but dominated by joints ranging in direction from a bearing of 210° to 270° subparallel to the graben. The graben is terminated on its north side by the Clough Gill Fault.

Clough Gill Fault

An outlier of Moor Grit is cut by the graben affecting Barker's Crags, and is terminated by the Clough Gill Fault with downthrow to the south of some 8 m and a bearing just north of west. Crags of the Crinoid Grit are clearly displaced west of Brian's Pond [5180 0073] and again north-west of High Crosslets [5290 0052]. A good indication of the throw is shown north of High Crosslets [5330 0044] where the Jet Rock Member is thrown against the basal sandstone of the Ravenscar Group. Farther east in the stream in Raisdale [5400 0040] (Fox-Strangways et al., 1886, p.58), shales of the Cleveland Ironstone Formation are thrown against the Redcar Mudstone Formation. The eastern end of the fault affects the Dogger Formation on Cold Moor End [5488 0022].

Carr Fault

A branch of the Clough Gill Fault trends north-eastwards through Raisdale Mill and terminates against the Raisdale Fault. The throw is small and down to the north.

Raisdale Fault

A fault converging with the Clough Gill Fault cuts out the Jet Rock Member north of Wath Hill [5390 0141]. Nearby, at Staindale Farm [5293 0171], the Jet Rock Member is displaced some 15 m down to the south. Small displacements are also mappable on Howe Moor to the north-west and Cold Moor to the south-east.

STRUCTURAL EVOLUTION

The Caledonian basement of the Northallerton district was finally consolidated in mid-Devonian times by the Acadian tectonic events (Soper et al., 1987). Subsequent to this, in late Devonian times, it is likely that the basement suffered severe erosion (though the local presence of Upper Devonian strata cannot be ruled out).

In earliest Carboniferous times, regional crustal extension (Leeder, 1982) led to development of an extensional basin-block system in northern England. One of the deepest basins was the Stainmore Trough (Collier, 1991), where very rapid early Dinantian subsidence was strongly influenced by large syndepositional normal displacements on the Butterknowle Fault System (Figure 10b). Extension diminished markedly in Namurian and Westphalian times which were characterised by more gradual, regional, post-extension subsidence, and much diminished contrasts between block and basin areas (Chadwick et al., 1995). In latest Carboniferous times, Variscan compressional stresses led to partial reversal of the Butterknowle Fault System and inversion of the Stainmore Trough. Minor folds developed south of the Butterknowle Fault System (Figure 10b) with more regional uplift of the Stainmore Trough itself. This uplift was followed, in early Permian times, by erosional removal of the Westphalian sequence and much of the Namurian sequence from the district (Figures 10b and 11). Judging from the thickness of preserved Westphalian and Namurian strata to the north of the district (Figure 10b), the total thickness of upper Carboniferous strata removed probably amounted to several hundred metres.

In late Permian times the district came again within a depositional regime, lying close to the western edge of the southern North Sea Permian basin. Subsidence continued through Triassic and Early Jurassic times as a peripheral effect of basin development in the North Sea. Subsidence at this time was of a regional nature, without widespread syndepositional normal faulting. Rates of subsidence were generally greater towards the east, which imparted an overall easterly or south-easterly structural dip. In late Jurassic and early Cretaceous

times, formation of the Cleveland Basin was accompanied by the development of both subplanar and listric normal faults (Kirby and Swallow, 1987). It is likely that the normal faults which cut the Permo-Triassic and Jurassic strata of the district also formed at this time. In late Cretaceous times faulting ceased, to give way to regional subsidence and deposition of the Upper Cretaceous Chalk (Whittaker, 1985). In Cainozoic times the Cleveland Basin suffered strong inversion, to form the Cleveland Anticline (Kent, 1980a); axial uplift on this anticline was well in excess of 2000 m (Kirby et al., 1987). Though uplifted less than this, the Northallerton district still underwent strong erosion with removal of the Cretaceous rocks and much of the Jurassic sequence.

The latest widespread movements took place some 18 000 to 13 000 years ago when up to 800 m of ice occupied the Tees and North Yorkshire lowlands, causing a temporary surface depression of perhaps 200 m. The district is now seismically quiet (Davison, 1924; Turbitt, 1990). In addition to regional earth movements, some recent foundering and dissolution of the Permian evaporites in the south-west part of the district near Leeming Bar and Catterick, has resulted in collapse hollows which behave like active sinkholes in present-day karst topography.

GEOPHYSICS

In addition to evidence from boreholes and from some seismic reflection surveys, information on the deeper structure in the district is available from extensive regional gravity and aeromagnetic survey data. Digital data from both types of surveys are available in the BGS database and were used to prepare the maps shown in Figures 17a, b.

Gravity data

The main part of the district is occupied by an area of low Bouguer gravity anomaly values (Figure 17a), which form part of an elongated anomaly extending southwards over the Mesozoic sedimentary rocks of the Vale of York. The increase in values to the west, and particularly to the north-west, mainly reflects the rise of the Carboniferous rocks from beneath the lower density Mesozoic cover. The explanation for the high to the east, over the Cleveland Hills, is less obvious; the Mesozoic continues to thicken eastwards towards the coast, and the gravity values would be expected to continue to decrease. The high extends eastwards over much of the North Yorkshire Moors and has been interpreted as being associated with inversion of the Cleveland Basin, the onshore extension of the Sole Pit inversion (Hemingway and Riddler, 1982). The increase in gravity values is considered to be due to the elevation of high density, compacted Mesozoic sedimentary rocks and of the underlying basement. It is also noted, however, that the axis of the central gravity low closely follows the outcrop pattern of the Permo-Triassic rocks and that it forms the northward continuation of the low

a.

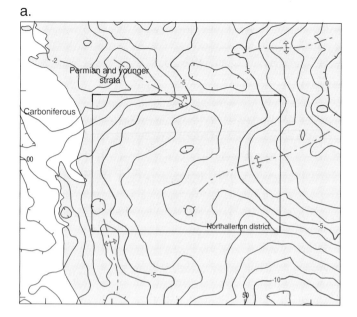

0   10 km

b.

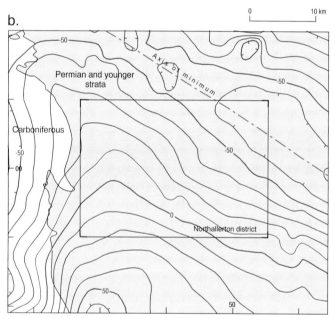

Figure 17a Bouguer gravity anomaly map with contours at 1 Mgal intervals based on a data coverage of 1 station/1.6 km sq. Data reduced using a density of 2.4 Mg/m^3. Local gravity features are indicated by dashed lines.

Figure 17b Aeromagnetic anomaly map with contours at 10nT interval based on data acquired at a mean terrain clearance of 305 m along north-south flight lines 2 km apart.

over the Vale of York, where it is associated with the basin of concealed Coal Measures. The observed gravity anomalies could therefore also include a contribution due to thickness variations in the Carboniferous rocks.

Superimposed on the main anomalies in Figure 17a are zones of steeper gradient and lower amplitude features of restricted extent. Several of the gradient zones have obvious relationships to surface structures, or their extensions, such as the east-south-east continuation of the anticline in Permian rocks at the northern margin of the district. Other features, such as the north–south feature in the south-west of the district, could reflect concealed structures. In the Thirsk district to the south, local gravity highs over Mesozoic rocks have been shown to be due both to concealed topographic features in the Carboniferous surface in the Ripon area (Allsop, 1985) and to grabens occupied by Mercia Mudstone, notably the Asenby–Coxwold structure (Powell et al., 1992). Farther south, in the Vale of York, gravity data have been used in the exploration for concealed basins of Coal Measures (Whetton et al., 1961).

Aeromagnetic data

The smooth, widely spaced contours on the aeromagnetic map (Figure 17b) indicate that the magnetic basement rocks must lie at considerable depth in the district, consistent with the seismic reflection evidence. The overlying rocks increase in depth to the north-north-east to form an elongated trough in the basement about 5 km north of the anomaly minimum indicated in Figure 17b. Hemingway and Riddler (1982) suggested that this basement low represents the original depositional basin axis beneath the Cleveland axis. To the south of the district, the magnetic basement forms a high in the Ripon and Harrogate areas (rising to within 4 to 5 km of the ground surface according to Kent (1966, fig.3). The magnetic high forms part of an extensive zone with the north-west to west-north-west trends characteristic of the Caledonian basement of eastern England.

There are no short wavelength aeromagnetic anomalies indicative of near-surface geological sources, apart from some minor features associated with the Cleveland–Armathwaite Dyke just to the north of the district.

SEVEN

Quaternary

About three quarters of the Northallerton district is covered by Quaternary deposits, the majority of which are glacial in origin. They were deposited during the Pleistocene (Dimlington Stadial, 26 000 to 13 000 BP, of the late Devensian stage; Rose, 1985), from an ice sheet which covered the district about 18 000 years ago and subsequently began to melt about 13 000 years ago (Penny, 1974). Older (pre-Devensian) deposits may also be present in buried valleys, and locally more recent Flandrian sediments overlie the Devensian deposits and modify the postglacial topography.

Powerful ice sheets streamed out eastwards and south-eastwards from the Lake District and south-west Scotland, and were joined by smaller less powerful glaciers from local centres in Wensleydale and Swaledale. Much of the ice came through the Stainmore gap with part continuing eastwards down the Tees and another branch swinging south through the Vale of Mowbray and into the Vale of York. The total thickness of ice in the central Tees lowland was probably about 800 m.

As the ice sheet melted and retreated from the Cleveland Hills, a complex sequence of glacial deposits was left behind, including till (boulder clay), sand and gravel, laminated clay, lacustrine clay, silt and sand, and loess. The average fill-line of the till against the flank of the Cleveland Hills is about 150 m in the north but decreases southwards; gravels have been recorded at over 300 m in the north-west of the Cleveland Hills near Osmotherley.

Generalised contours on the rockhead surface (the base of the Quarternary deposits) (Figure 18) show two major drift-filled, buried valleys; one drained northwards towards the Tees and the second drained southwards in a valley lying beneath the present-day alluvium of the River Swale. The major north-draining channel lies roughly along the line of the River Wiske and was originally considered to include part of the pre-glacial course of the River Swale (Raistrick, 1931; Radge, 1940). In addition, north-east-trending minor buried valleys mark the edge of the thick drift, adjacent to the scarp slope of the Cleveland Hills.

The rockhead surface falls northwards towards Teesside at a gradient of about 1 in 7, and the gradient is steeper and more irregular west of the Cleveland Hills. Rockhead lies below sea level in the vicinity of Sockburn [350 080], in the alluvial tract of the River Tees, and in the Swale valley.

Early work on the Quaternary deposits of the district includes a description of the superficial deposits by Fox-Strangways et al. (1886), and Kendall (1902), who described the glacial lakes in the Cleveland Hills. Elgee (1909), Radge (1940) and Best (1956) made passing reference to the district, and Raistrick (1931) described the preglacial course of the River Swale. More recent reviews of the region can be found in Taylor et al. (1971) and Penny (1974).

A threefold division of the Quaternary deposits was established by the early workers. This comprises Lower and Upper Boulder Clay separated by Middle Sands and Gravels. The Lower Boulder Clay is dark grey, stiff and stony with numerous erratics. The Upper Boulder Clay is reddish brown and largely devoid of stones. Kendall (1902) considered the Middle Sands to be a very unsatisfactory division, for in places they were absent and in other places they were interbedded with till at various levels. Despite this criticism, the threefold division of drift deposits in northern England has dominated the geological literature. The lower stony till of the district is correlated with the Lower Boulder Clay of County Durham and Tyneside.

Mitchell et al. (1973) correlate the Drab Till of Holderness (Catt and Penny, 1966) with the Durham Lower Boulder Clay (Smith and Francis, 1967). The Drab Till closely overlies the Dimlington Silts which have given a radiocarbon date of 18 240 ± 250 and 18 500 ± 400 years BP (Penny et al., 1969). Postglacial hollows in the Northallerton district contain peat which has been dated at 6450 ± 40 and 6355 ± 45. The glacial deposits of the district therefore belong to a relatively short-lived late Devensian glaciation. Catt (1991) noted that the area south of the Cleveland Hills seemed to have had a fairly simple Devensian glacial history related to a single coastal 'surge' (Boulton et al., 1977). North of the Cleveland Hills, however, there is evidence of two or more phases of ice movements, implying that the glacial period started earlier and consequently lasted longer.

At around 12 000 years BP the ice sheet stagnated, and as it began to melt it retreated northwards. There are no well-preserved terminal moraines in this district, comparable with the York and Eskrick moraines farther south, so the process may have been fairly uniform and relatively rapid. Radge (1940, pl.XX) interpreted deposits at Seamer [50 10] just north of the district to be of morainic origin. The pattern of superficial deposits within the district does enable a tentative interpretation of possible ice margins at successive retreat stages (Figure 19), for instance a marginal moraine is suggested in the Leeming Bar area. Other glacial landforms include drumlins, eskers and meltwater channels.

Sand and gravel bodies were deposited from meltwater during the retreat of the ice sheets and some formed as beaches and deltas at the margins of ice-dammed lakes. These glacial and glaciofluvial deposits range from small lenses, completely enclosed within till,

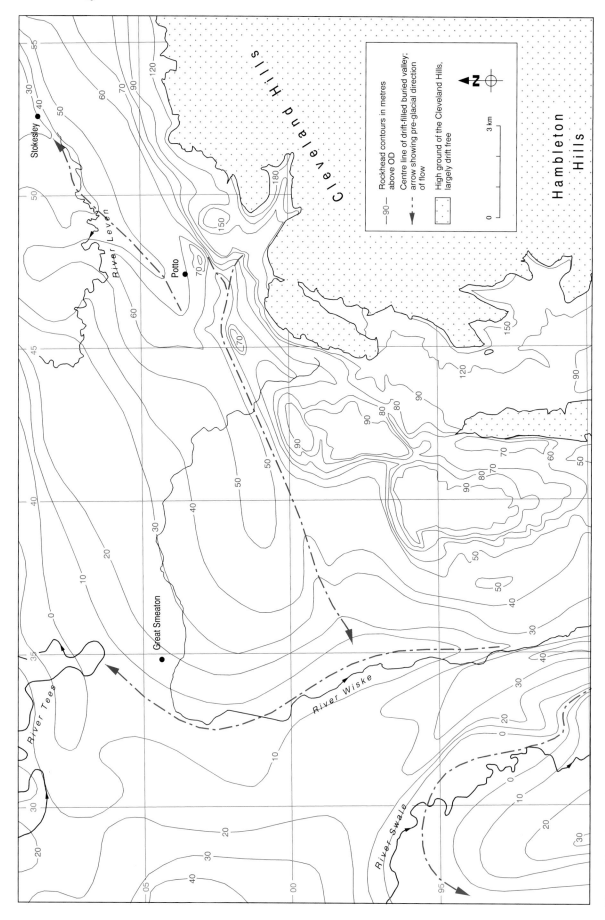

Figure 18   Generalised rockhead contours of the district showing the pattern of drift-filled buried valleys.

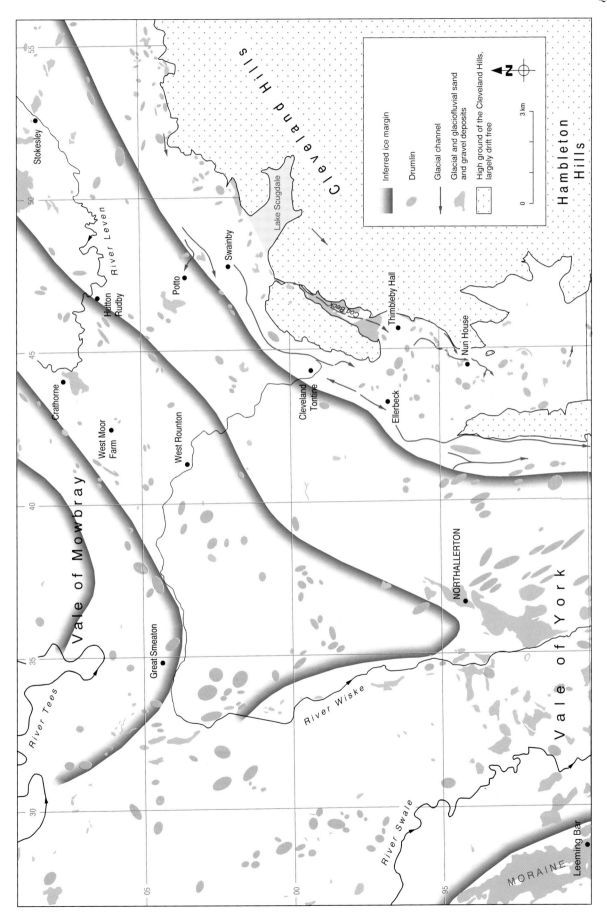

Figure 19 Glacial and glaciofluvial features of the district.

to extensive and complex sheets. Silts and clays were washed into the glacial lakes and formed laminated deposits.

Mounds of morainic debris are also referred to by Elgee (1909) for the area south of Swainby, [48 01] blocking the entrance to Scugdale.

A weak, red-brown, sparingly stony, silty clay is the youngest glacial deposit of the lowland area and has been correlated with the Teesside Clay or the Pelaw Clay of north-east England which may be a flow or ablation till.

Postglacial and late-glacial deposits are almost all water-laid and concentrated mainly in the valleys. They comprise alluvium, lacustrine alluvium and terrace deposits. Blown sand and peat are also present in small areas.

TILL (BOULDER CLAY)

Most of the north and west of the district is covered by a blanket of till. Sporadic drumlins are present (Figure 19) but rarely show evidence of alignment; elsewhere the ground is featureless, poorly drained and pock-marked by shallow depressions. The maximum proved thickness of the till is 30 m in a section at Rockcliffe Scar [3134 0860] in the Tees Valley near Eryholme; this includes some laminated clays and sands. A similar thickness was proved in a borehole at Hewitson Hill [299 998], north west of Danby Wiske. Many boreholes in the district have proved up to at least 18 m of till without reaching its base.

In the north and west of the district, the thickest (lowest) till is a tough, grey to dark brown silty clay containing pebbles, cobbles and boulders predominantly of locally derived Carboniferous cherts, sandstones, ganisters, ironstones and limestones, with sporadic far-travelled erratics including Shap Granite. The area south of Swainby [47 02] contains many large boulders of Shap granite, some up to 1 m long [4662 0198].

Farther east, the colour of the till reflects the underlying bedrock; it is red-brown and sandy overlying the Sherwood Sandstone Group, and red and purplish grey with a sparse sand content over the Mercia Mudstone Group. Erratics include pebbles of Permo-Triassic dolomites, limestones, sandstones as well as a few Carboniferous and Lower Palaeozoic examples. A dolerite boulder, 1 m × 0.5 m × 0.9 m, was found [4383 0755] just west of Crathorne. A cobble of fossiliferous Carboniferous limestone found [4404 9370] near Osmotherley was identified as containing *Linoprotonia dentifer*, typical of the species found in the Hardraw (Oxford) Limestone of the Pennines and northern England. Quartz and coal fragments are not uncommon.

The clasts in the till are variable in size, commonly subrounded and show signs of abrasion, with scratch marks, pitting and polishing. They are commonest in the lower parts of the till sheet.

The section quoted by Fox-Strangways (1886, p.53) in the River Tees at Rockliffe Scar (referred to as Rawcliffe Scar) near Eryholm [3130 0870] is now largely obscured by landslip. About 30 m of sediments were recorded, and is repeated below as it represents the best record of the drift deposits of the district. (Recent observations are in brackets, and thicknesses have been metricated.)

	Thickness m
Upper Boulder Clay with some sand. (The back of the landslip scar now exposes red-brown and grey, pebbly clay. The pebbles are small but up to 0.15 m near the surface and include Carboniferous siltstone, reddened sandstone, ganister, grit and cherty limestone. Dolerite (Whin Sill) is also present.	c.10.6 3.00
Bluish laminated clay without stones (Complex of laminated clay up to 1.35 m overlying red silt, micaceous sand and bedded gravel; some convolute lamination; 0.19 m impersistent unlaminated grey mudstone and silt near top.)	
Reddish Upper Boulder Clay with few stones (2.70 m of red-brown, silty sand and gravel, clayey, impersistent; passing laterally into till, 2.0 m, red-brown, silty stony clay).	up to 6.00
Sand	2.00
Bluish laminated clay without stones	2.00
Reddish Upper Boulder Clay with some stones	3.00
Lower Boulder Clay, base not seen	3.00

About 2 km farther east, sandstone of the Sherwood Sandstone Group is exposed in the river bed, which implies that most of the drift sequence is exposed in this locality.

GLACIAL SAND AND GRAVEL

In this district, glacial sand and gravel is intimately associated with the till. It occurs in small lenses, as larger areas forming sinuous ridges (eskers) or sheets of clayey sand extending over several square kilometres. The composition of the gravel clasts is similar to those of the till, but one exposure [4588 9790] near Osmotherley contains mainly limestone and ironstone in a concentration which is unusual in the district.

The sands and gravels occur at three levels within the district (Figure 19). The highest deposits form an isolated patch at 305 m [4860 9960] on the hillside south of Scugdale Beck, and two smaller areas occur slightly lower [4654 0000 and 4700 0000], 2 km west of Scarth Wood Moor at 260 m. They are rich in chert and sandstone pebbles. The nature and position of the deposit near Scugdale suggests a possible origin as a beach, marginal to the former glacial Lake Scugdale (Figure 19). The lower deposits are remnants of a major north–south-trending glacial channel through Scarth Nick [4721 0000] now occupied by Cod Beck.

At intermediate levels, sands and gravels occur between 150 m and 200 m on the Jurassic escarpment and penetrate the dales opening from it. These deposits were formed from glacial meltwater streams marginal to the ice sheet, as it lay banked against the escarpment. Many of these sands and gravels were reworked as the climate ameliorated.

The best exposures and provings by boreholes are to be found in the valley of the Cod Beck. The valley lies to the east of Osmotherley, and is aligned roughly north–south. It drains southwards, with a fall from about 223 m near Scarth Nick to 140 m south of Osmotherley, over a distance of some 3 km. In the centre of this valley, Cote Ghyll Youth Hostel Borehole [4614 9808] proved silty clay and gravel to a depth of 27 m and in the borehole OD is about 168 m below ground level, showing that the rockhead valley floor in the central part of the valley lies at a similar depth to that at the southern end, at Osmotherley Bridge.

A short distance north of the borehole, several exploratory bores were drilled along the site of a proposed dam for the Osmotherley Reservoir [4630 9845]. The rockhead profile proved to be similar to that of the existing valley profile. The boreholes showed that the valley contains up to 8 m of laminated clays and silts with interbedded and interlaminated sands, all underlying the sand and gravel deposits.

The Cod Beck valley has therefore had a complex Quaternary history. At the beginning of the period, it may have been scoured by southward-moving ice and was eventually completely covered by ice during the maximum of the Devensian glaciation. During ice retreat it would have contained a glacial lake, where laminated silts, clays and sands were deposited. As the ice melted from the surrounding hills, the proto-Cod Beck acted as a major spillway for water with outlets both at the northern end, at Scarth Nick and to the south, near Osmotherley. The sands and gravels were deposited during this fluviatile period and were reworked, sorted and dissected in postglacial times.

The lowest-lying deposits of sand and gravel are found associated with till in the Vale of Mowbray and Vale of York. Old sand pits near Leeming Bar [2785 9090] show sand interbedded with till, and in places the sand also contains laminae of red-brown stoneless clay, which show distortion of the bedding together with faulting (Figure 20). Faces nearby are composed largely of till but include flame structures of fine brown sand. Other features include overturned beds erosional contacts and washouts. Deposition at the margin of melting ice, within valleys cut into the surface of the ice, or in tunnels within or beneath the ice is indicated. Subsequent melting of the ice has inverted the topography leaving the sand and gravel as upstanding ridges or eskers. Evidence for the removal of ice support, and foundering following melting of buried ice, comes from the disruption, slumping and minor faulting visible in these beds. Cryoturbation may also have played a part in the formation of some of these structures.

The sands and gravels form a relatively high moraine-like ridge, aligned parallel to the A1 between Leeming Bar [287 901] and St Ann's Cross [266 935]. In Borehole SE 29SE27, beneath the old A1 road surface [2789 9144], near Leases Hall, 12 m of glacial sand and gravel rests on over 9.5 m of laminated clays (Lovell, 1982). A similar thickness of laminated clay resting on till was proved in nearby boreholes.

The low-lying area of the Swale valley, between Leeming Bar and Northallerton, contains many scattered remnants of glacial sand and gravel. The most continuous deposits trend north-eastwards through Northallerton and Romanby and have been dug in the past. A borehole near St James Church [3605 9320] proved gravel and strong clay to 6 m.

Boreholes, sunk along the line of the A19 By-pass for Crathorne, proved up to 5 m of sand and gravel overlying till. Nearby, running sand was reported during excavation and levelling for a playing field [439 074], and in the footings for a bungalow [4403 0752] in the village opposite the Post Office.

LAMINATED CLAY

Deposits of laminated clay are widespread in the Teesside area and continue into the northern part of the district. They are also common and extensive in the Leeming Bar area, and occur in many isolated hollows in the lowland part of the district.

The clays are stiff, slightly silty, almost stoneless, dark brown to purplish brown with some reddish colouration, and are plastic when wet. They occur in beds a few millimetres thick, separated by films of grey to pale brown, fine-grained, micaceous, silty sand. They pass, by interlamination, into fine-grained sands and may be overlain by thin sand or superficial till with, in places, a thin peat at the surface.

The laminated clays were laid down in lakes of various sizes, usually after the retreat of the ice. They are composed of reworked till and contain a similar suite of clay minerals. The sporadic occurrence of pebbles and boulders may be explained by release from melting ice floating on the lake surface.

Glacial lake deposits, up to 12 m thick have been proved at Crakehall Ings [265 905] east of Leeming Bar. (Lovell, 1982, fig. 2). They appear to be bounded on the west by glacial sands and gravels of the Hackforth–Langthorne and Patrick Brompton areas, just beyond the western margin of the district, and extend eastwards for about 5 km towards Northallerton. Borehole SE 27 [2789 9144] proved that the laminated clays pass beneath sand and gravel which forms the morainic ridge between Leeming Bar and Kirkby Fleetham. The clays occur between 20 m and 50 m above OD. If these clays are the result of deposition within lakes during the retreat of the ice sheet, then the overlying sands and gravels may represent local readvance of ice from the Yorkshire Dales to the west.

Laminated clays, silts and sands up to 19 m thick were proved in boreholes along the proposed line of the dam for Cod Beck Reservoir [462 985]. These deposits, although not recorded in detail, represent deposition in

a. [2786 9086]   View to the south

surface

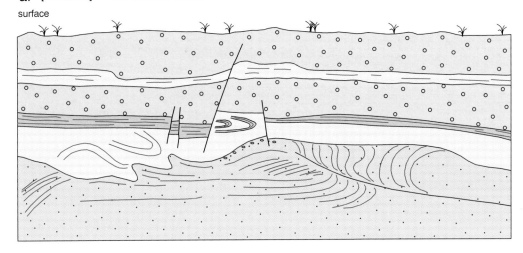

b. [2782 9088]   View to the south

lower bench

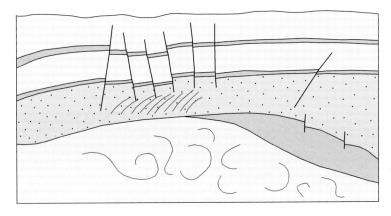

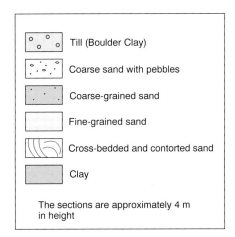

	Till (Boulder Clay)
	Coarse sand with pebbles
	Coarse-grained sand
	Fine-grained sand
	Cross-bedded and contorted sand
	Clay

The sections are approximately 4 m
in height

c. [2781 9092]   View to the west

surface

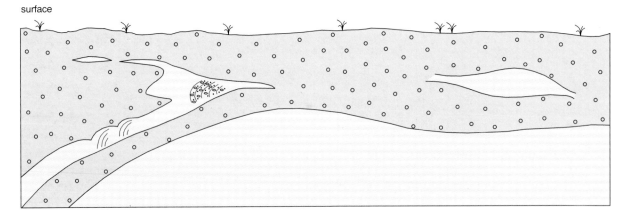

Figure 20   Structures in sand and gravel pits near Leeming Bar.

a glacial lake at a relatively high level, between 160 m and 180 m above OD.

The Teesside–Middlesbrough area is underlain by a nearly flat sheet of laminated clay, dissected by later erosion and partly concealed by alluvium. The laminated clay rarely exceeds 10 m in thickness, but extends southwestwards up the valley sides of the Tees and into the Northallerton district. It is exposed in the valley sides near Eryholm (see p.45), where two beds, up to 3 m thick, are separated by glacial deposits, up to 8 m thick, and are overlain by 11 m of the 'Upper Boulder Clay' of Gunn (1899).

At Eryholm Scar [318 089] the sequence is thinner:

	Thickness m
Till, red, stony, with sharp base	3.5 to 4.5
Sand, fine-grained, cross-bedded	4.5 to 6.0
Clay and laminated clay	1.5
Till, reddish brown, thinning eastwards	0 to 7.5
Till, grey	4.00

GEOMORPHOLOGICAL EVOLUTION OF THE DISTRICT

The rockhead contour map (Figure 18) shows two areas, in the valleys of the rivers Swale and Tees, where the base of the Quaternary deposits lies below sea level. Two other buried valleys, corresponding with the valleys of the rivers Wiske and Leven, show a reversed direction of flow. The former is aligned approximately north–south with a gradient of only 1 in 1000 northwards from near Romanby towards the Tees near Great Smeaton, where it swings north-eastwards towards the most southerly meander of the River Tees at Sockburn [3507]. The

latter has a gradient of 1 in 300 towards the north-eastwards from near Potto towards Stokesley, falling about 20 m over a distance of 6 km.

As the Devensian ice sheet retreated, meltwater escaped southwards across the Cleveland Hills, eroding channels into the solid rock. One high-level erosion channel, along Holy Well Gill (Plate 7), is now a dry valley. This drops from about 300 m above OD towards the south-west with a gradient of about 1 in 20; it is nearly 1 km in length and, up to 4 m deep. It may have drained the ice-marginal Lake Scugdale (Kendall, 1902) when it was dammed by ice to the north (Figure 19). Remnants of sand and gravel [489 996] adjacent to Holy Well Gill are probably the relics of outwash material along the shores of Lake Scugdale.

Further deposits of sand and gravel [4700 9990] are associated with the sides of a glacial channel at Scarth Nick (Plate 8) and are 60 m lower in altitude. The highest point in the channel is just our 220 m, and it is floored by peat, sand and gravel and alluvium. The gradient is largely to the south but a small section of the channel may have once drained northwards for a short period. The main channel followed the present line of the Cod Beck and reached about 168 m OD just north of Thimbleby Hall [4544 9626]. Similar channels farther south in the proximity of Nun House [446 940], at about 150 m OD, may represent a southern continuation of flow around the ice margin, to the north-west of the Cleveland Hills [Figure 19]. The Nun House channel bifurcated at Over Silton and discharged into the Leake Stell to the west and the Broad Beck to the east.

Towards the end of the Devensian, the ice sheet occupied only the lowland area of Teesside and the Vale of York plains. Several glacial spillways have been described (Elgee, 1909), which formed features around the north-west of the Cleveland Hills. They may have

Plate 7 Glacial drainage channel of Holy Well Gill [4895 9920] on the south side of Scugdale, near Osmotherley. The channel is cut into sandstones and mudstones of the Ravenscar Group at an elevation of c.297 m above OD. (L2463)

Plate 8 Glacial drainage channel at Scarth Nick [4715 9957] near Osmotherley. The bottom of the channel, at about 230 m above OD, is filled with peat and drift deposits. The sides are cut into sandstones and mudstones of the Saltwick Formation and the alignment is fault controlled. (L2464)

been cut by subglacial streams or represent periods of stillstand as the ice retreated northward. These channels occur near Swainby, Ellerbeck (Figure 19) and Cotcliffe, lying between about and 60 and 75 m above OD; and drain largely to the south. When the drainage had reached these levels, water flowing in the Cod Beck channel bypassed the Nun House section and followed the present course of the Cod Beck, westwards from Thimbleby Hall, eventually turning south past Cotcliffe.

A glacial lake was formed for a time in the Cleveland Tontein area [44 99] where several channels and spillways converged. From this lake, the headwaters of the River Wiske flowed north and north-westwards to West Rounton (Figure 19). A likely direction from here was north and north-eastwards along the Carr Bridge Stell [411 043] and into the area of alluvium around West Moor Farm [426 060]. The present River Tees is only 6 km north of this location; the River Leven is 2 km to the north-east and probably follows a similar course to the proto-Leven.

The accumulation of superficial deposits, together with isostatic readjustment after the great weight of ice had been removed from the area, caused a major reversal in drainage directions. The initial response of the River Tees and River Leven would have been rapid downcutting, resulting in entrenched meanders, for example in the Tees at Eryholm and in the Leven at Hutton Rudby. The ponded waters of the Leven between Stokesley and Hutton Rudby escaped northwards at Hutton Rudby by cutting a gorge through to Crathorne and on to the Tees near Yarm [415 117]. The original erosion was into soft Mercia Mudstones, but north of Crathorne the more resistant Sherwood Sandstone Group probably caused the change in direction of the river. This new section of the River Leven captured the

headwaters of the River Wiske, which then meandered gently westwards to join and follow the lower reaches of the river now draining southwards.

The River Swale crosses the south-west of the district. Raistrick (1931) considered that the preglacial Swale flowed north-eastwards to the sea at Teesmouth in a valley trending north-east from near Catterick [24 98] and crossing the present Tees at Sockburn [350 070]. Radge (1940, fig.1) indicated that this valley crossed the present Tees farther west and north at Hurworth [310 100]. The rockhead contour map (Figure 18) for the northern and eastern part of the district does not support these theories.

The pattern of glaciofluvial deposits in the district gives an indication of ice margins at successive retreat stages (Figure 19). For example, an early stage of ice front at an altitude of just over 80 m OD influenced the position of the spillways near Swainby and Cotcliffe. A secondary boundary at about 70 m above OD, north of Northallerton, influenced the Brompton Beck and the fluvioglacial gravels of the Leven. A tertiary feature at about 60 m above OD influenced the course of the Wiske and another at about 50 m above OD south of High Worsall [380 070] may have contributed to the course of the Staindale Beck which parallels the Wiske in this area. The topography and drainage was further modified by postglacial processes.

POSTGLACIAL DEPOSITS

The early postglacial history resulted in the formation of river terraces and the accumulation of peat in kettle holes. Most of the head deposits and some landslips may also date from this period. Formation of peat mosses and alluvium on the lowlands and hill peat on the Cleveland

and Hambleton hills completed the Quaternary history of the district.

Figure 21 shows the pattern of alluvium and terrace deposits of the district. The most striking alignment is that of the north-north-west-trending section of the River Wiske and its tributaries, linking the meanders of the Tees southwards through the Vale of Mowbray. The upper reaches show two other alignments again hinting at possible river capture during Quaternary times (see p.71).

RIVER TERRACE DEPOSITS

The river terraces are represented on the geological map by an undiffentiated terrace symbol and form a series of step-like features formed by coarse gravels and sands with subordinate clays and silts. They are thickest in the Leven valley where they form a major source of aggregate up to 21 m thick (see p.79).

Although the terraces of the Tees are broad, their thickness does not exceed 4.5 m. The lithology varies from coarse gravel to clayey sand. There are at least four separate levels of terrace above the alluvium over the entire length of Tees, but the highest terrace is present only beyond the limits of the district (Mr D H Land, personal communication, 1992) downstream from where the river crosses the outcrop of the Cleveland Dyke. In the vicinity of Eryholme, [310 092] the alluvium is at a level of 24 m above OD. The first terrace at 27 m, the second at 29 m and a third at 30 m above OD.

Diversion of the River Leven south-east of Stokesley into the Broughton Bridge Beck, by means of a manmade channel parallel with Love Lane, proved that the top 4 m or so consist mostly of sand and gravel with sporadic red-brown clay partings and lenses. A thin peat was recorded 2 m beneath the surface [540 084].

Site investigation boreholes at Garden House [538 088], in the terrace of the Leven, proved 10.5 m as follows:

	Thickness m
Soil	0.6
Sand, clayey	1.2
Clay, sandy	0.8
Sand, clayey	1.0
Sand	3.2
Gravel	2.2
Clay, silty	1.5

ALLUVIUM

All the streams and rivers of the district are flanked to a large extent by alluvium, and, by definition, alluvial areas are subject to flooding. The Stokesley area in the valley of the River Leven has until recently been subject to damaging floods. The River Tees regularly rises 6 m above normal low water, and the valley of the

Swale, in the south-west of the district, is subject to rapid run-off from the high ground of the Pennines to the west.

The alluvial deposits are up to about 6 m thick. The most extensive area of alluvium is associated with the River Swale and its tributaries (Figure 21). Silts and clays predominate, with sporadic sands and pockets of peat (see p.68). Bedding is commonly near horizontal, and the more arenaceous fraction is usually cross-bedded. Cryoturbation is also typical.

Exposures of river deposits are common in the valley of the River Leven between Stokesley and Hutton Rudby (Plate 1). The alluvial deposits usually comprise silt and sand and gravel. The gravels are commonly ferruginous but contain sporadic near horizontal carbonaceous laminae. The base of the gravel on rockhead is irregular and in this area [484 067] the underlying Mercia Mudstone Group shows considerable disturbance of the bedding over a thickness of 2 to 3 m.

Near Crathorne Hall, the river deposits are only 3 m thick, and rest on red sandstone of the Sherwood Sandstone Group. The areas of alluvium are small and have an irregular top surface. They are approximately 1 or 2 m above the water level. The main areas of terrace are 3 to 5 m above this level.

The wide alluvial tracts near Stokesley have been proved both in boreholes and temporary sections. A mineral assessment borehole (NZ50NW/11) proved sand, clayey sand and gravel to a depth of 9.2 m, on red stony and laminated clay. To the south, near Broughton Bridge [541 082], a section exposes 2 m of clay overlying 1.5 m sand and gravel, and passes southwards into the following section, 4.18 m thick.

	Thickness m
Soil; brown silty loam	0.50
Clay, red-brown, silty	0.30
Sand, silty, laminated	0.13
Clay, mottled orange-brown and grey	0.05
Sand, coarse-grained	0.05
Sand, fine-grained	0.25
Gravel	0.40
Clay, purplish red, with pebbles	0.50
Sand, yellow-brown, laminated; coarse-grained at base, with gravel	2.00

Traced 10 m westwards these beds pass laterally into clayey gravel 4 m in thickness.

Large areas of alluvium, up to 1 km wide in places, have been mapped along the banks of the Swale. At Kiplin a mineral assessment borehole (SE29NE/19) (Gozzard and Price, 1982) proved 7.2 m of sand and gravel beneath a thin, brown, silty, loamy soil. The gravel comprises well-rounded limestone, chert, sandstone and quartzite with some igneous rock, possibly derived from the Lake District, and small amounts of Permian limestone. The intervening sand is medium to coarse grained, comprising rounded quartz and rock fragments. The alluvium rests on 1 m of reddish brown to dark grey, stiff, pebbly till which in

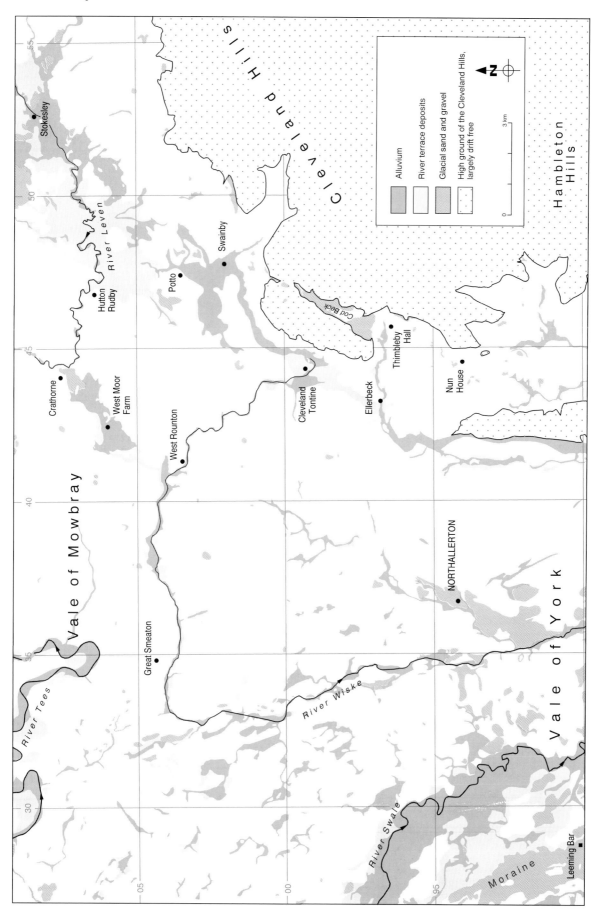

Figure 21 Postglacial deposits of the district.

turn rests on red sandstone of the Sherwood Sandstone Group.

PEAT

Extensive deposits of peat cover much of the high moorland of the Cleveland and Hambleton hills, particularly around Arden Great Moor and Black Hambleton. This hill peat is heavily dissected and eroded, and appears to be wasting (Plate 9). Maximum proved thickness is 2 m. On Bilsdale West Moor [551 955], black peat with silver birch stumps and trunks is being eroded down to limestone bedrock at about 365 m above OD. Other upland localities with delineated peat deposits occur at Meggy Mire [547 963], near Wiley Howe, and Brians Pond [522 006] on Whorlton Moor at Clough Gill Top.

Scattered patches of peat are common on the low-lying ground of the district and show no signs of denudation. The largest area of lowland peat [436 932], about 1 km^2 in extent, occurs 1 km north east of Landmoth. The peat, about 1 m thick, rests on 0.2 m of pale grey shell marl containing gastropods. Some 0.4 m of peat were proved by augering at Ainderby Bottoms [339 928], 4 km south-west of Northallerton.

A peat bed, 0.1 m thick [4525 0081], was noted about 1 m below the surface in the alluvium of Carr Beck near Ingleby Arncliffe. The locality has been described by Best (1956) as a 'gutter' which lies on the inner, northern edge of the Scugdale Moraine. The 'gutter' is attributed to glaciofluvial erosion (see p.72). Radiocarbon dates for the peat samples vary between 6450 ± 40 years BP and 6355 ± 45 years BP. This may indicate the date of a landslip on the northern scarp of the Cleveland Hills, which resulted in the local ponding of the drainage in the vicinity of the 'gutter' of Carr Beck. A thin peat bed was recorded [540 084] south-east of Stokesley in terrace gravels of the River Leven.

CALCAREOUS TUFA

Calcareous tufa consists largely of calcium carbonate which has formed by evaporation from spring water, and commonly coats or encrusts vegetation over which the water has passed. It forms a soft, greyish white rock with a spongy or cellular texture.

Within the district, tufa is associated mainly with springs flowing from the base of the permeable Lower Calcareous Grit, for example at Dunsforth's Hill [4866 9189], Limekiln House Gill [4996 9156] and Thorodale [5003 9156] where mound-like aprons up to 3 m high are formed. Smaller deposits are located near springs issuing from the base of the Dogger Formation or the Staithes Sandstone Formation, for example near Howes Hill [4604 9051].

HEAD AND SCREE

Head, a solifluction deposit, comprises weathered shallow bedrock or drift which is mobilised during repeated freezing and thawing, and moves downslope. Most of the head dates from a period of periglacial conditions, following the retreat of the ice.

Solifluction deposits, consisting of silt and clay with angular fragments of Jurassic bedrock, mantle many of the slopes of the Cleveland and Hambleton hills. They have been omitted from the maps, in places, for the sake of clarity.

Screes resulting from frost-shattering of exposed bedrock usually rest immediately below the steep

Plate 9   Accelerated erosion of peat after heather burning, exposing the weathered top of the Lower Calcareous Grit Formation near the crest of Black Hambleton [4915 9367]. (L2668)

Jurassic escarpments, and grade imperceptibly down-slope into head deposits.

Details

The western flanks of Easterside Hill are masked by a large area [5525 9040] of scree consisting of mostly angular fragments of the Lower Calcareous Grit Formation.

The north-eastern slopes of Black Hambleton [49 94] are covered by large areas of scree and head. These deposits lie just below the escarpment, from an altitude of just over 350 m above OD downslope to around just over 300 m above OD, in a 100 m wide belt for several kilometres along most of the feature. In places they form a featureless slope masking the outcrop of the Oxford Clay and other formations lower in the geological sequence. Some areas are extensively gullied and others show active soil creep.

Certain areas near the top of Black Hambleton [4915 9367] show the weathered surface of the Lower Calcareous Grit Formation with incipient scree formation taking place along the contact with the immediately overlying hill peat. Acid waters percolating down from the peat rapidly dissolve the limestone which, combined with the seasonal burning of the peat, is leading to accelerated erosion along this section of the hills.

BLOWN SAND AND SILT (LOESS)

Thin, structureless, yellow-brown silt, probably picked up by the prevailing westerly winds, may have originated from the glacial deposits occupying the low ground in the west of the district. Such deposits are too thin to warrant mapping but have been recorded as thin patches overlying the Hambleton Oolite Member on Little Moor, in the south east of the district [490 910].

Loess overlain by peat also occurs in a dry valley [4973 9269] north-east of Limekiln House. The section is as follows:

	Thickness m
Peat	1.2
Silt, pale grey with sporadic sand and rootlets	0.1
Silt, yellow sandy	0.2
Limestone fragments (Hambleton Oolite Member)	

LANDSLIPS

Landslips are common in the south-eastern part of the district, on the steep slopes of the Jurassic rocks of the Cleveland and Hambleton hills. Rock-cored slides around the northern and western scarps of the Cleveland Hills largely affect the Redcar Mudstone Formation and the overlying Staithes Sandstone Formation.

Farther south, the Hambleton Hills are ringed by landslips, where soft plastic clays of the Oxford Clay Formation have been unable to support the overlying Lower Calcaceous Grit and Coralline Oolite formations.

Slides involving superficial deposits (mainly till and head) are also present in areas affected by slips of the rock-cored type.

The larger slides are rotational in type, with failure occurring along a concave surface forming an arcuate scar at the back of the slip. The angle of dip in Jurassic rocks is rarely steep and the slides are closely related to the joint or fault directions. Many slips were probably initiated in the late Devensian when the rockhead was saturated with groundwater and weakened by the repetitive freeze-thaw process. Slips still occur where the strata are undercut by stream and river action or destabilised by human activities such as excavations or overloading of slopes.

Details

Carlton Bank, Busby Moor and Dromonby Bank

An impressive landslip, 4 km long, drapes the north face of the Cleveland Hills near Carlton [515 025 to 645 036] (see Frontispiece). The back face varies between about 200 m and 360 m above OD. The main cause of slippage has been the movement of water down through the permeable Staithes Sandstone Formation until its passage was blocked by the underlying Redcar Mudstone Formation, which forms the basal section of this part of the Cleveland Hills. The water was then either ponded back or escaped and found its way out via joints to form a spring. Repetition of this process together with repeated freezing and thawing eventually led to slope failure. East of Dromonby Bank, the erosion has worked upwards to affect the Middle Jurassic strata. The arcuate scar of Kirby Bank, comprising largely sandstones of the Saltwick Formation, forms the backwall of a classic landslip.

Exposures of the Lias Group mudstones in Tom Gill [5274 0357] show considerable disturbance, with dip directions bearing no resemblance to the trend of the district. The slips are rock-cored. The toe of the slip reaches down to near 150 m above OD providing a width of about 1 km. Some parts of the toe of this slip comprise wet yellow and brown clays. They may have incorporated till during their movement, and later been modified by mud-flows.

Wath Hill [534 012]

Although small, covering less than half a square kilometre, the landslip at Wath Hill, at the head of Raisdale, contains most features typical of landslips in this district. The movement has been in mudstones of the Redcar Mudstone Formation, which now form irregular hummocky ground beneath the arcuate scar — a feature comprising the basal sandstone of the Saltwick Formation. The toe of the slip has reached the Raisdale Beck and so is systematically eroded and removed, ensuring reactivation of the slip. A small but significant slip in a newly constructed forestry track provides such evidence of very recent movement.

Hawnby Hill [540 905] and Easterside Hill [554 904]

The most extensive landslips in the district lie either side of Hawnby Hill. Several generations of landslip can be recognised, and the rotational slips are partly covered by large boulders of the Hambleton Oolite Member. These block-falls were initiated by the widening of joints as the escarpment weathered back. The small cap of Upper Jurassic rock is heavily cambered giving the strata anomalous dips of up to 70° (Plate 10). Small debris-flows have occurred recently, and the Hawnby to Osmotherley road has been blocked by such deposits in the last decade, during periods of heavy rain.

Plate 10 Cambering in the Lower Calcareous Grit Formation near Hawnby [5397 9070]. (L2465)

The slips on either side of Hawnby Hill and Easterside Hill have reached the Ladhill Beck and coalesced, thus ensuring continued erosion and further slippage. The eastern side of Easterside Hill is, by comparison, only in the initial stages of slip, with a small area of movement developing [558 905] just beyond the margin of the district. The River Seph is sufficiently far away from the slip not to accelerate the erosion. However, the area above Timber Holme [5615 9050] is a potential slip zone. The ground already shows small slips, the outcrop of the Moor Grit Member is cambered and shows signs of valley bulging and may provide the district with another major landslip during the next decade.

Landslips farther west in Ryedale appear to have stabilised. Arden Hall [5195 9060], built in the last century, is situated upon a slip and shows no sign of movement.

Kirby Sigston – Cotcliffe

A 2 km-long landslip was surveyed on the west side of the Kirby Sigston–Cotcliffe graben (see p.60) stretching from Sigston Wood through Landmoth Wood [42 93]. All the classic features of a slip are well displayed. Most of the rotational/gravitational movement has been in mudstones of the Whitby Mudstone Formation and the Redcar Mudstone Formation, which are faulted and lie adjacent along the length of the slip. The fault line has been a major influence in the development of the slip, firstly by weakening the inherent strength of the mudstones, and secondly by providing avenues of access for percolating ground water.

The slip has a backwall formed by the lowest sandstones of the Saltwick Formation — a major zone of spring formation. The Cod Beck continually activates the toe of the slip along its length. Recent movement in the region of Wood House [4220 9340] is suspected because of the highly irregular and wet terrain between the house and the river, and the virtual absence of alluvial flats in this vicinity, due to encroachment of the slip towards the river. Old workings for jet in the Whitby Mudstone Formation have exacerbated the instability of the slope. They would also have provided a very dangerous zone of shale in which to mine.

MUD FLOWS, SLUMPS AND SLIPS

Hutton Rudby

The right bank of the River Leven, upstream from Hutton Rudby Church [474 067] consists of an irregular area of wet clay stretching from the top of the steep river bank down to the alluvial plain, or in places to the river itself. The area to the north of the river is overlain by a hummocky till plain, proved in a nearby borehole [4781 0717] to consist of firm red-brown clay with silt and sand laminae, and is at least 18 m thick.

In the past the river has undercut the valley sides on the outer bank of the meander. Water seepage through the sand and silt laminae has helped to lubricate the deposit and provide further lines of weakness along which slips may occur.

Cod Beck Reservoir

In 1955, site investigation boreholes were drilled in connection with the construction of a dam across the valley of the Cod Beck. Interlaminated silt, sand and clay of glaciofluvial origin were recorded, up to 19 m thick, along the dam line, and mudflows were indicated on plans of the area just south of the proposed construction. This area is now incorporated into the dam, earthworks and the made ground occupying a landscaped zone some 100 m south of the dam.

Raisdale

Two areas of landslip on West Bank [544 992 and 549 991] were probably initiated by rotation of the mudstones beneath the lowest sandstone of the Saltwick Formation. These have subsequently been lubricated by percolation of groundwater, and have flowed down the valley side from an elevation of about 312 m above OD to about 180 m above OD, almost reaching the bottom of the slope. The slip therefore spans a geological sequence of strata from the highest beds of the Whitby Mudstone Formation, across the Jet Rock Member, the Cleveland Ironstone and Staithes Sandstone formations and on to the Redcar Mudstone Formation.

MADE GROUND

Small areas of made ground comprising quarry spoil occur in front of many of the abandoned faces of quarries in the district. Most are small areas associated with sandstone and limestone quarries, but significant spoil is mapped at Kepwick Quarry [485 914] and unnamed quarries to the east [486 915].

Tips of mudstone have been recorded at the entrance to ironstone mines in Scugdale [470 007, 485 008 and 494 008] and near Faceby [494 028]. Hundreds of small trials for jet have left a distinctive trail of individual tips, particularly in Scugdale, Raisdale and Bilsdale.

The largest and most significant areas of made ground have originated from the alum workings. The burnt red shales covering much of Carlton Bank [520 030] remain a permanent eyesore on the northern scarp of the Cleveland Hills.

Numerous old sand pits in the Leeming area have been filled in and some landscaping has taken place west of the A1 [278 911] near Leases Hall. Sand and gravel pits, shown on the original survey maps of the late 19th century, have been filled and built over in Northallerton, for example [370 944 and 267 938].

Old clay pits, for example near Stokesley [504 079], have been filled and levelled. Large pits adjacent to the Yafforth Road [357 947], west of Northallerton, have been used for domestic refuse and then covered by soil and landscaped.

The unconsolidated and uncompacted nature of made ground, its varied content and the imprecise limits of its margins, make it a potential engineering hazard.

EIGHT

Economic geology

ALUM

The alum industry of the Cleveland district was active for some 300 years until the mid 19th century.

Aluminium sulphate was discovered at the end of the 16th century, according to the North York Moors National Park Committee, in shales towards the top of the Lower Jurassic strata in the Whitby Mudstones.

The Alum Shales, as they were then known, were worked from three quarries in the district. The earliest recording was from Carlton Bank [520 028], worked between about 1680 and 1809. Other sites worked were at Oakdale [464 963] near Osmotherley, between 1752 and 1774, and Dromonby Bank [535036] south east of Carlton, around the 1730s.

The mudstones containing the aluminium sulphate are 15 m thick, and the most suitable were found to contain the bivalve *Nuculana ovum*, which was a good indicator of those mudstones low in calcium carbonate. Anything from 50 to 120 tons of shale were required to produce one ton of alum. The process was long, complex and rather unsavoury. It began by burning the shale over brushwood fires in the floor of the quarry. The pile of alternating shale and brushwood reached heights of up to 30 m and was left to roast or calcine for about 9 months. The air pollution in the district was obviously considerable. The quarries were sited however on the flanks of the Cleveland escarpment and the local updraughts of air were utilised to keep the fires burning. The roasted shale was transferred to pits, where it was steeped in water to produce liquid alum. If the solution was too weak (an egg would float in the solution of ideal specific gravity) it was pumped back over new shale for further concentration. The solution was then run into cisterns and allowed to settle, after which it was conveyed by troughs to where it was boiled in lead pans over open coal fires for 24 hours.

To the concentrated liquor, an alkali was added which after a few days reduced the specific gravity to the point of crystallisation of crude alum. The alkali used in this process was ammonia or potash. The former was obtained from human urine which was shipped from London at a cost of one penny per gallon. Potash was won by burning seaweed and possibly bracken. The retention on the map of names such as 'Hell Holes' for these unique locations of basic chemistry on such a massive scale is an impressive reminder of the conditions in which the workers in this industry had to survive.

Rough salt was a by-product of the process, selling at £3 per ton. Carlton Bank formed the largest inland working, producing 250 tons per year. Its peak of activity was in the 1760s. The alum was used in the tanning, dyeing and papermaking industries. It was also used for hardening candles, for fireproofing materials and for medicinal purposes. The alum industry in Cleveland predated the railways and so transportation was largely by packhorse and boat. Alum was originally imported into the United Kingdom at a cost of £52 per ton — a price levied by the Pope. The alum from this district, despite the complex production, cost only £11 per ton.

AGGREGATES AND BUILDING MATERIALS

Sand and gravel

Sand and gravel is not widespread in the district (Figure 19), and the present survey has shown far less extensive areas delineated as sand and gravel than on the 1883 edition of the geological map.

Intensive resource studies by the BGS Mineral Assessment Unit involving drilling and grading of samples have been made of areas in the north of the district (Crofts, 1981; Gozzard and Price, 1982) and in the south-west (Lovell, 1982).

Few working quarries remain but gravel is occasionally dredged from the bed of the River Swale near Kiplin [280 971].

The sand and gravel deposits of the district vary in age from recent alluvial accumulations to glaciofluvial and glacial deposits. The best reserves have been proved in the alluvial and terrace deposits of the rivers Swale, Tees and Leven. The most extensive are associated with the River Leven near Stokesley but the thickest deposits occur in the Swale Valley in the south-west of the district. The deposits are variable, in the gravel/sand ratio, the clay content and also in thickness. The vast spreads of till in Teesside and in the Vale of York contain lenses of glacial sand and gravel, but are usually either too thin or contain too high a clay content to justify exploitation.

A recently abandoned series of sand and gravel pits [28 91] at Leeming Bar shows the complex interrelationships of the sand, gravel and red and brown clay beds (see p.69) which make prediction of quality, and method of working, extremely difficult (Figure 20).

The thickest sand and gravel deposits were proved in the valley of the River Swale near Kiplin. A borehole [2771 9679] penetrated 6.6 m of alluvial sand and gravel. The gravel comprises well-rounded limestone, chert, sandstone and quartzite pebbles of Carboniferous age, some igneous and volcanic rocks (possibly from the Lake District) and a small amount of 'Magnesian Limestone'. The sand is medium to coarse grained, comprising rounded quartz and rock fragments.

Many of the undifferentiated terraces of the rivers Tees, Swale and Leven contain pebbles and cobbles, but are usually too clayey and too thin to warrant exploitation. A borehole at Sockburn [3478 0684] in a large southward meander of the River Tees proved up to 3.6 m of sand and gravel. The gravel is clayey at the top and comprises subangular to sub-rounded Carboniferous sandstone, limestone, mudstone and siltstone together with Permian dolomite and Triassic red sandstone.

The thickest proving of glacial sand and gravel in the south-west of the district was at Tickergate Lane Borehole [2692 9362], 3 km north of Leeming Bar. An overburden of 5 m of clay rests on 15 m of sand and gravel. A disadvantage of deposits of glacial origin, in this district, is a high clay content. Farther north, at West End Well [4962 1046], near Stokesley, a thin sandy gravel 1.3 m thick overlies 9 m of clayey sand. The sand passes downwards into very clayey sand mixed with laminated clays for at least a further 13 m before drilling was stopped. A discontinuous ridge of sand and gravel west of great Smeaton was proved by boring [3223 0467] to be up to 6 m in thickness. The pebbles and cobbles comprised subangular sandstone, limestone, quartz, quartzite, tuff, basic igneous rock, coal and mudstone.

Numerous old gravel pits, in the west of Northallerton town, have now been filled and built over, for example, near the hospital at the side of Brompton Road [370 944], near the Cattle Market on Springwell Lane [3673 9375] and beneath the garage on Malpas Road [3650 9340]. These sands and gravels form a north–south-trending series of lenses proved by boring to be up to 8 m in thickness.

Clay

Both solid and drift deposits have been used in the past to provide the basic material for brick and tile manufacture. Just north of Snilesworth Lodge [510 957], old clay pits and an adjacent kiln exploited shales from the Ravenscar Group, and the Cobshaw Brick and Tile works [262 915] on the western margin of the district worked blue-grey laminated clays of glacial origin.

The laminated clays, formed in glacial lakes, provide the most widely utilised source within the district. An old brickworks [502 080], just west of Stokesley, was recorded during the original survey of 1886 to have a kiln and worked a 5 m section of clay. A borehole [5028 0776] adjacent to the old pits proved 14 m of brown, weakly laminated clay overlying the till. These clays were the major source of bricks for Stokesley during the Victorian era.

Old Clay pits [456 058] in till south-west of Hutton Rudby remain as flooded workings and were shown on the original survey maps as brick and tile works. An old, now flooded, clay pit [4250 0820] west of Crathorne was reported to have been reopened in the 1950s for use in lining the Cod Beck Reservoir [4650 9900] near Osmotherley. A large area of ground [358 946] on the Yafforth Road, west of Northallerton, now used as a refuse tip, was primarily excavated as a clay pit, the diggings postdate the first survey. Near Brompton [3675 9635] a 'Brick Field' was delineated on the 1886 Survey Map adjacent to an excavation. A shallow depression is all that remains of this former working in till.

South-east of Northallerton [306 919], till provided a source for bricks and tiles, although the low-lying situation may indicate that a pocket of laminated lake-clays provided the original raw material.

Limestone

Although limestone is a common lithology in many of the geological formations within the district and the potential reserves are considerable, its accessibility and economic value is seriously limited. The Carboniferous limestones could only be mined, largely at uneconomic depths, and much of the rock nearest to the surface is rich in chert. The Permian limestones are overlain by a thick overburden of superficial deposits which would make quarrying expensive and the unique position of the district, lying across the 'Cleveland High' (see p.8) results in the absence of Permian carbonates over a large area. The best prospect for economic exploitation is the Jurassic limestone in the Cleveland Hills. Much of this area falls in the National Park so planning permission to work new quarries would be difficult to obtain.

In the past, however, the three major divisions of the Jurassic have been exploited for the limestone either as building stone, road aggregates or for agricultural purposes. The Hambleton Oolite provides the purest calcium carbonate rock of all the Jurassic formations. It was formerly worked in numerous small shallow quarries along the outcrop. The thin-bedded nature of the limestone makes it ideal for use as a walling stone. Much of the stone was burnt locally to produce lime for use on the acidic upland peaty soils. The largest quarry at Kepwick [486 914] may have been used to supply road metal and building stone.

Disused small-scale diggings in the Brandsby Roadstone on Watherhouse Moor [551 949] indicate the remnants of a local industry which supplied agricultural lime. Several ruined limekilns [5433 9498 and 5159 9457] are present nearby. The hard, siliceous and flaggy nature of some of the limestone has enabled its use as a walling stone.

Limestones within the Lower Calcareous Grit have not been worked. They are thin, impersistent, variable in composition and have a significant quartz and chalcedonic silica content.

Many small disused quarries are present along the outcrop of the Brandsby Roadstone. Some have ruins of old limekilns nearby [5433 9498 and 5159 9557], where the stone was burnt for the production of agricultural lime. The hard argillaceous flaggy beds have been utilised for walling stone in the Snilesworth and Hawnby Moors areas.

Sandstone

The sandstones of the Middle Jurassic were formerly quarried for building stone at many localities throughout the Cleveland Hills, but brick was the preferred building material away from the Cleveland Hills.

Cottages in villages such as Osmotherley and Over Silton, the stately halls and manors, as well as farmhouses on the higher moorland, were all built of the local sandstone. The stone used can commonly be matched with that in a nearby quarry. The sandstone weathers into a mellow, warm yellowish brown hue, but is susceptible to exfoliation as the cement is invariably weak and in places calcareous.

The most significant quarries occur along Thimbleby Bank [458 947] above Over Silton [4517 9375], Nab Plantation [4725 9184], and from Kepwick [4713 9062] along Atlay Bank [4680 9054] to Cowesby Quarry [4711 9021].

The largest quarries occur on the northern flank of the Cleveland Hills near Osmotherley [46 99] (Priests Spa and Black Shore quarries), at Cop Loaf Quarry [462 003], on Carlton Bank (Carlton Quarry) [520 027], and on Cringle Moor [5355 0270].

The Moor Grit has been used locally for flagstones. The sandstones of the Ravenscar Group remain a huge resource of building stone in the district.

COAL

The possible presence of concealed Westphalian (Coal Measures) strata in the south-eastern part of the district has been inferred from commercial seismic data. Little is known of these rocks, although their occurrence midway between the Durham and Yorkshire coalfields makes them of some stratigraphical interest. They appear to occur over a restricted and as yet ill-defined area, at depths of up to around 1 km. The maximum thickness preserved is around 200 m, probably insufficient for the main productive parts of the Coal Measures, with thick workable seams, to have been preserved.

Coal was widely exploited in the Cleveland area in the 18th and 19th centuries mostly from the Saltwick and Cloughton formations of the Middle Jurassic. In the Northallerton district the coals are mostly thin and laterally variable. The most extensive workings, in the form of shallow bell-pits, occur on the eastern side of Hawnby Moor and on either side of Ladhill Beck [550 930]. The horizon exploited, known as the Moor Coal(s), is high in the Cloughton Formation, 10 m to 20 m below the Brandsby Roadstone.

The coal was reported (Fox-Strangways, 1886, p.37) to be 10 in (0.25 m) thick. The scatter of old pits and diggings suggests that possibly several seams were won at slightly different horizons. The coal was dug for firing the kilns which burnt the locally quarried Brandsby Roadstone. Fox-Strangways (1886 p.37) noted several disused adits and pits for coal below Swinestone Cliff east of Kepwick. Collapsed bell-pits are still present in Butcher's Wood [480 903] and are considered to be at the horizon of the Moor Coals farther east.

A borehole reported by Winch (1821) and put down on Osmotherley Moor, [47 98] proved a 0.15 m (6 inch) coal at a depth of 15 m (50 ft), possibly a correlative of the Moor Coal.

No evidence remains of the coal workings referred to by Fox-Strangways (1886, p.36) on Coal Ridge [5002 9780], but an old pit [5097 9725] near the horizon of the Moor Coal in the valley of Moor Sike,

1 km to the south-east, presumably provided fuel for the limekiln [5095 970] nearby.

Two old pits [5126 9592 and 5128 9583], near Snilesworth Lodge on the west bank of the River Rye, and two drifts [5151 9514 and 5152 9517] farther south, on the east bank of the river, near Hill End Farm, reveal coaly shale and ganister fragments on their spoil heaps. A section in the river nearby [5140 9536] (see p.39) exposes two thin coals and coaly shales, up to 0.3 m thick, separated by 2 m of measures. These coals closely overlie the Dogger Formation.

In the nearby tributary of Arns Gill, a section of the Saltwick Formation [5322 9653] showed coal and dirt to total nearly 2 m with a further thin seam, 0.16 m thick, about 1 m higher in the sequence.

A 0.2 m-thick coal, 15 m above the base of the Middle Jurassic, was recorded at Carlton Bank [521 027] (see p.41) and crops out on the path over the moor.

EVAPORITES

The term evaporites includes the mainly soluble salts of calcium, sodium and potassium which have been chemically precipitated from marine brines. The principle salts in the Cleveland Basin are gypsum ($CaSO_4.2H_2O$), anhydrite ($CaSO_4$), halite ($NaCl$), and sylvite (KCl). They occur mostly in Upper Permian and Triassic strata and are usually thickest in the east, wedging out westwards. Potassium deposits have not been proved in this district.

Gypsum

The mineral occurs either as a primary vein-filling or as a hydration product of bedded or nodular anhydrite. It is common in many Permian formations, particularly the Roxby and Edlington formations, and near the top of the Mercia Mudstone Group.

Smith (1989, fig.8) recorded 5 m of sulphate rock at about 642 m depth in Harlsey Borehole, towards the top of the first Zechstein cycle (Figure 4); this may be a correlative of the Hayton Anhydrite of the Yorkshire Province. Overlying dolomitic rocks also include anhydrite which implies a possible further correlation with the Hayton Anhydrite for a thickness of some 35 m.

The sulphate phase of Cycle EZ3 (Teesside Group) is represented by the Billingham Anhydrite (Table 1; Figure 4). It reaches a maximum of about 19 m in the Cleveland Hills Borehole but dies out rapidly westwards.

Halite (Salt)

In the Cleveland Hills Borehole, 6 m of salt were proved at a depth of some 994 m (3260 ft) in the Aislaby Group (EZ2) (Figure 4).

HYDROCARBONS

The petroleum geology of the Cleveland Basin has been reviewed by Kirby et al. (1987), Scott and Colter (1987)

and Fraser et al. (1990). Despite considerable exploratory activity for hydrocarbons over many decades, only limited success has been achieved to date in the basin with the discovery of a few minor gas fields. The western margin of the basin, including the Northallerton district, has received much less attention than elsewhere. Two exploratory wells, Cleveland Hills (Gulf Exploration 1940-1) and Harlsey (Home Oil 1965), both with no significant shows, have been drilled within the district, and only restricted seismic reflection surveys, using both dynamite and vibroseis sources, have been carried out.

Potential hydrocarbon source rocks of Jurassic and Carboniferous age are present within the district. Organic-rich, oil-prone source rocks occur in the Lias Group, particularly in the Whitby Mudstone Formation, but these are believed to be immature (Barnard and Cooper, 1983; Kirby et al., 1987). This, and their restricted and relatively shallow occurrence, precludes the possibility of economic accumulations being derived from such sources within the district.

Comparison with neighbouring districts suggests that the concealed Carboniferous rocks are probably dominantly gas-prone, despite the near complete absence of coal-bearing Westphalian (Coal Measures) rocks. The late Dinantian–Namurian rocks, proved in Harlsey Borehole, are largely within the oil window (vitrinite reflectance values between 0.9 and 1.62 per cent), but the more deeply buried, thick, Dinantian sequence, here and elsewhere in the district, is likely to be in the gas zone or overmature. Oil-prone, late Brigantian–Namurian shales of pro-delta facies, which sourced the oilfields of the East Midlands, are believed to be absent in North Yorkshire (Fraser et al., 1990). However, as so little is known of the Carboniferous rocks beneath the district, and of their sedimentary and structural controls, the presence of oil-prone sources cannot yet be totally discounted.

As well as local sources of hydrocarbons, westerly migration of gas from Carboniferous rocks in the deeper parts of the Cleveland Basin is probable (Kirby et al., 1987). Unfortunately, suitable trapping structures seem to be absent in the Permian and Mesozoic rocks of the district. In the Cleveland Basin, gas accumulations occur typically in the Kirkham Abbey and Brotherton formations, where thick halites form tight seals. In the district, the Kirkham Abbey Formation is thin and not separated from the Edlington Formation, and the district lies largely to the west of halite deposition and preservation. It must be doubted whether the marginal Permian clastic rocks of the Edlington and Roxby formations can form suitable seals even in closed structures.

From the evidence of the Harlsey and Cleveland Hills boreholes, Carboniferous sandstones are not abundant in the district, and are generally relatively thin and have a significant shale content. Moreover, the reservoir properties of Carboniferous sandstones in the Cleveland Basin are generally poor because of the effects of the two phases of deep burial and inversion that they have undergone (Kent, 1980a). However, around the basin margins, including the Northallerton district, such effects are likely to be less severe, and more favourable

porosity and permeability may have been locally preserved. Carboniferous limestones and cherts have little reservoir potential except where fractured.

The presence of structural or even stratigraphical traps in Carboniferous rocks of the district cannot be discounted given the present lack of detailed knowledge of these rocks. The occurrence of thick shale sequences should ensure adequate sealing of such structures. The main period of deformation of these rocks, and hence of structural trap formation, was in Late Carboniferous (Variscan) times; well before the time of maximum burial and hydrocarbon generation at the end of the Cretaceous, prior to uplift and inversion of Tertiary times.

It must be concluded that on present evidence the prospects of finding major hydrocarbon accumulations within the district do not seem great. However, as so few exploratory boreholes have yet been drilled, and as so little is known of the concealed Carboniferous strata of the district, this conclusion may yet prove premature.

OIL SHALE

The Jet Rock Member of the Whitby Mudstones is a fissile and slightly flexible brown shale, weathering to a pale purple colour. Its characteristics are similar to a Carboniferous oil shale of the Midland Valley of Scotland or the Doupster Oil Shale of the Berwickshire coast. Some 60 litres of oil have been obtained from about one ton of shale on distillation.

Attempts to extract oil on a commercial basis were once made at Kettleness on the Yorkshire coast but these proved unprofitable. The oil was reported to be very sulphurous (Anon., 1920, p.63).

In 1953 an explosion occurred in the Lingdale Ironstone Mine, in the Cleveland Hills east of the district. It was considered to have been caused by oil in the overlying 'Jet Shales'. Experiments made on the jet itself found that 100 gm of jet gave off 30 cc of gas at 100°C. The chemical composition was given as: carbonic anhydride 11 per cent, 'quartane' or 'ethyl' 87 per cent, nitrogen 2 per cent (Thomas, 1876).

IRONSTONE

The industry based upon the Cleveland Ironstone deposits began, possibly, in the 14th century, and rose to prominence in the 17th century only to fade and finally die in 1964. The population of Middlesbrough, which comprised a hamlet of 25 people in the early 19th century rising through 6000 in 1841, to 56 000 in 1880, mirrors the importance of the industry. Early records suggest that the nuns of Rosedale were the first to discover the Jurassic ores, followed by the monks belonging to the different abbeys in the Cleveland Hills.

Those Carboniferous ironstones which had the cost benefit of close association with the coal seams for smelting were approaching exhaustion in the 1880s. The invention of new furnaces and blasting methods made considerable savings on fuel, with the result that location on a coalfield was not a critical economic factor. Transportation was also improving, with new railway routes, making easier distribution of the smelted iron.

The Jurassic ironstones, however, were first exploited in the 1790s on the Yorkshire coast, in the Robin Hoods Bay area, by gathering the nodules and transporting them by sea to the River Tyne and then on to Chester-le-Street in Co. Durham. Such nodules were presumably clay ironstones from the Whitby Mudstones and not from the Cleveland Ironstone Formation.

During the first half of the 19th century, bedded ores were not exploited on a large scale because of the low quality of the ore. There were then few railway links and although the geological sequence was known along the well-exposed coast, inland exposures were poor and the geological structure imperfectly known. The first major development inland was made by the Whitby Stone Company who leased mines at Grosmont and shipped the ore to the Tyne from Whitby in 1837. A purpose-built harbour was constructed in 1838 at Port Mulgrave to enable the shipment of ore won from the coast section between Staithes and Mulgrave. The venture was short lived, however, because of the difficulties of navigation during the winter months from the exposed coastline.

In 1840, rolling mills, near Bishop Auckland in Co. Durham, used ore from Eskdale and Grosmont. Ten years later the Main Seam was discovered inland and the Eston Mines opened in 1851. In 1866 the Middlesbrough–Guisborough railway opened and quarrying reached as far west as Roseberry Topping.

By 1881, maximum output was attained making the cheapest pig iron in the world, and production was maintained at about $5\frac{1}{2}$ million tons per annum until 1914. After the First World War production rapidly declined, but it has been calculated that some 232 million tons of untouched ore still remain.

The ironstones in the district were therefore some of the last deposits of Cleveland to be exploited. The seams were of poorer quality, with increased silica content and thinner than farther east. Mines near Swainby in Scugdale, known as the Ailesbury Mines [47950062], proved the 'top block or dogger' of the Main Seam to be just under a metre thick (Tate and Blake, 1876, p.141), with a bottom seam only half as thick, some 5 m beneath. The position of the Main Seam was known by trials over much of this area and was mined by drifts at Huthwaite [4947 0080] near Scugdale End.

Conglomeratic nodules of ironstone were worked from drifts into the Dogger Formation on the north-west side of Cold Moor [5495 0335] (see p.38).

JET

Jet is hard, black, fossilised, araucarian wood used for ornaments and jewellery which became particularly fashionable during the Victorian period. It was found in some 10 m of dense, finely laminated dark brown-grey mudstones not far above the Cleveland Ironstone Formation (see p.34). The industry was centred upon Whitby, but exploitation in this district was on a very extensive scale. Mining of jet was not allowed on good agricultural land so the steep slopes and high moorland areas of this district were ideal locations for the mining operations.

A necklace of jet beads was discovered in a Bronze Age burial mound in East Yorkshire (1969, North York Moors National Park, HMSO), and jet is known to have been worked in Roman times in the Whitby area. The industry was established in 1800, and reached a peak during the 1870s when over 1500 people were employed in some 200 workshops in Whitby. Several manufacturers were still in business during the 1920s, but its desirability as jewellery had by then waned. Attempts were made in the 1960s to revive the industry by combining jet with diamonds and silver. The Duchess of Kent was presented with a jet pendant inlaid with silver when re-opening the North Yorkshire Moors Railway.

The jet was mined from drifts into the hillside. The jet shales are overlain by the Top Jet Dogger, a hard bed of argillaceous limestone, which acted as an ideal roof to the excavations, removing the need for timber props or supports. Operators paid rent of £15 per annum to the local estates for the right to work the jet, leaving behind a landscape scarred by lines of shale tips. Jet was worth about one pound per pound weight. A by-product of the mines was to burn the shale to produce red clinker for road metal. The shales were found to ignite very easily by virtue of their oil content (see p.82). According to the Venerable Bede, if the jet shales were heated it drove away serpents!

MINERALISATION

No deposits of economic importance are known in the district but boreholes through the Carboniferous and Permo-Triassic strata, where cored, have proved the presence of small quantities of metallic ores (Hurworth Place Borehole [2902 0953]). It is possible to infer that the concealed area of the Askrigg Block, in the west of the district, contains workable quantities of lead, zinc, and copper by extrapolating evidence from the exposed part of the block to the north-west and south of the district.

The highest Carboniferous limestones cored in the Cleveland Hills Borehole were reported as 'fissured' with chert nodules. In the cores from the Harlsey Borehole, scattered glauconite grains and pyrite crystals were recorded at a depth of 920 m (3020 ft) and 924 m (3030 ft) in grey-brown siliceous limestone.

Potentially important new mineral deposits may be present at depth, associated with the faults of the Kirby Sigston–Cotcliffe Graben, which is interpreted as forming the eastern boundary of the Askrigg Block. Similar mineral concentrations may be present at depth along the north–south fractures which affect the Jurassic strata at outcrop along the north-western edge of the Cleveland Hills.

Calcite veining was recorded in the Cadeby Formation in the Cleveland Hills Borehole between the depths of 1082 m (3550 ft) and at 1170 m (3840 ft) at the base of the Permian succession.

RADDLE AND OCHRE

Earthy haematite, variously known as raddle, ruddle, reddle or rudd, was worked over a long period, possibly dating back to Roman times. The raddle was used for marking sheep, staining floors, making paint, polishing lenses and even as a cosmetic in earlier times (Smith *in* Hemingway, 1974).

Jurassic raddle was noted by Fox-Strangways (1892, p.475) at Rud Scar near Ingleby Greenhow [58 06], 2 km north-east of the district. Many streams and springs in the district emanate from or pass over ferruginous-rich strata, resulting in an ochreous colour to the water which forms deposits on vegetation and other solid objects downstream.

WATER RESOURCES

The western two thirds of the district form a low-lying northward extension of the Vale of York drained by tributaries of the River Tees, to the north, and the River Swale, to the south-west. The eastern third of the area includes the scarp-bounded Cleveland Hills which are drained to the east by the River Rye.

Average annual rainfall varies from less than 650 mm in the low western area to more than 900 mm over the Cleveland Hills. Evapotranspiration levels vary between 680 and 720 mm per annum.

The main producing aquifers of the district are the Sherwood Sandstone Group and the sandy horizons of the Ravenscar Group that include elements of the Middle Lias and Upper Jurassic in this description. Small quantities of groundwater are obtained from the Mercia Mudstone and Lias groups, these strata forming regional aquicludes. The distributions of aquifer units and groundwater flow pattern within the Sherwood Sandstone Group are shown on Figure 22.

The relative importance of the aquifer units is illustrated by the licenced abstraction rates (Table 7). More than 85 per cent of the total licenced abstraction is for public water supply. Yorkshire Water plc obtain up to 1 760 000 m³/annum from the Sherwood Sandstone aquifer via its wellfield located at Ainderby Steeple, adjacent to the River Swale. In addition this company also obtains up to 3 318 600 m³/annum from two groups of springs issuing from permeable sandstone horizons within the Ravenscar Group in the Osmotherley Moor and Kepwick areas of the Cleveland Hills. The Northumbrian Water Group plc is licenced to obtain part of its public water supply from the Ravenscar Group of the Cleveland Hills, abstracting up to 345 000 m³/annum from two groups of springs, although this source was replaced by a new supply during 1990–91. Individual farms and agriculture-related industries form the bulk of the other licenced abstractors of groundwater within the district.

Sherwood Sandstone Group

Within the western third of the district the 250 m thick Sherwood Sandstone aquifer is overlain and confined by a variable thickness of till and drift deposits. This aquifer unit dips to the east beneath the Mercia Mudstone Group by which it is confined. Most hydrogeological data available from the district derive from the Sherwood Sandstone Group, the district's major aquifer unit.

The presence of a north-west–south-east-trending groundwater divide across the northern half of the area is indicated by the water table contours of the aquifer (Figure 22). The water table falls from 45 m above OD at the groundwater divide to 20 m at the River Tees 5 km to the north. To the south, the water table declines from 45 m to less than 25 m above OD towards the River Swale over a distance of 10 km there is an area of groundwater recharge to the north-west of the district with infiltration taking place through sandy horizons within the till along the line of the groundwater divide. The presence of several springs, for example near Warlaby (SE 335/914 and SE 344/915), and artesian boreholes, for example at Scurton (SE 2509/9999) and Kirkby Fleetham (SE 286/941), along the River Swale valley, indicate that the Sherwood Sandstone aquifer probably contributes to the base flow of the River Swale.

Studies of the hydrogeological nature of the Sherwood Sandstone aquifer have been undertaken at RAF Leeming, a site just south of the district (SE 335/890), and Ainderby Steeple (SE 332/925) by Yorkshire Water plc and the British Geological Survey. The results indicate that intergranular flow, sometimes enhanced by fracture flow, occurs within this aquifer. The porosity ranges between 20 and 24 per cent; horizontal permeability varies between 0.2 and 0.4 m/day for intergranular flow, increasing to more than 1 m/day where enhanced by fracture flow. Aquifer transmissivities of 20 to 45 m²/day were determined. Pumping borehole specific capacities varied from 0.01 to 0.5 l/sec/metre of drawdown for intergranular flow conditions to 7.8 l/sec/metre for fracture-enhanced flow conditions. Borehole discharge rates are largely dependent upon the requirements of the users, farm boreholes being pumped at discharges up to 2 l/sec while public supply boreholes are pumped at flow rates up to 40 l/sec.

Boreholes constructed for farm use rarely exceed 50 m depth at 100 to 125 mm completed diameter, usually only partially penetrating the aquifer system. In contrast those constructed for public supply or large-scale commercial abstraction are usually 70 to 100 m deep at 305 mm completed diameter, fully penetrating the aquifer.

Long-term changes in water level within the Sherwood Sandstone aquifer have been monitored at the Scruton Village site (SE 3004/9244) since 1969. Average monthly maximum and minimum water levels over that period vary from 28.6 to 27.2 m above OD. Maximum water levels prevailed in 1970 and 1980, whereas minimum levels were recorded in 1976 and were exceeded during

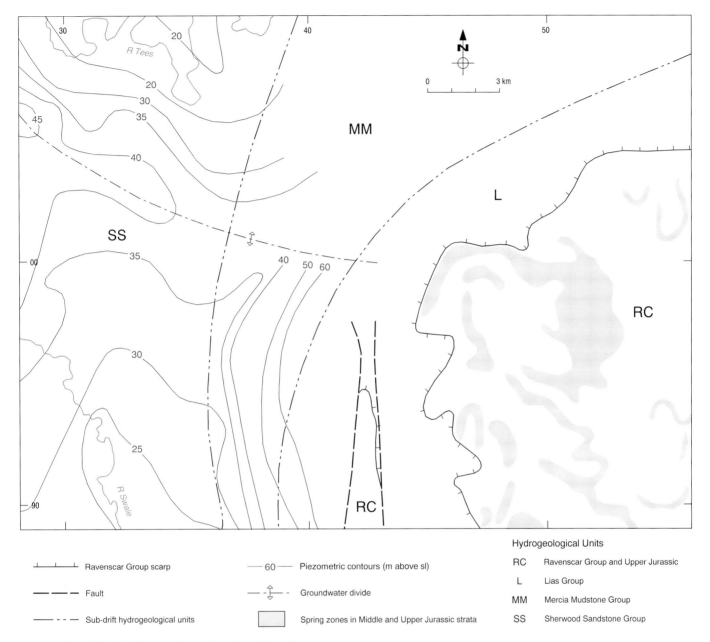

Figure 22 Main hydrogeological units of the district.

the 1990–92 drought period with the water table declining to an all time low of 26.9 m above OD during September 1992.

Groundwaters contained within the Sherwood Sandstone aquifer of the calcium bicarbonate type with significant total hardness contents (Table 8). Relatively few whole ion analyses are available. Partial analysis data indicate that groundwater quality deteriorates from west to east especially towards the River Tees. Total dissolved solids increase from less than 500 mg/l along the valley of the River Swale to more than 2500 mg/l in the vicinity of the River Tees. This deterioration in quality is mirrored by an increase in chloride content from less than 20 mg/l along the Swale Valley to greater than 70 mg/l along the Tees, and an increase in total

hardness from below 400 mg/l to more than 1500 mg/l to the east and north.

Mercia Mudstone Group

Within the central third of the district, strata of the Mercia Mudstone Group are overlain by a variable thickness of till and drift except where exposed to the east of Northallerton. These strata dip to the east, overlying and confining the Sherwood Sandstone aquifer. Although primarily composed of impermeable red and grey shaley marls with much gypsum, the Mercia Mudstone Group can include discontinuous bodies of permeable sandstones from which small quantities of very hard, fairly good-quality, groundwater can

Table 7 Groundwater abstraction licence data for the district.

Water use Aquifer	*Agriculture*		*Spray irrigation*		*Industrial*		*Public supply*		*Private supply*		Totals	
	m³/year	No. licences	m³/year	No. licences	m³/year	No. licences	m³/year	No. licences	m³/year	No. licences	m³/year	No. licences
Ravenscar Group and Upper Jurassic	73 360	22					3 664 085	5	40 834	8	3 778 279	35
Lias	26 830	7							1 820	1	28 650	8
Mercia Mudstone Group	7 771	4									7 771	4
Sherwood Sandstone Group	99 260	26	120 450	2	352 300	2	1 760 000	1			2 332 010	31
Totals	207 221	59	120 450	2	352 300	2	5 424 085	6	42 654	9	6 146 710	78

Derived from data supplied by the National Rivers Authority, Northumbria and Yorkshire regions

be abstracted. Several boreholes and wells located within the vicinity of Northallerton are used by licensed abstractors to obtain small quantities of groundwater (less than 1 l/sec) mainly for agricultural usage. Yields more than 1 l/sec have been obtained but these are rare.

Lias Group

The lower part of the Lias Group is composed of dark slightly sandy shales that form the Redcar Mudstone Formation. Groundwater abstraction from this formation is limited to a few boreholes supplying farms, with tested yields of 0.5 to 1 l/sec. Groundwater quality is generally good with high total-hardness levels.

The middle part of the Lias Group includes the Staithes Sandstone and Cleveland Ironstone formations. Significant springs issue from these formations which crop out on the lower parts of the escarpment. The Northumbrian Water Group plc are licenced to abstract up to 345 000 m³/annum from springs located at Scugdale (between NZ 510/003 and SE 517/992) and Kildale (NZ 517/022). The latter spring was used to supply villages located between Swainby and Kildale, but this supply has been discontinued in favour of a trunk mains supply; neither colour nor quality standards could be ensured without expensive treatment. Other springs issuing from the same formations along the escarpment supply small quantities of water to farms. The total licenced abstraction from the Lias Group is included within the Ravenscar Group totals within Table 7. This aquifer unit is confined by the mudstones of the Whitby Mudstone Formation.

Ravenscar Group

The upper parts of the escarpment and dip slope to the east are composed mainly of elements of the Ravenscar Group. The lower part of the group including the Saltwick and Cloughton formations are composed of shaly sandstones with interbedded permeable sandstone units. A multitude of springs issue from the latter and form the sources of the headwaters of the River Rye and water supplies to numerous farms.

The upper parts of the Ravenscar Group includes two very porous gravelly grits, the Crinoid Grit and Moor Grit members. These are the source strata of a number of strongly flowing springs, as at Kepwick Moor (between SE 479/932 and SE 484/915) where the Yorkshire Water plc are licenced to abstract 3 318 600 m³/annum from a series of 16 springs. The water produced is of good enough quality to be passed into the distribution mains without treatment other than chlorination. At Osmotherley, a large spring issuing from faulted Moor Grit forms the source of the Cod Beck. Recharge to this aquifer is from the moors above.

Upper Jurassic

The Oxford Clay and Osgodby formations form an aquiclude below the Lower Calcareous Grit Formation; numerous springs are found along the base of the latter. Potential yields and water quality are not known. An adit excavated into the Kellaways Rock at Kepwick Moor (SE 487/919) encountered groundwater at a distance of 80 m into the formation. The adit was completed at a distance of 87 m, a discharge rate of 26 l/sec being determined.

Till

Till, deposits from 10 to 15 m thick, mantles the Sherwood Sandstone aquifer in the western part of the district. These deposits thin from north to south, and the thickest deposits, more than 30 m, are found within an east–west trending belt just south of the River Tees. Boreholes drilled for groundwater abstraction are usually cased through the till sequence, much larger volumes of water being found in the Sherwood Sandstone aquifer beneath. It is possible that groundwater may be recharged to the Sherwood Sandstone aquifer from sandier

Table 8
Hydrochemical analyses for the district.

Location		South Cawton Grange	Ravensworth	Warlaby Nook	RAF Leeming
National Grid reference		NZ 289 012	NZ 412 084	SE 353 904	SE 315 890
Type of source		Borehole	Borehole	Borehole	Borehole
Aquifer		Sherwood Sandstone	Sherwood Sandstone	Sherwood Sandstone	Sherwood Sandstone
Date of analysis		21.2.83	13.1.92	22.2.83	9.7.85
pH		7.38	7.45	7.73	7.30
Cond μmhos	mg/1	802.00	488.00	778.00	670.00
Calcium Ca^{2+})	mg/1	89.00	68.00	110.00	88.00
Magnesium (Mg^{2+})	mg/1	30.60	18.20	28.20	30.00
Sodium (Na$^+$)	mg/1	43.30	14.60	11.10	12.00
Potassium (K$^+$)	mg/1	2.95	1.37	4.26	1.40
Bicarbonate (HCO$_3^-$)	mg/1	405.00	286.00	358.00	190.00
Sulphate (SO$_4^{2-}$)	mg/1	67.10	25.00	45.40	32.00
Chloride (Cl$^-$)	mg/1	15.00	29.00	23.00	17.00
Nitrate (NO$_3^-$)	mg/1	0.44	<0.20	23.50	6.80

elements of the till as indicated by the east-west-trending groundwater divide shown in Figure 22. The later mechanism may be responsible for the higher sulphate contents with groundwaters obtained at South Cowton Grange borehole (NZ 289/012) (Table 8).

Landfill and waste disposal sites

Of the 12 currently licenced landfill sites located within the district, one has not been used, another receives only topsoil and six receive generally inert construction material, for example builders' rubble. Domestic waste is dumped at sites near Leeming Bar (SE 293/902) and Yafforth Road (SE 385/945 and SE 358/946), where a confining layer of till and drift deposits limit risk to groundwater within the underlying Sherwood Sandstone aquifer. At Osmotherley (SE 446/972), a waste wood dump from a local sawmill is similarly protected from the local spring line abstraction from the Ravenscar Group.

REFERENCES

Most of the references listed below are held in the Library of the British Geological Survey at Keyworth, Nottingham. Copies of the references can be purchased subject to the current copyright legislation.

ALLSOP, J M. 1985. Geophysical indications of the sub-Permian geology beneath the Ripon area, Northern England. *Proceedings of the Geologists' Association*, Vol. 96, 161–169.

ANON. 1920. *Special Report Mineral Resources of Great Britain*, 3 (2nd edition).

BARNARD, P C, and COOPER, B S. 1983. A review of geochemical data related to the northwest European gas province. 19–33 in *Petroleum geochemistry and exploration of Europe*. BROOKS, J (editor). *Special Publication of the Geological Society of London*, Vol. 12.

BEST, R H. 1956. Westward proglacial drainage in Cleveland. *Proceedings of the Yorkshire Geological Society*, Vol. 30, 301–319.

BEWICK, J. 1861. *Geological treatise on the district of Cleveland, in north Yorkshire, its ferruginous deposits, Lias and Oolites; with some observations on ironstone mining.* (London: Weale.)

BLACK, M. 1929. Drifted plant-beds of the Upper Estuarine Series of Yorkshire. *Quarterly Journal of the Geological Society of London*, Vol. 85, 389–437.

BLAKE, J F. 1872. The Yorkshire Lias and the distribution of its ammonites. *Report of the British Association for 1871.*

BOTT, M H P. 1967. Geophysical investigations of the northern Pennine basement rocks. *Proceedings of the Yorkshire Geological Society*, Vol. 36, 139–168.

BOTT, M H P. 1988. The Market Weighton gravity anomaly — granite or graben? *Proceedings of the Yorkshire Geological Society*, Vol.47, 47–53.

BOTT, M H P, LONG, R E, GREEN, A S P, LEWIS, A H J, SINHA, M C, and STEVENSON, D L. 1985. Crustal structure south of the Iapetus suture beneath northern England. *Nature, London*, Vol. 314, 724–726.

BOULTON, G S, JONES, A S, CLAYTON, K M, and KENNING, M J. 1977. A British ice-sheet model and patterns of glacial erosion and deposition in Britain. 231–246 in *British Quaternary studies, recent advances*. SHOTTON, F W (editor). (Oxford: Clarendon Press.)

BRADSHAW, M J, and seven others. 1992. Jurassic. 107–129 in Atlas of palaeogeography and lithofacies. COPE, J C W, INGHAM, J K and RAWSON, P F (editors). *Memoir of the Geological Society of London*, No 13.

BUCKMAN, S S. 1915. A palaeontological classification of the Jurassic rocks of the Whitby District; with a zonal table of Lias ammonites. 59–102 in Geology of the country between Whitby and Scarborough. FOX-STRANGWAYS, C E, and BARROW, G. *Memoir of the Geological Survey of England and Wales* (2nd edition).

CALVER, M A. 1958. 47 in *Summary of progress of the Geological Survey of Great Britain*. (London: HMSO.)

CAMERON, A G. 1881. Subsidences over the Permian boundary between Hartlepool and Ripon. *Proceedings of the Yorkshire Geological Polytechnic Society*, Vol. 7, 342–351.

CATT, J A. 1991. Late Devensian glacial deposits and glaciations in eastern England and the adjoining offshore region. 61–69 in *Glacial deposits in Great Britain and Ireland*. EHLERS, J. GIBBARD, P L, and ROSE, J (editors). (Rotterdam, Balkema.)

CATT, J A, and PENNY, L F. 1966. The Pleistocene deposits of Holderness, East Yorkshire. *Proceedings of the Yorkshire Geological Society*, Vol. 35, 375–420.

CHADWICK, R A, and HOLLIDAY, D W. 1991. Deep crustal structure and Carboniferous basin development within the Iapetus convergence zone, northern England. *Journal of the Geological Society of London*, Vol. 148, 41–53.

CHADWICK, R A, HOLLIDAY, D W, HOLLOWAY, S, and HULBERT, A G. 1995. The structure and evolution of the Northumberland–Solway Basin and adjacent areas. *Subsurface Memoir of the British Geological Survey.*

CHOWNS, T M. 1966. Depositional environment of the Cleveland Ironstone. *Nature, London*, Vol. 211, 1286–1287.

CHOWNS, T M. 1968. Environmental and diagenetic studies of the Cleveland Ironstone Formation of north-east Yorkshire. Unpublished PhD thesis, University of Newcastle upon Tyne.

CHRINTZ, T, and CLEMMENSEN, L B. 1993. Draa reconstruction, the Permian Yellow Sands, northeast England. 151–161 in Aeolian sediments. PYE, K, and LANCASTER, N (editors). *Special Publication of the International Association of Sedimentologists*, No. 16.

CLARKE, R F A. 1965. British Permian saccate and monosaccate miospores. *Palaeontology*, Vol. 8, 322–354.

COLLIER, R E L L. 1991. The Lower Carboniferous Stainmore Basin, N England: extensional basin tectonics and sedimentation. *Journal of the Geological Society of London*, Vol. 148, 379–390.

COOPER, A H. 1986. Foundered strata and subsidence resulting from dissolution of Permian gypsum in the Ripon and Bedale area, North Yorkshire. 127–139 in The English Zechstein and related topics. HARWOOD, G M, and SMITH, D B (editors). *Special Publication of the Geological Society of London*, No. 22.

COOPER, A H. 1995. Subsidence hazards due to the dissolution of Permian gypsum in England: investigation and remediation. 23–29 in *Karst geohazards — engineering and environmental problems in karst terrane*. Proceedings of the fifth multidisciplinary conference on sinkholes and environmental impacts, of karst, Gutlinburg, Tennessee. BECK, B F (editor). (Rotterdam: A A Balkema.)

COOPER, A H, and BURGESS, I. 1993. Geology of the country around Harrogate. *Memoir of the British Geological Survey*, Sheet 62. (England and Wales).

COPE, J C W, GETTY, T A, HOWARTH, M K, MORTON, N, and TORRENS, H S. 1980a. A correlation of Jurassic rocks in the British Isles. Part one: Introduction and Lower Jurassic. *Special Report of the Geological Society of London*, No. 14.

COPE, J C W, DUFF, K L, PARSONS, C F, TORRENS, H S, WIMBLEDON, W A, and WRIGHT, J K. 1980b. A correlation of Jurassic rocks in the British Isles. Part two: Middle and Upper Jurassic. *Report of the Geological Society of London*, No 15.

CROFTS, R G. 1981. The sand and gravel resources of the country around Stokesley, North Yorkshire. Description of sheets NZ40 and 50, and parts of NZ 41 and 51. *Mineral Assessment Report Institute of Geological Sciences*, No. 75.

DAVISON, C. 1924. *A history of British earthquakes.* (Cambridge: Cambridge University Press.)

DUNHAM, K C. 1951. Recent work on the Cleveland Ironstone. *Proceedings of the Yorkshire Geological Society*, Vol. 28, 66.

DUNHAM, K C. 1959. Epigenetic mineralization in Yorkshire. *Proceedings of the Yorkshire Geological Society*, Vol. 32, 1–30.

DUNHAM, K C. 1974. Granite beneath the Pennines in north Yorkshire. Proceedings of the Yorkshire Geological Society, Vol. 40, 191–194.

DUNHAM, K C. and WILSON, A A. 1985. Geology of the Northern Pennine Orefield: Volume 2, Stainmore to Craven. *Economic Memoir of the British Geological Survey*, Sheets 40, 41 and 51 and parts of 31, 32, 51, 60 and 61 (England and Wales).

ELGEE, F. 1909. The glaciation of north Cleveland. *Proceedings of the Yorkshire Geological Society*, Vol. 16, 372–382.

FISHER, M J, and HANCOCK, N J. 1985. The Scalby Formation (Middle Jurassic, Ravenscar Group) of Yorkshire: reassessment of age and depositional environment. *Proceedings of the Yorkshire Geological Society*, Vol. 45, 293–298.

FORSTER, S C, and WARRINGTON, G. 1985. Geochronology of the Carboniferous, Permian and Triassic. 99–117 *in* The chronology of the Geological Record. SNELLING, N J (editor). *Memoir of the Geological Society of London*, No. 10.

FOWLER, A. 1944. A deep bore in the Cleveland Hills. *Geological Magazine*, Vol. 81, 193–206.

FOX-STRANGWAYS, C. 1880. The geology of the Oolite and Cretaceous rocks south of Scarborough. *Memoir of the Geological Survey of England and Wales.* (Quarter sheets 85 SN and 95 SE).

FOX-STRANGWAYS, C. 1892. The Jurassic rocks of Britain. Vols. 1 and 2, Yorkshire. *Memoirs of the Geological Survey of the United Kingdom.*

FOX-STRANGWAYS, C. 1908. The geology of the country north and east of Harrogate. *Memoir of the Geological Survey of Great Britain* (Sheet 62).

FOX-STRANGWAYS, C. and BARROW, G. 1915. The geology of the country between Whitby, and Scarborough. *Memoir of the Geological Survey of Great Britain* (2nd edition).

FOX-STRANGWAYS, C. CAMERON, A G, and BARROW, G. 1886. The geology of the country around Northallerton and Thirsk. *Memoirs of the Geological Survey, England and Wales.* Explanation of Quarter-sheets 96NW and 96SW, New Series, Sheets 42 and 52.

FRASER, A J, NASH, D F, STEELE, R P, and EBDON, C C. 1990. A regional assessment of the infra-Carboniferous play of northern England. 417–440 *in* Classic petroleum provinces. BROOKS, J (editor). *Special Publication of the Geological Society of London*, No. 50.

GAUNT, G D. 1981. Quaternary history of the southern part of the Vale of York. 82–97 in *The Quaternary of Britian.* NEALE, J, and FLENLEY, J (editors). (Oxford: Pergammon Press.)

GAUNT, G D, IVIMEY-COOK, H C, PENN, I E, and COX, B M. 1980. Mesozoic rocks proved by I G S boreholes in the Humber and Acklam areas. *Report of the Institute of Geological Sciences,* No. 79/13, 1–34.

GAUNT, G D, FLETCHER, T D, and WOOD, C J. 1992. Geology of the country around Kingston upon Hull and Brigg. *Memoir of the British Geological Survey*, Sheets 80 and 89 (England and Wales).

GEORGE, T N. 1958. Lower Carboniferous palaeogeography of the British Isles. *Proceedings of the Yorkshire Geological Society*, Vol. 31, 227–318.

GLENNIE, K W. 1972. Permian Rotliegendes of NW Europe interpreted in light of modern desert sedimentation studies. *Bulletin of the American Association of Petroleum Geologists*, Vol. 56, 1048–1071.

GOZZARD, J R, and PRICE, D. 1982. The sand and gravel resources of the country east and south-east of Darlington, Durham: Description of 1:25 000 resource sheet NZ 31 and 30. *Mineral Assessment Report Institute of Geological Sciences*, No. 111.

GUNN, W. 1886 *in* FOX-STRANGWAYS et al.. The geology of the country around Northallerton and Thirsk. *Memoirs of the Geological Survey of England and Wales.* Explanation of Quarter-sheets 96NW and 96SW, New Series, Sheets 42 and 52.

GUNN, W. 1899. Correlation of Lower Carboniferous of England and Scotland. *Transactions of the Edinburgh Geological Society*, Vol. 7, 361–367.

HALLIMOND, A F. 1925. Iron ores: bedded ores of England and Wales. Petrography and chemistry. *Memoir of the Geological Survey Special Report on Mineral Resources, Great Britain*, Vol. 29.

HANCOCK, N J, and FISHER, M J. 1981. Middle Jurassic North Sea deltas with particular reference to Yorkshire. 186–195 *in Petroleum geology of the continental shelf of North-West Europe.* ILLING, L V, and HOBSON, G D (editors). (London: Institute of Petroleum.)

HEMINGWAY, J E. 1949. A revised terminology and subdivision of the Middle Jurassic rocks of Yorkshire. *Geological Magazine,* Vol. 86, 67–71.

HEMINGWAY, J E. 1974. Jurassic. 161–223 in The geology and mineral resources of Yorkshire. RAYNOR, D H, and HEMINGWAY, J E (editors). (Leeds: Yorkshire Geological Society.)

HEMINGWAY, J E, and KNOX, R W O'B. 1973. Lithostratigraphical nomenclature of the Middle Jurassic strata of the Yorkshire basin of north-east England. *Proceedings of the Yorkshire Geological Society*, Vol. 39, 527–535.

HEMINGWAY, J E, and RIDDLER, G P. 1982. Basin inversion in north Yorkshire. *Transactions of the Institution of Mining and Metallurgy*, Vol. 91, (Section B: Applied earth sciences), B175–B186.

HOWARD, A S. 1984. Palaeoecology, sedimentology and depositional environments of the Middle Lias of North Yorkshire. Unpublished PhD thesis, University of London.

HOWARD, A S. 1985. Lithostratigraphy of the Staithes Sandstone and Cleveland Ironstone formations (Lower Jurassic) of north-east Yorkshire. *Proceedings of the Yorkshire Geological Society*, Vol. 45, 261–275.

HOWARTH, M K. 1955. Domerian of the Yorkshire coast. *Proceedings of the Yorkshire Geological Society*, Vol. 30, 147–175.

HOWARTH, M K. 1962. The Jet Rock Series and the Alum Series of the Yorkshire Coast. *Proceedings of the Yorkshire Geological Society*, Vol. 33, 381–422.

IVIMEY-COOK, H C. 1992a. On Triassic and Jurassic material from the Cleveland Hills No. 1 Borehole Yorkshire. *British Geological Survey Technical Report*, WH/92/234R.

IVIMEY-COOK, H C. 1992b. The Upper Triassic of the Winton Manor Borehole, Brompton, North Yorkshire and correlation of the Penarth Group in this area. *British Geological Survey Technical Report*, WH/92/236R.

IVIMEY-COOK, H C. 1992c. The Lower Jurassic of the Northallerton area. *British Geological Survey Technical Report*, WH/92/253R.

IVIMEY-COOK, H C. and POWELL, J H. 1991. Late Triassic and early Jurassic biostratigraphy of the Felixkirk Borehole, North Yorkshire. *Proceedings of the Yorkshire Geological Society*, Vol. 48, 367–374.

JEANS, C V. 1978. The origin of the Triassic clay assemblages of Europe with special reference to the Keuper Marl and Rhaetic of parts of England. *Philosophical Transactions of the Royal Society of London*, Vol. 289, 549–639.

KENDALL, P F. 1902. A system of glacier-lakes in the Cleveland Hills. *Quarterly Journal of the Geological Society of London*, Vol. 58, 471–571.

KENDALL, P F. and WROOT, H E. 1924. Geology of Yorkshire 1 (Vienna.)

KENT, P E. 1966. The structure of the concealed Carboniferous rocks of north-eastern England. *Proceedings of the Yorkshire Geological Society*, Vol. 35, 323–352.

KENT, P E. 1980a. Subsidence and uplift in East Yorkshire and Lincolnshire: a double inversion. *Proceedings of the Yorkshire Geological Society*, Vol. 42, 505–524.

KENT, P E. 1980b. *British regional geology: Eastern England from the Tees to The Wash* (2nd edition). (London: HMSO for Institute of Geological Sciences.)

KING, W. 1850. *A monograph of the Permian fossils of England.* (Palaeontological Society.)

KIRBY, G A, SMITH, K, SMITH, N J P, and SWALLOW, P. 1987. Oil and gas generation in eastern England. 171–180 in *Petroleum geology of north west Europe.* Vol. 1. BROOKS, J, and GLENNIE, K W (editors). (London: Graham and Trotman.)

KIRBY, G A, and SWALLOW, P. 1987. Tectonism and sedimentation in the Flamborough Head region of north-east England. *Proceedings of the Yorkshire Geological Society*, Vol. 46, 301–309.

KIRKBY, J W. 1861. On the Permian rocks of south Yorkshire and on their palaeontological relations. *Quarterly Journal of the Geological Society of London*, Vol. 17, 287–325.

KNOX, R W O'B. 1973. The Eller Beck Formation (Bajocian) of the Ravenscar Group of NE Yorkshire. *Geological Magazine*, Vol. 110, 511–534.

KNOX, R W O'B. 1984. Lithostratigraphy and depositional history of the late Toarcian sequence at Ravenscar, Yorkshire. *Proceedings of the Yorkshire Geological Society*, Vol. 45, 99–108.

LEEDER, M R. 1982. Upper Palaeozoic basins of the British Isles — Caledonide inheritance versus Hercynian plate margin processes. *Journal of the Geological Society of London*, Vol. 139, 479–491.

LEEDER, M R. and ALEXANDER, M R. 1985. *In* Discussion of Fisher, M J, and Hancock, N J. 1985. The Scalby Formation (Middle Jurassic, Ravenscar Group) of Yorkshire: reassessment of age and depositional environment. *Proceedings of the Yorkshire Geological Society*, Vol. 45, 293–298.

LEEDER, M R, and NAMI, M. 1979. Sedimentary models for the non-marine Scalby Formation (Middle Jurassic) and the evidence for late Bajocian/Bathonian uplift of the Yorkshire Basin. *Proceedings of the Yorkshire Geological Society*, Vol. 42, 461–482.

LIVERA, S E, and LEEDER, M R. 1981. The Middle Jurassic Ravenscar Group ('Deltaic Series') of Yorkshire: recent sedimentological studies as demonstrated during a Field Meeting, 2–3 May, 1980. *Proceedings of the Geologists' Association*, Vol. 92, 241–250.

LOTT, G K, and WARRINGTON, G. 1988. A review of the latest Triassic succession in the UK sector of the southern North Sea Basin. *Proceedings of the Yorkshire Geological Society*, Vol. 47, 139–147.

LOVELL, J H. 1982. The sand and gravel resources of the country around Catterick, North Yorkshire. Description of 1:25 000 resource sheet SE 29. *Mineral Assessment Report Institute of Geological Sciences*, No. 120.

LOVELL, J P B. 1977. *The British Isles through geological time; a northward drift.* (London: Allen and Unwin.)

MARLEY, J. 1857. *In* General meeting. WOOD, N. *North of England Institute of Mining Engineers*, Vol. 6, 187–196

MARLEY, J. 1864. The discovery of rock salt in the New Red Sandstone at Middlesbrough. *North of England Institute of Mining Engineers*, Vol. 13, 17–25 and 92.

MITCHELL, G F, PENNY, L F, SHOTTON, F W, and WEST, R G. 1973. A correlation of Quaternary deposits in the British Isles. *Special Report of the Geological Society of London*, No. 4.

NAMI, M. 1976. An exhumed meander belt from Yorkshire, England. *Geological Magazine*, Vol. 113, 47–52.

NAMI, M, and LEEDER, M R. 1978. Changing channel morphology and magnitude in the Scalby Formation (M. Jurassic) of Yorkshire, England. 431–440 *in* Fluvial sedimentology. MIALL, A D (editor). *Memoir of the Canadian Society of Petroleum Geologists*, No. 5.

NORTH YORK MOORS NATIONAL PARK COMMITTEE. 1969. a) Alum; b) Jet.

PAGE, K N. 1989. A stratigraphical revision for the English Lower Callovian. *Proceedings of the Geologists' Association*, Vol. 100, 363–382.

PARSONS, C F. 1977. A stratigraphic revision of the Scarborough Formation. *Proceedings of the Yorkshire Geological Society*, Vol. 41, 203–221.

PATTISON, J. 1978. Upper Permian palaeontology of the Aiskew Bank Farm Borehole, north Yorkshire. *Report of the Institute of Geological Sciences*, No. 78/14.

PENNY, L F. 1974. Quaternary. 245–284 in *The geology and mineral resources of Yorkshire.* RAYNOR, D H, and HEMINGWAY, J E (editors). (Leeds: Maney and Son Ltd for Yorkshire Geological Society.)

PENNY, L F, COOPE, G R, and CATT, J A. 1969. Age and insect fauna of the Dimlington Silts, East Yorkshire. *Nature, London*, Vol. 224, 65–67.

PHELPS, M. 1985. A refined ammonite biostratigraphy for the Middle and Upper Carixian (ibex and davoei zones, Lower Jurassic) in North-west Europe and stratigraphical details of the Carixian–Domerian boundary. *Geobios*, No. 18, 21–362.

PHILLIPS, J. 1829. *Illustrations of the geology of Yorkshire, or a description of the strata and organic remains. Part I. The Yorkshire Coast*, 199, printed privately, York.

PHILLIPS, J. 1858. On some comparative sections of the Oolite and Ironstone Series of Yorkshire. *Quarterly Journal of the Geological Society of London*, Vol. 14, 84.

POWELL, J H. 1983. The geology of the country around Thirsk, North Yorkshire, with particular reference to the sand and gravel deposits: description of 1:25 000 Sheet SE 48. (Keyworth, Nottingham: British Geological Survey.)

POWELL, J H. 1984. Lithostratigraphical nomenclature of the Lias Group in the Yorkshire Basin. *Proceedings of the Yorkshire Geological Society*, Vol. 45, 51–57.

POWELL, J H. and RATHBONE, P A. 1983. The relationship of the Eller Beck Formation and the supposed Blowgill Member (Middle Jurassic) of the Yorkshire Basin. *Proceedings of the Yorkshire Geological Society*, Vol. 44, 365–373.

POWELL, J H. COOPER, A H, and BENFIELD, A C. 1992. Geology of the country around Thirsk. *Memoir of the British Geological Survey.* Sheet 52 (England and Wales).

RADGE, G W. 1940. The glaciation of north Cleveland. *Proceedings of the Yorkshire Geological Society*, Vol. 24, 180–205.

RAISTRICK, A. 1931. The pre-glacial Swale. *Naturalist* for 1931, 233–237.

RATHBONE, P A. 1987a. Geological notes and local details for 1:10 000 sheets: SE 49 SE (Kepwick). (Keyworth: British Geological Survey.)

RATHBONE, P A. 1987b. Geological notes and local details for 1:10 000 sheets: SE 59 SW (Hawnby Moor). (Keyworth: British Geological Survey.)

RAYMOND, L R. 1955. The Rhaetic Beds and Tea Green Marl of North Yorkshire. *Proceedings of the Yorkshire Geological Society*, Vol. 30, 5–23.

RAYNER, D H. 1953. The Lower Carboniferous rocks in the north of England. *Proceedings of the Yorkshire Geological Society*, Vol. 28, 231–315.

RAYNER, D H. and HEMINGWAY, J E (editors). 1974. *The geology and mineral resources of Yorkshire.* (Leeds: Yorkshire Geological Society.)

RICHARDSON, L. 1912. The Lower Oolitic Rocks of Yorkshire. *Proceedings of the Yorkshire Geological Society*, Vol. 17, 184–215.

RIDING, J B, and WRIGHT, J K. 1989. Palynostratigraphy of the Scalby Formation (Middle Jurassic) of the Cleveland Basin, north-east Yorkshire. *Proceedings of the Yorkshire Geological Society*, Vol. 47, 349–354.

ROSE, J. 1985. The Dimlington Stadial/Dimlington Chronozone: a proposal for naming the main glacial episode of the Late Devensian in Britain. *Boreas*, Vol. 14, 225–230.

SCOTESE, C R, and MCKERROW, W S. 1990. Revised world maps and introduction. 1–21 in Palaeozoic palaeogeography and biogeography. MCKERROW W S, and SCOTESE, C R (editors). *Memoir of the Geological Society of London*, No. 12.

SCOTT, J, and COLTER, V S. 1987. Geological aspects of current onshore Great Britain exploration plays. 95–107 in *Petroleum geology of North West Europe.* BROOK, J, and GLENNIE, K W (editors). (London: Graham and Trotman.)

SEDGWICK, A. 1829. On the geological relations and internal structure of the Magnesian Limestone and the lower portions of the New Red Sandstone Series, in their range through Nottinghamshire, Derbyshire, Yorkshire and Durham, in the southern extremity of Northumberland. *Transactions of the Geological Society of London*, (2) Vol. 3, 37–124.

SIMPSON, M. 1855. *The fossils of the Yorkshire Lias described from nature with a short outline of the Yorkshire Coast.* (London: Whittaker; Whitby: Reed.)

SMITH, B. 1910. The Upper Keuper Sandstones of East Nottinghamshire. *Geological Magazine*, Vol. 7, 302–311.

SMITH, D B. 1968. The Hampole Beds — a significant marker in the Lower Magnesian Limestone of Yorkshire, Derbyshire and Nottinghamshire. *Proceedings of the Yorkshire Geological Society*, Vol. 36, 463–477.

SMITH, D B. 1970. Submarine slumping and sliding in the Lower Magnesian Limestone of Northumberland and Durham. *Proceedings of the Yorkshire Geological Society*, Vol. 38, 1–36.

SMITH, D B. 1972. Foundered strata, collapse-breccias and subsidence features in the English Zechstein. 255–262 in *Geology of saline deposits.* RICHTER-BERNBURG, G (editor). Proceedings of the Hanover Symposium organised by UNESCO (Paris: UNESCO.)

SMITH, D B. 1974. Permian. 115–144 in *The geology and mineral resources of Yorkshire.* RAYNER, D H, and HEMINGWAY, J E (editors). (Leeds: Maney and Son Ltd for Yorkshire Geological Society.)

SMITH, D B. 1980. The evolution of the English Zechstein. *Contributions to Sedimentology*, Vol. 9, 7–34.

SMITH, D B. 1989. The late Permian palaeogeography of north-east England. *Proceedings of the Yorkshire Geological Society*, Vol. 47, 285–313.

SMITH, D B, and FRANCIS, E A. 1967. Geology of the country between Durham and West Hartlepool. *Memoir of the Geological Survey of Great Britain*, Sheet 27 (England and Wales).

SMITH, D B, and MOORE, P J. 1973. Deposits of gypsum at Hurworth Place, Darlington. *Report of the Institute of Geological Sciences*, No. 73/16, 4.

SMITH, D B, BRUNSTROM, R G W, MANNING, P I, SIMPSON, S, and SHOTTON, F W. 1974. A correlation of Permian rocks in the British Isles. *Special Report of the Geological Society of London*, No. 5.

SMITH, D B, and HARWOOD, G M, PATTISON, J, and PETTIGREW, T. 1986. A revised nomenclature for Upper Permian strata in eastern England. 9–17 *in* The English Zechstein and related topics. HARWOOD, G M, and SMITH D B (editors). *Special Publication of the Geological Society of London*, No. 22.

SMITH, D B, and TAYLOR, J C M. 1992. Permian. 87–96 in Atlas of palaeogeography and lithofacies. COPE, J C W, INGHAM, J K, and RAWSON, P F (editors). *Memoir of the Geological Society of London*, No. 13.

SMITH, E G et al. 1973. Geology of the country around East Retford, Worksop and Gainsborough. *Memoir of the Geological Survey of Great Britain.*

SMITHSON, F. 1934. The petrography of Jurassic sediments in Yorkshire. *Proceedings of the Yorkshire Geological Society*, Vol. 22, 188–198.

SMITHSON, F. 1941. The alteration of detrital minerals in the Mesozoic rocks of Yorkshire. *Geological Magazine*, Vol. 78, 97.

SMITHSON, F. 1954. The petrography of dickitic sandstones in North Wales and Northern England. *Geological Magazine*, Vol. 41, 177–188.

SNELLING, N J. 1985. The chronology of the geological record. *Memoir of the Geological Society of London*, No. 10.

SOPER, N J, WEBB, B C, and WOODCOCK, N H. 1987.   Late Caledonian (Acadian) transpression in north-west England: timing, geometry and tectonic significance.   *Proceedings of the Yorkshire Geological Society*, Vol. 46, 175–192.

SORBY, H C. 1857.   On the origin of the Cleveland Hills ironstone.   *Proceedings of the Yorkshire Geological Polytechnic Society*, Vol. 3, 457–461.

SORBY, H C. 1906.   The origin of the Cleveland ironstone. *Naturalist*, 354–357.

STEELE, R P. 1981.   Aeolian sands and sandstones. Unpublished PhD thesis, University of Durham.

TATE, R, and BLAKE, J F. 1876.   *The Yorkshire Lias.*   (London: Voorst John van.)

TAYLOR, B J, and five others. 1971.   *British regional geology: Northern England* (4th edition).   (London: HMSO for Institute of Geological Sciences.)

THOMAS, J. 1876.   *Chemical Journal*, New Series, Vol. 14, 150.

TUKE, J. 1794.   *General view of the agriculture of the North Riding of Yorkshire. (Map and account of soils.)* London.

TURBITT, T. (editor). 1984.   Catalogue of British earthquakes recorded by British Seismograph Network, 1979, 1980, 1981. *Global Seismology Unit, British Geological Survey*, No. 210.

TURBITT, T. 1990.   Bulletin of British Earthquakes 1988. *British Geological Survey, Global Seimology Series*, Technical Report, WL/90/3.

VAN BUCHEM, F S P, and McCAVE, I N. 1989.   Cyclic sedimentation patterns in Lower Lias mudstones of Yorkshire (GB).   *Terra Nova*, Vol. 1, 461–667.

VAN BUCHEM, F S P, MELNYK, D H, and McCAVE, I N. 1992. Chemical cyclicity and correlation of Lower Lias mudstones using gamma ray logs, Yorkshire, UK.   *Journal of the Geological Society of London*, Vol. 149, 991–1002.

VAN WAGONER, J C, POSAMENTIER, H W, MITCHUM, R M, VAIL, P R, SARG, J F, LOUTIT, T S, and HARDENBOL, J. 1988.   An overview of the fundamentals of sequence stratigraphy and key definitions.   39–45 *in* Sea level changes: an integrated approach. WILGUS, C K, HASTINGS, B S, KENDALL, C St C, POSAMENTIER, H W, ROSS, C A, VAN WAGONER, J C (editors). *Special Publication of the Society of Economic Paleontologists and Mineralogists*, No. 42.

VERSEY, H C. 1928.   Geology of the Malton area.   *Naturalist*, 269–270.

WARRINGTON, G. 1970.   The stratigraphy and palaeontology of the Keuper Series of the central Midlands of England. *Journal of the Geological Society of London*, Vol. 126, 183–227.

WARRINGTON, G. 1974.   Triassic.   145–160 in *The geology and mineral resources of Yorkshire*.   RAYNER, D H, and HEMINGWAY, J E (editors). (Leeds: Maney and Son Ltd for Yorkshire Geological Society.)

WARRINGTON, G, and eight others. 1980.   A correlation of Triassic rocks in the British Isles.   *Special Report of the Geological Society of London*, No. 13.

WARRINGTON, G, and IVIMEY-COOK, H C. 1992.   Triassic. 97–106 *in* Atlas of palaeogeography and lithofacies. COPE, J C W, INGHAM, J K, and RAWSON, P F (editors). *Memoirs of the Geological Society of London*, No.13.

WHETTON, J T, MYERS, J O, and BURKE, K B S. 1961.   Tracing the boundary of the concealed coalfield of Yorkshire using the gravity method.   *Mining Magazine*, 657–674.

WHITTAKER, A (editor).   1985.   *Atlas of onshore sedimentary basins in England and Wales: post-carboniferous tectonics and stratigraphy.*   (Glasgow and London: Blackie.)

WILLAN, R. 1782.   *Observations on the sulphur–water at Croft, near Darlington.*   London.   Ed.2 under a different title, in 1786.

WILSON, A A, and EVANS, W B. 1990.   Geology of the country around Blackpool.   *Memoir of the British Geological Survey*, Sheet 66 (England and Wales).

WINCH, N J. 1817.   Observations on the geology of Northumberland and Durham.   *Transactions of the Geological Society of London*, Vol. 4, 1–101.

WINCH, N J. 1821.   Observations on the eastern part of Yorkshire.   *Transactions of the Geological Society*, Vol. 5, 545–557.

WRIGHT, J K. 1968.   The stratigraphy of the Callovian rocks between Newtondale and the Scarborough coast, Yorkshire. *Proceedings of the Geologists' Association*, Vol. 79, 363–399.

WRIGHT, J K. 1977.   The Cornbrash Formation (Callovian) in North Yorkshire and Cleveland.   *Proceedings of the Yorkshire Geological Society*, Vol. 41, 325–346.

WRIGHT, J K. 1978.   The Callovian succession (excluding Cornbrash) in the western and northern parts of the Yorkshire Basin.   *Proceedings of the Geologists' Association*, Vol. 89, 259–261.

WRIGHT, J K, 1980.   Oxfordian correlation chart.   61–76 in A correlation of Jurassic rocks in the British Isles. Part 2: Middle and Upper Jurassic. COPE, J C W et al. (editors). *Special Report of the Geological Society of London*, No. 15.

WRIGHT, J K. 1983.   The Lower Oxfordian (Upper Jurassic) of North Yorkshire.   *Proceedings of the Yorkshire Geological Society*, Vol. 44, 249–281.

WRIGHT, T. 1860.   On the subdivisions of the Inferior Oolite in the South of England, compared with equivalent beds of that formation on the Yorkshire coast.   *Quarterly Journal of the Geological Society of London*, Vol. 16, 1–48.

YOUNG, G, and BIRD, J. 1822.   *A geological survey of the Yorkshire coast.*   (Whitby: Clark.)

APPENDIX 1

List of boreholes

At the time of going to press, 889 borehole records of the Northallerton district are held in BGS archives, and additional information is constantly being added as it becomes available.

This appendix lists, by six-inch maps, the main borehole records for the district. For each record the permanent record number, location and the stratigraphical formation is given, together with the starting level (where known), the total depth, and the thickness of drift. Copies of the complete records may be obtained from the National Geoscience Records Centre, British Geological Survey, Keyworth, Nottingham NG12 5GG at a fixed tariff.

Abbreviations are as follows:

LCG   Lower Calcareous Grit Formation
OXC   Oxford Clay Formation
OSY   Osgodby Formation
CRG   Crinoid Grit Member
BYR   Brandsby Roadstone
CLF   Cloughton Formation
RG   Ravenscar Group
WHM   Whitby Mudstone Formation
CDI   Cleveland Ironstone Formation
STA   Staithes Sandstone Formation
REM   Redcar Mudstone Formation
PNG   Penarth Group
MMG   Mercia Mudstone Group
SSG   Sherwood Sandstone Group
ROX   Roxby Formation
BTH   Brotherton Formation
C   Confidential
c.   circa (approximately)

Name	Reference number	Grid reference	Starting level (m)	Depth to base of drift (m)	Total depth (m)	Stratigraphy
Ainderby Well	SE39SW/18	3326 9252	c.37	14.3	91.4	SSG
Ainderby Steeple	SE39SW/19	3320 9250	c.33	13.5	100.1	SSG, ?ROX
Ainderby	SE39SW/5	3268 9246	c.32	6.7	18.3	SSG
Angleham House	SE29SE/4	2692 9310	c.52	—	52.0	—
Arden Arms	NZ20SE/5	2861 0246	c.64	38.7	50.3	SSG
Arden Hall	SE59SW/1	5037 9157	c.316	0.3	67.8	LCG, OXC, OSY
Ashfield House	NZ40SE/7	4624 0253	70.1	—	18.0	—
Atley Hill	NZ20SE/7	2870 0229	c.55	35.7	46.0	SSG
Atley Hill Farm	NZ20SE/9	2881 0192	c.61	38.4	51.2	SSG
Bay Horse	NZ20NE/11	2913 0820	51	16.1	C	SSG, ROX, BTH
Beggar My Neighbour Farm	NZ50NW/20	5169 0742	64.0	—	21.0	—
Bense Bridge	NZ50NW/6	5201 0775	c.67	—	15.4	—
Birkby Manor	NZ30SW/25	3327 0248	42.7	—	18.0	—
Birkby Farm	NZ30SW/21	3345 0343	44.5	—	18.0	—
Birkby	NZ30SW/5	3284 0241	40	—	9.1	—
Birkby Gate House	NZ30SE/9	3605 0220	60.4	—	18.0	—
Birkby Grange	NZ30SW/11	3439 0174	54	—	—	—
Black Bridge Farm	NZ30SW/2	3235 0001	40	30.5	41.2	SSG
Black Swan	NZ40SW/9	4428 0376	70.1	—	18.0	—
Blackhills	SE39SE/2	3891 9291	c.85	4.9	72.9	REM, PNG, MMG
Blow Houses	SE29SE/32	2962 9056	34.2	10.5	11.0	SSG
Blow Houses	SE29SE/1	2961 9044	35.7	10.36	21.34	SSG

Name	Reference number	Grid reference	Starting level (m)	Depth to base of drift (m)	Total depth (m)	Stratigraphy
Bowlturner House	NZ30SW/7	3088 0458	54	42.7	52.7	SSG
Brampton Farm	SE39SW/6	3136 9369	c.34	39.3	48.8	SSG
Brecken Hill	NZ40SW/11	4313 0143	76.8	—	18.0	—
Brickyard Wood	NZ40SW/10	4161 0197	75.3	—	18.0	—
Broad Carr Farm	NZ40NE/16	4514 0519	76.8	—	18.0	—
Broadmire	NZ40NE/12	4867 0708	59.7	—	18.0	—
Brompton Hill House 4	SE39NE/18	3947 9659	76	1.5	C	C
Brompton Hill House 3	SE39NE/15	3920 9646	100	2.1	C	C
Brompton Hill House 2	SE39NE/14	3962 9652	c.99	3.0	C	C
Brompton Hill House 1	SE39NE/13	3957 9632	99	1.8	C	C
Brompton	SE39NE/1	3737 9642	c.45	24.1	52.4	MMG
Broughton Bridge	NZ50NW/32	5392 0800	c.70	—	17.6	—
Broughton Bank	SE50SE/2	5550 0451	136.6	—	18.0	—
Bullamooe British Gypsum	SE39SE/13	3932 9432	110	C	—	C
Bullamoor Reservoir	SE39SE/7	3927 9424	c.110	3.8	17.7	REM
Busby House (East)	NZ50NW/25	5103 0635	66.8	—	18.0	—
Busby House	NZ50NW/24	5049 0692	62.8	—	18.0	—
Butterhill Plantation	NZ50SW/7	5139 0369	133.8	—	5.8	—
Calf Close Hill	NZ50NW/28	5036 0580	69.8	—	20.0	—
Carlton	NZ50SW/6	5042 0367	104.5	—	18.0	—
Carlton Grove	NZ40NE/18	4959 0536	73.2	—	5.5	—
Carr Bridge Farm	NZ40NW/20	4187 0572	50.3	—	18.0	—
Carr Hill	SE29SE/23	2736 9229	63.5	—	24.0	—
Carr House	NZ40NE/7	4865 0871	77.1	23.5	26.0	MMG
Church Farm	NZ20SE/8	2918 0274	c.41	23.8	33.8	SSG
Cinnamire Farm	SE39NE/5	3596 9757	c.54	29.0	72.5	MMG, SSG
Cleveland Tontine Inn	SE49NW/4	4441 9930	72	4.3	30.5	REM
Cleveland Hills No. 1 Oil	SE59NW/1	5354 9844	384	—	744.8	MIDDLE JURASSIC to CARBONIFEROUS
Cock Holme	NZ30SW/28	3490 0110	55.5	—	18.0	—
Cockbush Hall Farm	SE49NW/2	4423 9999	79	17.7	27.4	REM
Cod Beck Reservoir	SE49NE/4	462 985	—	Several bores	—	REM
Cote Ghyll Youth Hostel	SE49NE/7	4615 9811	c.170	22.8	45.7	STA, REM
Cote House	NZ50SW/5	5258 0459	c.107	—	18.0	—
Crabtree Farm	NZ50NW/15	5154 0876	64.3	—	20.5	—
Crakehall Ings Lane	SE29SE/30	2683 9062	36.5	—	18.2	—
Cramble Cross	NZ20SE/18	2748 0432	c.64	26.8	60.9	SSG
Crathorne Grange	NZ40NW/4	4397 0783	c.55	12.2	54.9	SSG
Crathorne Hall	NZ40NW/3	4449 0856	c.55	?c.40	45.4	SSG
Croft Airfield	NZ20NE/8	2811 0681	c.55	39.6	73.1	SSG
Crow Foot Farm	SE39NE/2	3558 9835	c.55	41.5	45.7	SSG
Dales Farm	NZ30NE/3	3635 0625	46	37.0	46.9	SSG
Dalton upon Tees	NZ20NE/3	2964 0816	c.52	36.6	76.2	SSG
Danby Hill	SE39NW/3	3348 9744	c.45	27.4	39.6	SSG
Danby Plantation	NZ30SW/3	3038 0012	43	21.0	231.65	SSG, PERMIAN FORMATIONS UNDIFFERENTIATED
Danby Hill Farm	NZ30SW/9	3043 0135	62	50.3	67.4	SSG
Danby Wiske Railway	SE39NW/1	3477 9778	c.37	—	5.2	—
Deepdale	NZ40SW/14	4199 0049	78.9	—	18.0	—
Deighton Grange	NZ30SE/10	3757 0090	c.75	—	18.0	—
Dromonby House	NZ50NW/30	5341 0553	96.3	—	18.0	—
East Cowton Pumping Station	NZ30SW/14a–e	3150 0273		—	3.65	—
		3118 0310		—	4.57	—
		3060 0340	c.38	—	—	—
		3086 0329		—	—	—
		3112 0311		—	—	—
East Sockburn Farm	NZ30NE/18	3518 0737	15.5	19.8	20.0	SSG
East Rounton	NZ40SW/8	4217 0358	65.8	—	19.0	—
East Harlsey Manor	NZ40SW/1	4301 0005	c.99	8.2	45.6	REM, PNG
East Harlsey No. 2	SE49NW/3	4213 9980	111	7.3	24.0	REM
East Harlsey No. 1	SE49NW/1	4233 9976	115	—	24.4	REM
Eryholme	NZ30NW/20	3210 0873	38	67.4	203.0	SSG

Name	Reference number	Grid reference	Starting level (m)	Depth to base of drift (m)	Total depth (m)	Stratigraphy
Faceby Lodge	NZ40SE/4	4958 0425	78.5	—	18.0	—
Farfield House	SE29SE/31	2865 9056	35.4	13.3	14.0	SSG
Fence Dike Lane	SE29SE/24	2853 9216	35.5	11.0	11.3	SSG
Field House	NZ50NW/23	5453 0798	73.2	—	20.0	—
Fir Trees Farm	NZ50NW/21	5235 0710	71.0	—	20.5	—
Fire Station Northallerton	SE39SE/9	3720 9381	c.40	?1.7	10.7	MMG
Firtree House	NZ30SW/15	3056 0485	53	—	21.0	—
Five Mile Bank Farm	NZ30SE/3	3548 0138	c.66	?29.1	61	MMG, SSG
Fog Close	NZ50SW/9	5062 0046	185.7	—	22.0	—
Folly Hill	NZ40NE/10	4781 0717	78.0	—	18.0	—
Frigidale Wood	NZ30SW/20	3233 0381	43.9	—	18.0	—
Garden House Farm	NZ50NW/31	5382 0874	c.70	—	15.1	—
Girsby Hall	NZ30NE/8	3559 0881	44	39.6	61.0	SSG
Girsby Green	NZ30NE/19	3619 0749	43.3	—	18.0	—
Girsby Green	NZ30NE/7	3592 0783	45	41.2	57.9	SSG
Girsby House	NZ30NE/6	3557 0832	47	16.5	44.2	SSG
Goslingmire	NZ40NE/6	4742 0832	75.6	—	18.0	—
Goulton Grange	NZ40SE/3	4772 0412	70.1	—	18.0	—
Grange Farm	NZ20SE/10	2896 0123	c.52	30.8	39.9	SSG
Grange Farm	NZ30NE/25	3640 0510	59.4	—	18.0	—
Granville Farm	SE39NW/5	3228 9642	c.46	27.4	40.8	SSG
Greenberry Farm	SE29NE/4	2960 9880	c.49	28.7	43.3	SSG
Greenhills	SE39SW/20	3402 9103	c.36	16.5	100.6	SSG
Greenhills	NZ30SE/11	3881 0153	80.3	—	18.0	—
Greythorne Flatts	SE49SW/1	4247 9045	113	4.0	23.0	RG
Grimescar Farm	SE39SW/4	3073 9031	c.30	12.8	24.7	SSG
Gulf Exploration G6	NZ50SW/4	5410 0420	c.153	8.2	132.6	REN, PNG, MMG
Gulf Exploration G5	NZ50SW/3	5405 0475	c.129	12.8	58.5	REM, PNG, MMG
Gulf Exploration G7	NZ50SW/11	5410 0450	c.139	19.8	183	REM, PNG, MMG
Gulf Exploration G1	NZ50SW/1	5255 0415	c.125	5.2	121.6	REM, PNG, MMG
Gulf Exploration G11	NZ50NW/33	5155 0595	72.3	42.7	64.0	MMG
Gulf Exploration G3	NZ50NW/2	5404 0537	100.3	39.6	61.0	MMG
Gulf Exploration G4	NZ50NW/1	5400 0515	112.7	17.0	42.7	REM, PNG, MMG
Gulf Exploration G2	NZ50SW/2	5245 0410	104.1	29.3	122.0	?REM, ?PNG, MMG
Haggitt Hill	NZ40NW/21	4314 0524	67.1	—	18.0	—
Hailstone Moor	SE39SE/12a-f	3902 9391	95	0.7	12.0	PNG, MMG
Half Round Plantation	NZ30SE/2	3733 0194	c.77	22.9	41.2	MMG, SSG
Hall Farm	NZ30SW/13	3435 0020	c.45	28.9	52.4	SSG
Hallikeld House	SE39NE/4	3943 9690	c.56	7.9	68.0	MMG
Harlsey No. 1 Oil Bore	SE49NW/6	4224 9806	113	—	1082.0	JURASSIC−CARBONIFEROUS
High Entercommon (Windpump)	NZ30NW/3	3383 0585	55	—	6.1	—
High Barn	SE39SW/1	3235 9493	c.49	11.0	18.3	SSG
High Foxton Farm	NZ40NE/4	4604 0820	68	—	18.0	—
High Entercommon	NZ30NW/18	3423 0570	52	—	18.0	—
High Magdalen	NZ30NW/19	3352 0537	70	—	21.0	—
High Whinholme	NZ30SW/26	3056 0076	46.6	—	18.0	—
High Worsall Moor	NZ30NE/20	3819 0754	46.3	—	18.0	—
Hill House	NZ30SE/8	3987 0355	58.8	—	18.0	—
Hillilees Farm	NZ40NW/5	4103 0821	c.55	—	36.1	—
Holtby Hall	SE29SE/22	2689 9254	47.9	—	5.4	—
Holtby Grange	SE29SE/6	2676 9326	c.52	—	—	—
Hook Carr Hill	SE29NE/24	2753 9559	51.8	—	22.5	—
Hornby Green	NZ30SE/5	3745 0452	c.58	—	18.0	—
Huthwaite Green Farm	NZ40SE/14	4901 0081	137.5	—	18.0	—
Hutton Bridge	NZ40NE/14	4712 0664	46.6	6.5	7.5	MMG
Hutton Rudby	NZ40NE/19	4655 0695	50	—	6.1	—
Hutton Rudby	NZ40NE/24	4662 0643	c.73	—	4.0	—
Hutton Rudby	NZ40NE/20	4699 0655	46	—	6.1	—
Hutton Bonville	NZ30SW/4	3361 0026	40	—	33.8	—
Hutton Rudby	NZ40NE/21	4717 0660	c.46	—	6.1	—
Hutton Rudby	NZ40NE/23	4713 0691	c.66	—	4.3	—

Name	Reference number	Grid reference	Starting level (m)	Depth to base of drift (m)	Total depth (m)	Stratigraphy
Hutton Rudby	NZ40NE/22	4694 0616	c.69	—	4.0	—
Ingleby By-pass 12	NZ40SE/17	4521 0068	c.73	—	5.92	—
Ingleby By-pass 14	NZ40SE/19	4535 0084	c.74	—	16.75	—
Ingleby By-pass 20	NZ20SE/21	4550 0100	c.75	—	5.0	—
Ingleby By-pass 21	NZ40SE/22	4557 0107	c.75	—	5.0	—
Ingleby By-pass 22	NZ40SE/23	4565 0114	c.76	—	7.90	—
Ingleby By-pass 7	NZ40SW/17	4481 0015	c.75	—	5.0	—
Ingleby By-pass 10	NZ40SE/15	4506 0051	c.73	—	10.5	—
Ingleby By-pass 6	NZ40SW/16	4476 0004	c.76	—	8.7	—
Ingleby By-pass 8	NZ40SW/18	4493 0033	c.75	—	5.5	—
Ingleby Arncliffe	NZ40SW/2	4431 0059	c.84	14.3	31.7	REM
Ingleby By-pass 9	NZ40SW/19	4500 0044	c.75	—	7.0	—
Ingleby By-pass 2	SE49NW/9	4462 9975	74	—	3.0	—
Ingleby By-pass 1	SE49NW/7	4448 9954	73	—	3.0	—
Ingleby By-pass 3	SE49NW/11	4471 9993	76	—	5.22	—
Kiplin	SE29NE/19	2771 9679	37.6	8.2	8.5	SSG
Kiplin Beck	SE29NE/16	2832 9703	38.2	14.7	15.0	SSG
Kirkby Wood	SE29NE/25	2858 9504	49.1	15.5	15.7	SSG
Kirkby Fleetham Mill Farm	SE29SE/3	287 942	32.6	26.52	33.36	SSG
Kirkby Fleetham	SE29SE/14	2825 9438	39.6	—	20.5	—
Kirkby Bridge Farm	NZ50NW/22	5357 0761	74.1	—	18.0	—
Kirkby Lane Farm (North)	NZ50NW/26	5352 0683	81.7	—	18.0	—
Langton Grange Farm	SE39NW/16	3081 9706	45	28.34	52.4	SSG
Langton Cottages	SE39NW/6	3106 9522	c.45	—	30.6	—
Langton Hall	SE39NW/4	3033 9531	c.38	—	36.6	—
Lark Hall	SE39SW/41	3497 9267	c.31	7.0	45.7	SSG
Lazenby Grange	SE39NW/2	3496 9909	c.52	39.3	57.9	SSG
Leap Close Wood	NZ40NE/15	4867 0622	68.0	—	18.0	—
Leases Grange	SE29SE/33a	2780 9155	61.5	—	16.1	—
Leases Hall	SE29SE/27	2789 9144	62.3	—	22.5	—
Leases Grange	SE29SE/33b	2791 9154	59.9	—	10.5	—
Linden Grove	NZ40NE/17	4681 0539	71.3	6.5	7.5	MMG
Little Fencote	SE29SE/19	2849 9326	37.3	—	22.5	—
Lovesome Hill	SE39NE/3	3586 9969	c.69	—	10	—
Low Field Farm	NZ30NE/22	3828 0633	46.3	—	18.0	—
Low Magdalen	NZ30SW/17	3308 0445	43.6	—	21.0	—
Lucky Barn	SE29SE/25	2952 9226	34.6	16.8	17.7	SSG
Main Line Bridge	NZ30SW/1a-c	3311 0195	38	—	50.2	—
Manor Farm	NZ30SW/8	3463 0456	62	—	—	?
Manor Farm	NZ40NW/18	4491 0633	64.9	—	18.0	—
Manor House	NZ30SW/24	3110 0236	36.4	—	18.0	—
Manor House	SE29NE/8	2821 9923	c.52	24.1	36.6	SSG
Middle Brockholme Farm	SE39NW/7	3161 9779	c.40	28.0	41.5	SSG
Mill Vale	NZ50NW/18	5499 0868	76.8	—	18.0	—
Moat Farm	NZ40NW/19	4057 0595	60.0	—	18.0	—
Moor House Farm	SE39SW/3	3338 9491	c.52	21.0	39.6	SSG
Moor House Farm	SE29SE/28	2905 9159	32.6	—	10.3	—
Moor House Farm	NZ30NW/7	3073 0525	55	46.9	61.3	SSG
Morton Grange	SE39SW/42	3264 9128	c.32	35.5	90.0	SSG
Mount Flatts	NZ40NW/17	4338 0630	52.7	—	18.0	—
New Spa	NZ20NE/10	2893 0900	42	C	C	SSG, ROX
New Inn	NZ50NW/3	5271 0878	c.68	—	36.6	—
New Church Romanby	SE39SE/3	3605 9320	c.40	—	6.1	—
Newstead Grange	SE39NE/7	3799 9890	c.57	16.5	45.7	MMG
North of Picton Station	NZ40NW/14	4235 0821	49.7	—	18.0	—
North Bridge	SE39SW/40	3260 9368	c.30	28	53.4	SSG
North Lowfield	SE29NE/26	2977 9522	31.2	12.0	12.0	SSG
North of Crathorne Grange	NZ40NW/15	4407 0822	56.4	—	20.0	—
North Lowfield	SE29NE/20	2921 9602	35.4	—	13.0	—
North Bore	SE39SW/45	3310 9240	c.35	7.0	100.0	SSG
Northallerton Prison	SE39SE/6	371 939	c.40	5.5	28.4	MMG, SSG
Northallerton Library	SE39SE/14a–d	3697 9357	40	—	15.0	—

Name	Reference number	Grid reference	Starting level (m)	Depth to base of drift (m)	Total depth (m)	Stratigraphy
Northallerton Alverton Factory	SE39SE/4	3652 9358	c.40	8.2	25.6	?MMG
Northallerton Cow & Gate Factory	SE39SE/8a	3626 9349	c.38	2.7	123.4	MMG, SSG
Northeast of Thorn Hill Farm	NZ40SE/5	4703 0316	76.8	12.9	14.0	REM
Northfields Farm	SE39NE/6	3836 9949	c.56	32.0	53.6	MMG
Norwood Farm	NZ40SE/11	4546 0054	85	—	18.0	—
Oak Hill	NZ40NE/8	4940 0820	70.7	—	19.5	—
Oakland House	NZ50NW/4	5219 0830	c.67	30.48	56.09	MMG
Old Hall, Yafforth	SE39SW/14	3450 9458	c.37	18.9	30.8	SSG
Osmotherley Moor	SE49NE/2	?	?	?	52.0	RG
Osmotherley	SE49SE/1	4864 9178	247	2.6	31.4	RG
Over Whitwell Farm	SE29NE/1	2808 9930	c.52	13.7	36.6	SSG
Palms Hall Farm	NZ30SE/1	3638 0078	c.69	28.4	104.0	MMG, SSG
Park House 3	SE49NW/17	4151 9725	102	6.1	C	PNG
Park House 2	SE49NW/16	4143 9707	91	7.9	C	PNG
Park House 1	SE49NW/15	4143 9683	93	9.5	C	PNG
Pepper Arden	NZ20SE/6	2971 0180	c.57	49.4	61.0	SSG
Pepper Hall	NZ20SE/2	2942 0190	c.58	—	20.1	—
Pepper Arden Hall	NZ20SE/17	2967 0202	c.58	49.4	67.7	SSG
Peter Hill Bridge	NZ40SE/28	4539 0459	c.82	18.6	146.0	MMG
Picton Junction	NZ40NW/2	4225 0794	c.52	?39.6	39.6	SSG
Plane Tree Farm	NZ50SW/8	5062 0269	129.8	—	18.0	—
Plantation Farm	NZ30NW/4	3217 0602	47	38.7	51.8	SSG
Potto Hill Farm	NZ40SE/6	4809 0308	85.3	4.8	6.0	REM
Prospect House	NZ30NE/24	3900 0563	61.2	—	25.0	—
Radby Lane	NZ30SW/19	3114 0417	46.9	—	18.0	—
RAF Leeming	SE39SW/46	3051 9016	30.5	10.5	12.0	SSG
RAF Leeming	SE39SW/43	3061 9010	c.31	11.6	75.0	SSG, ROX, PERMIAN FORMATIONS
Railway Bridge Farm	NZ50NW/27	5459 0699	87.5	—	18.0	—
Railway crossing	SE39SE/17a–d	3666 9243	39	2.9 to 7.2	9.0	MMG
Raisdale	NZ50SW/10	5320 0012	c.253	3.7	32.6	WHM, CDI, STA
Rawcar Bridge	SE29NE/30	298 986	c.43	31.1	60.1	SSG
Rocky Plain Farm	SE49NE/5	467 979	c.52	—	51.81	RG
Roman Road	NZ30SE/7	3823 0363	56.3	—	18.0	—
Rudley Wood	NZ40NE/9	4605 0728	70.1	—	18.0	—
Scarth Wood Farm	NZ40SE/12	4659 0083	111.9	—	18.0	—
Scourton Road Farm	NZ20SE/4	2788 0210	c.63	26.0	33.5	SSG
Scruton Grange	SE29SE/20	2970 9317	29.5	—	19.1	—
Scruton	SE39SW/17	3004 9243	c.31	18.3	137.2	SSG, ROX
Seamer Hill	NZ50NW/14	5052 0902	73.1	—	20.0	—
Shepherd Hill	NZ40SE/13	4772 0100	127.7	—	25.0	—
Silton	SE49SE/2	4722 9469	270	1.7	29.4	CRG, BYR, CLF
Smeaton Manor	NZ30SW/18	3414 0443	54.6	—	18.0	—
Smithy House Farm	NZ30NW/21	332 055	c.69	54.8	63.1	SSG
Sockburn	NZ30NW/17	3478 0684	17	—	19.8	—
Somerset House	NZ40SW/15	4427 0056	82.9	19.0	19.5	REM
South Bore	SE39SW/44	3310 9240	c.35	11.0	100.0	SSG
South Walmire	NZ20NE/4	2861 0570	c.66	40.5	47.5	SSG
South Lowfields Farm	SE29SE/15	2914 9405	30.6	8.9	9.2	SSG
Southmoor Farm	NZ20SE/3	2975 0079	c.46	36.6	39.6	SSG
Spyknave Hill Farm	NZ40NE/5	4722 0899	77.4	—	21.5	—
Staindale	NZ30NE/23	3925 0675	49.7	—	19.0	—
Staindale Grange	NZ30NE/21	3641 0642	43.9	—	18.0	—
Staindale Hill	NZ40NW/13	4030 0767	56.1	—	18.0	—
Stanhowe Farm	SE29NE/5	2954 9798	c.47	—	36.6	?SSG
Station Well Northallerton	SE39SE/5	3644 9316	c.40	?	8.8	MMG
Stell Plantation	NZ30SE/6	3616 0347	45.6	—	20.0	—
Stokesley Brewery	NZ50NW/5	5226 0862	c.67	32.3	33.1	MMG
Stokesley	NZ50NW/16	5273 0816	66.8	—	25.0	—
Stones Rigg	NZ30SW/16	3223 0467	46.3	—	2	—

Name	Reference number	Grid reference	Starting level (m)	Depth to base of drift (m)	Total depth (m)	Stratigraphy
Summerfield House	NZ40SE/9	4523 0178	78.3	7.8	8.5	REM
Swainby 1	NZ40SE/24	4780 0284	c.75	—	4.5	—
Swainby 3	NZ40SE/26	4761 0223	c.77	—	3.8	—
Swainby 2	NZ40SE/25	4764 0240	c.77	—	4.5	—
Swainby 4	NZ40SE/27	4776 0203	c.77	—	3.8	—
Tewit Castle	NZ30NW/14	3054 0769	47	—	20.0	—
The Green Romanby	SE39SE/11	3587 9356	c.40	0.60	39.6	MMG, SSG
The Stell	NZ30SW/23	3087 0201	37	—	22.0	—
The Forest	NZ20SE/1	?271 013	c.63	29.3	36.6	SSG
Thimbleby Moor	SE49NE/1	4782 9551	c.274	2.6	31.4	RG
Thimbleby	SE49SE/3	4541 9469	186	9.40	45.55	JRB, WHM, CDI, STA
Thoraldby Hall	NZ40NE/13	4922 0720	67.1	—	18.0	—
Thorn Farm	NZ40SE/2	4561 0420	79.8	—	18.0	—
Thorntree Farm	NZ30NW/16	3122 0673	46	—	18.0	—
Thorntree 1	SE39NE/16	3887 9615	101	2.4	C	C
Thorntree 2	SE39NE/17	3895 9620	103	5.5	C	C
Thrintoft Park Farm	SE39SW/8	3172 9450	c.38	42.7	56.7	SSG
Thrush Nest Farm	NZ40SW/7	4123 0416	52.1	—	18.0	—
Tickergate Lane	SE29SE/18	2747 9333	53.7	—	22.0	—
Tickergate Lane	SE29SE/17	2692 9362	52.9	—	25.0	—
Trenholm Farm	NZ40SW/12	4451 0261	73.8	—	18.0	—
Trenholme Farm	SE49NE/6	4681 9709	c.216	0.6	51.8	RG
Vale of Mowbray Brewery Leeming Bar	SE29SE/2	2872 9015	36.6	6.45	69.34	SSG, ROX, PERMIAN
Viewley Hill	NZ30NE/17	3841 0849	35.4	—	18.0	—
Viewley Hill Farm	NZ30NE/5	3839 0858	32	32.0	43.3	SSG
Viewly Hill	NZ50NW/29	5151 0541	77.7	—	18.0	—
Villa Farm	NZ50NW/17	5342 0858	70.1	—	21.0	—
Violet Hill	NZ40SW/13	4050 0046	64.6	—	18.0	—
Warlaby Grange	SE39SW/7	3442 9036	c.39	19.5	39.9	SSG
Warlaby Nook	SE39SE/1	3528 9037	c.4.3	3.7	38.4	SSG
West Worsall Farm	NZ30NE/4	3766 0699	48	46.0	55.6	SSG
West Lees Farm	NZ40SE/8	4739 0225	76.2	—	18.0	—
West Thorpe	NZ30SW/6	3469 0351	46	—	10.4	—
West of Hunter Banks	NZ40NW/16	4492 0881	24.7	5.2	6.0	SSG
Westfield Farm	NZ30NW/1	3194 0764	47	47.6	51.8	SSG
Westhorpe Hall	NZ30SW/22	3450 0315	41.3	—	18.0	—
Westlands	SE49NE/3	?	?	4.8	20.73	RG
White House Farm	SE39NW/9	3027 9828	c.46	23.0	34.1	SSG
White Houses	NZ30NW/15	3477 0814	44	—	18.0	—
White Houses	NZ30NW/5	3468 0811	46	45.1	61.0	SSG
Whorlton House	NZ40SE/10	4881 0199	123.4	—	20.0	—
Willowtree Farm	SE39NW/8	3226 9641	c.38	—	—	—
Winton Manor	SE49NW/12	4021 9655	101	4.9	C	REM, PNG, MMG
Wiske House Farm	NZ30SW/27	3254 0105	37	—	18.0	—
Yafforth Village Pump	SE39SW/2	3425 9449	c.40	7.3	7.3	SSG
Zetland Bridge	SE39SE/10	3581 9461	c.39	10.3	12.2	MMG

APPENDIX 2

Open-file reports

Open-file reports containing geological details additional to those shown on the 1:10 000 maps are listed here. They can be consulted at BGS libraries or purchased from the same outlets as the dyeline maps.

SE 49 SE	(Kepwick)	P A Rathbone	WA/87/76
SE 59 SW	(Hawnby Moor)	P A Rathbone	WA/87/77

APPENDIX 3

Geological Survey photographs

Forty-eight photographs illustrating the geology of the Northallerton district are deposited for reference in the headquarters library of the British Geological Survey, Keyworth, Nottingham NG12 5GG; in the library at the BGS, Murchison House, West Mains Road, Edinburgh EH9 3LA; and in the BGS Information Office at the Natural History Museum Earth Galleries, Exhibition Road, London SW7 2DE. They belong to the L Series and were taken between April 1978 and September 1981 during the survey. The photographs depict details of the various rocks and sediments exposed and also include general views and scenery. The photographs can be supplied as black and white or colour prints and 2 × 2 colour transparencies, at a fixed tariff.

LIST OF GEOLOGICAL SURVEY PHOTOGRAPHS FOR THE AREA OF THE NORTHALLERTON DISTRICT (SHEET 42)

Photo No.

L 1981	Carlton Bank, near Carlton, Northallerton
L 1982	Garden House, near Stokesley
L 1983	Broughton Bridge, Eller Beck, near Stokesley
L 1984	Left bank of River Leven near Sutterskelfe Hall
L 1985	North bank of River Leven near Hutton Rudby
L 1986	Left bank of River Leven, Sutterskelfe Hall, Nr Stokesley
L 1987	Left bank of River Leven, Sutterskelfe Hall, Nr Stokesley
L 1988	Left bank of River Leven, Sutterskelfe Hall, Nr Stokesley
L 1989	River Leven south bank near Hutton Rudby
L 2436	Northern scarp of the Cleveland Hills
L 2437	Northern scarp of the Cleveland Hills
L 2438	Northern scarp of the Cleveland Hills
L 2439	Upper Raisdale to Roseberry Topping
L 2440	Cringle Moor — an outlier of Middle Jurassic
L 2441	Lowest sandstone beds of the Middle Jurassic
L 2442	Lowest sandstone beds of the Middle Jurassic
L 2443	Hambleton Oolite and Lower Calcareous Grit

L 2444	Northern scarp of the Cleveland Hills
L 2445	Northern scarp of the Cleveland Hills
L 2446	Eastern side of Tom Gill
L 2447	Western side of Scugdale showing the Jet Rock Member
L 2448	General view across Raisdale from Harten Gill
L 2449	Basal beds of the Middle Jurassic
L 2450	Basal beds of the Middle Jurassic
L 2451	Old adit driven into the Dogger Formation at the base of the Middle Jurassic
L 2452	Northern scarp of the Cleveland Hills showing Middle Jurassic sandstones
L 2453	Middle Jurassic sandstones
L 2454	The Eller Beck Formation, Middle Jurassic
L 2455	Doming and dislocations of the Crinoid Grit Member
L 2456	Penecontemporaneous structures in sandstone of Middle Jurassic age
L 2457	Concretion-like structures in the Lower Calcareous Grit
L 2458	The Hambleton Oolite, Upper Jurassic
L 2459	Concretion-like structures in the Lower Calcareous Grit
L 2460	Silicified *Thalassinoides* burrows in the Lower Calcareous Grit Formation
L 2461	Silicified *Thalassinoides* burrows in the Lower Calcareous Grit Formation
L 2462	High level (825 ft) 251 m sand and gravel
L 2463	Glacial drainage channel
L 2464	Glacial drainage channel at c.780 ft (230 m)
L 2465	Extreme cambering in the Lower Calcareous Grit Formation
L 2466	Large area of slipped strata beneath Middle Jurassic sandstones
L 2467	Landslip in Middle and Lower Jurassic strata
L 2468	Landslip in Whitby Mudstone Formation
L 2668	Black Hambleton, erosion of peat after burning
L 2669	Black Hambleton, general view of Rye Dale
L 2670	Rye Dale, general view
L 2671	Hawnby and Rye Dale
L 2672	Easterside, Hawnby, scarp features
L 2673	Kepwick Quarries, general view

AUTHOR CITATIONS FOR FOSSIL SPECIES

To satisfy the rules and recommendations of the international codes of botanical and zoological nomenclature, authors of cited species are listed below.

Chapter 2   Devonian

Cravenoceras cowlingense Bisat, 1926
Eomarginifera tissingtonensis (Sibly, 1912)
Eumorphoceras bisulcatum Girty, 1909
Productus hemisphaericus J Sowerby, 1822
Productus redesdalensis Muir-Wood, 1928

Chapter 3   (Permian)

Calcinema permiana (King) Podemski, 1970
Crustaesporites globosus Leschik, 1956
Falcisporites zapfei (Potonié & Klaus) Leschik, 1956
Klausipollenites schaubergeri (Potonié & Klaus) Jansonius, 1962
Labiisporites granulatus Leschik, 1956
Lueckisporites virkkiae Potonié & Klaus emend. Clarke, 1965
Paravesicaspora splendens (Leschik) Klaus, 1963
Perisaccus granulosus (Leschik) Clarke, 1965
Protohaploxypinus chaloneri Clarke, 1965
Protohaploxypinus jacobii Jansonius emend.
  Hart, 1964
Protohaploxypinus microcorpus (Schaarschmidt) Clarke, 1965
Striatopodocarpites antiquus (Leschik) Potonié 1958
Taeniaesporites albertae Jansonius, 1962
Taeniaesporites angulistriatus (Klaus) Clarke, 1965
Taeniaesporites labdacus Klaus, 1963
Vittatina hiltonensis Chaloner & Clarke, 1962

Chapter 4   (Triassic)

Acanthotriletes ovalis Nilsson, 1958
Acanthotriletes varius Nilsson, 1958
Alisporites circulicorpus Clarke, 1965
Alisporites grauvogeli Klaus, 1964
Alisporites toralis (Leschik) Clarke, 1965
Angustisulcites gorpii Visscher, 1966
Angustisulcites grandis (Freudenthal) Visscher, 1966
Angustisulcites klausii Freudenthal, 1964
Aratrisporites palettae (Klaus) Schulz, 1967
Beaumontella caminuspina (Wall) Below, 1987

Beaumontella langii (Wall) Below, 1987
Calamospora mesozoica Couper, 1958
Camarozonosporites golzowensis Schulz, 1967
Carnisporites anteriscus Morbey, 1975
Carnisporites lecythus Morbey, 1975
Carnisporites spiniger (Leschik) Morbey, 1975
Chasmatosporites apertus (Rogalska) Nilsson, 1958
Chasmatosporites magnolioides (Erdtman) Nilsson, 1958
Cingulizonates rhaeticus (Reinhardt) Schulz, 1967
Classopollis torosus (Reissinger) Balme, 1957
Contignisporites problematicus (Couper) Döring, 1965
Converrucosisporites luebbenensis Schulz, 1967
Convolutispora microrugulata Schulz, 1967
Cyathidites australis Couper, 1953
Cyathidites minor Couper, 1953
Cymatiosphaera polypartita Morbey, 1975
Dapcodinium priscum Evitt, 1961 emend. Below, 1987
Ellipsovelatisporites plicatus Klaus, 1960
Eotrapezium concentricum (Moore, 1861)
Geopollis zwolinskae (Lund) Brenner, 1986
Gliscopollis meyeriana (Klaus) Venkatachala, 1966
Granuloperculatipollis rudis Venkatachala & Góczán emend. Morbey, 1975
Klausipollenites schaubergeri (Potonié & Klaus) Jansonius, 1962
Kraeuselisporites reissingeri (Harris) Morbey, 1975
Kuglerina meieri Scheuring, 1978
Kyrtomisporis laevigatus Mädler, 1964
Kyrtomisporis speciosus Mädler, 1964
Leptolepidites argenteaeformis (Bolkhovitina) Morbey, 1975
Limbosporites lundbladii Nilsson, 1958
Lunatisporites discrepans (Visscher) Warrington, 1974
Lunatisporites rhaeticus (Schulz) Warrington, 1974
Lycopodiacidites rhaeticus Schulz, 1967
Lycopodiacidites rugulatus (Couper) Schulz, 1967
Micrhystridium lymense Wall, 1965
Microreticulatisporites fuscus (Nilsson) Morbey, 1975
Natica oppelii Moore, 1861
Nevesisporites bigranulatus (Levet-Carette) Morbey, 1975
Osmundacidites wellmanii Couper, 1953
Ovalipollis pseudoalatus (Thiergart) Schuurman, 1976
Perinopollenites elatoides Couper, 1958
Perinosporites thuringiacus Schulz, 1962
Polycingulatisporites bicollateralis (Rogalska) Morbey, 1975
Porcellispora longdonensis (Clarke) Scheuring emend. Morbey, 1975
Protocardia rhaetica (Merian, 1853)

Protodiploxypinus fastidiosus (Jansonius) Warrington, 1974
Protohaploxypinus microcorpus (Schaarschmidt) Clarke, 1965
Quadraeculina anellaeformis Maljavkina, 1949
Retitriletes austroclavatidites (Cookson) Döring, Krutzsch, Mai & Schulz, 1963
Rhaetavicula contorta (Portlock, 1843)
Rhaetipollis germanicus Schulz, 1967
Rhaetogonyaulax rhaetica (Sarjeant) Loeblich & Loeblich emend. Below, 1987
Ricciisporites tuberculatus Lundblad, 1954
Semiretisporis gothae Reinhardt, 1962
Semiretisporis maljavkinae Schulz, 1967
Striatoabieites balmei Klaus emend. Scheuring, 1978
Todisporites major Couper, 1958
Todisporites minor Couper, 1958
Triadispora plicata Klaus, 1964
Triadispora staplini (Jansonius) Klaus, 1964
Tsugaepollenites pseudomassulae (Mädler) Morbey, 1975
Tsugaepollenites oriens Klaus, 1964
Vallasporites ignacii Leschik, 1956
Vesicaspora fuscus (Pautsch) Morbey, 1975
Vitreisporites pallidus (Reissinger) Nilsson 1958
Voltziaceaesporites heteromorpha Klaus, 1964
Zebrasporites interscriptus (Thiergart) Klaus, 1960

Chapter 5   (Jurassic)

Amaltheus gibbosus (Schlotheim, 1820)
Amaltheus margaritatus de Montfort, 1808
Amaltheus subnodosus (Young & Bird, 1828)
Ammonites armatus J Sowerby, 1815
Androgynoceras maculatum (Young & Bird, 1822)
Arnioceras semicostatum (Young & Bird, 1828)
Avicula [Meleagrinella] braamburiensis (Phillips, 1829)
Beaniceras luridum (Simpson, 1855)
Camptonectes laminatus (J Sowerby, 1818)
Camptonectes subulatus (Münster, 1836)
Cardinia laevis (Young & Bird, 1828)
Chlamys fibrosus (J Sowerby, 1816)
Cucullaea reticulata Bean *in* Young & Bird, 1828
Dactylioceras (Orthodactylites) semicelatum (Simpson, 1843)
Dactylioceras (Orthodactylites) tenuicostatum (Young & Bird, 1822)
Dimorpharaea defranciana (Michelin, 1840)
Enallocoenia richardsoni (Milne Edwards & Haime, 1851)
Entolium lunare (Roemer, 1839)
Equisetum columnare Brongniart, 1828
Gervillia praecursor Quenstedt, 1856
Gliscopollis meyeriana (Klaus) Venkatachala, 1966

Goniomya hybrida (Münster *in* Agassiz, 1842)

Gryphaea dilobotes Duff, 1978

Gryphaea gigantea J de C Sowerby, 1823

Gryphaea incurva J Sowerby, 1815

Gryphaea maccullochii J de C Sowerby, 1827

Harpoceras falciferum (J Sowerby, 1820)

Kraeuselisporites reissingeri (Harris) Morbey, 1975

Liostrea hisingeri (Nilsson, 1831)

Meleagrinella fallax (Pflücker, 1868)

Modiolus bipartitus J Sowerby, 1818

Modiolus laevis J Sowerby, 1812

Modiolus minimus J Sowerby, 1818

Myophorella phillipsii (Morris & Lycett, 1853)

Oxytoma inequivalve (J Sowerby, 1819)

Palaeoneilo galatea (d'Orbigny, 1850)

Palmoxytoma cygnipes (Young & Bird, 1822)

Piarorhynchia rostellata (Quenstedt, 1871)

Pinna sexcostata Terquem & Piette, 1865

Platymyoidea concinna (Tate, 1876)

Pleuromya costata (Young & Bird, 1828)

Plicatula numismalis (Quenstedt, 1856)

Polymorphites costatus (Quenstedt, 1884)

Polymorphites lineatus (Quenstedt, 1884)

Protocardia philippiana (Dunker, 1847)

Protocardia truncata (J de C Sowerby, 1827)

Pseudohastites charmouthensis (Mayer, 1863)

Pseudolimea acuticostata (Münster *in* Goldfuss, 1836)

Pseudolimea pectinoides (J Sowerby, 1815)

Pseudomytiloides dubius (J de C Sowerby, 1828)

Pseudopecten equivalvis (J Sowerby, 1816)

Pteromya tatei (Richardson & Tutcher, 1914)

Reophax helvetica (Haeusler, 1881)

Rhaxella perforata Hinde, 1890

Rollieria bronni (Andler, 1858)

Rudirhynchia huntcliffensis Ager, 1958

Spirillina infima (Strickland, 1846)

Steinmmania bronni (Voltz, 1833)

Tetrarhynchia dunrobinensis (Rollier, 1917)

Tetrarhynchia subconcinna (Davidson, 1852)

Trochammina sablei Tappan, 1955

Trochammina topogorukensis Tappan, 1955

Uptonia jamesoni (J de C Sowerby, 1827)

Chapter 7   (Quaternary)

Linoprotonia dentifer (Prentice, 1949)

Chapter 8   (Economic geology)

Nuculana ovum (J de C Sowerby, 1824)

INDEX

BRITISH GEOLOGICAL SURVEY

Keyworth, Nottingham NG12 5GG
0115 936 3100

Murchison House, West Mains Road, Edinburgh
EH9 3LA   0131-667 1000

London Information Office, Natural History Museum
Earth Galleries, Exhibition Road, London SW7 2DE
0171-589 4090

The full range of Survey publications is available through the Sales Desks at Keyworth and at Murchison House, Edinburgh, and in the BGS London Information Office in the Natural History Museum (Earth Galleries). The adjacent bookshop stocks the more popular books for sale over the counter. Most BGS books and reports can be bought from The Stationery Office and through Stationery Office agents and retailers. Maps are listed in the BGS Map Catalogue, and can be bought together with books and reports through BGS-approved stockists and agents as well as direct from BGS.

The British Geological Survey carries out the geological survey of Great Britain and Northern Ireland (the latter as an agency service for the government of Northern Ireland), and of the surrounding continental shelf, as well as its basic research projects. It also undertakes programmes of British technical aid in geology in developing countries as arranged by the Department for International Development and other agencies.

The British Geological Survey is a component body of the Natural Environment Research Council.

Published by The Stationery Office and available from:

The Publications Centre
(mail, telephone and fax orders only)
PO Box 276, London SW8 5DT
General enquiries 0171 873 0011
Telephone orders 0171 873 9090
Fax orders 0171 873 8200

The Stationery Office Bookshops
59–60 Holborn Viaduct, London EC1A 2FD
temporary until mid 1998
(counter service and fax orders only)
Fax 0171 831 1326
68–69 Bull Street, Birmingham B4 6AD
0121 236 9696   Fax 0121 236 9699
33 Wine Street, Bristol BS1 2BQ
0117 9264306 Fax 0117 9294515
9–21 Princess Street, Manchester M60 8AS
0161 834 7201 Fax 0161 833 0634
16 Arthur Street, Belfast BT1 4GD
01232 238451 Fax 01232 235401
The Stationery Office Oriel Bookshop
The Friary, Cardiff CF1 4AA
01222 395548 Fax 01222 384347
71 Lothian Road, Edinburgh EH3 9AZ
(counter service only)

Customers in Scotland may
mail, telephone or fax their orders to:
Scottish Publications Sales
South Gyle Crescent, Edinburgh EH12 9EB
0131 228 4181 Fax 0131 622 7017

The Stationery Office's Accredited Agents
(see Yellow Pages)

and through good booksellers